STREET OCCUPATIONS

STREET OCCUPATIONS

Urban Vending in Rio de Janeiro, 1850–1925

PATRICIA ACERBI

UNIVERSITY OF TEXAS PRESS *Austin*

Printed in the United States of America
First edition, 2017

Requests for permission to reproduce material from this work should be sent to:

Permissions
University of Texas Press
P.O. Box 7819
Austin, TX 78713-7819
http://utpress.utexas.edu/index.php/rp-form

∞ The paper used in this book meets the minimum requirements of ANSI/NISO Z39.48-1992 (R1997) (Permanence of Paper).

LIBRARY OF CONGRESS CATALOGING-IN-PUBLICATION DATA

Names: Acerbi, Patricia, author.
Title: Street occupations : urban vending in Rio de Janeiro, 1850/1925 / Patricia Acerbi.
Description: First edition. | Austin : University of Texas Press, 2017. | Includes bibliographical references and index.
Identifiers: LCCN 2016052407
ISBN 978-1-4773-1355-8 (cloth : alk. paper)
ISBN 978-1-4773-1356-5 (pbk : alk. paper)
ISBN 978-1-4773-1357-2 (library e-book)
ISBN 978-1-4773-1358-9 (non-library e-book)
Subjects: LCSH: Street vendors—Brazil—Rio de Janeiro—History—19th century. | Street vendors—Brazil—Rio de Janeiro—History—20th century. | Street vendors—Brazil—Rio de Janeiro—Social conditions. | Peddling—Brazil—Rio de Janeiro—History—19th century. | Peddling—Brazil—Rio de Janeiro—History—20th century. | Slavery—Brazil—Rio de Janeiro—History. | Urban policy—Brazil—Rio de Janeiro.
Classification: LCC HF5459.B6 A23 2017 | DDC 381/.1809815309034—dc23
LC record available at https://lccn.loc.gov/2016052407

doi:10.7560/313558

FOR ELISABETH

TABLE OF CONTENTS

ILLUSTRATIONS

FIGURES

MAPS

ACKNOWLEDGMENTS

This book may be the fruit of one author's persistence, but it does not reflect the work of just one individual. Participants in this collective effort are many, and I ask forgiveness if from poor memory I have overlooked anyone's contribution. Foremost, I am grateful to Barbara Weinstein and Andor Skotnes. Barbara's firm belief in this project and great ability to guide me through the academic experience has kept me engaged since my early days at the University of Maryland. My thanks to Andor for consistently valuing my research.

I thank James Woodard for his many readings of my work and for his remarkable expertise. I am grateful also to the anonymous reviewer who helped me clarify this work's unique perspectives. I appreciate the academic support I found in the Department of History at the University of Maryland. Daryle Williams's dedicated advising guided my research process since this project's inception. Mary Kay Vaughan raised important questions and helped me establish a crucial viewpoint from the start. Laura Lenci, Mary Junqueira, and Sarah Sarzynski were also great sources of support for this project in Maryland. I am also very thankful to Amy Chazkel, whose innovative historical analysis of Rio's underground economy has been a great influence.

Funding from of a Fulbright IIE fellowship in 2006 helped me carry out the bulk of the research for this book. I remain immensely grateful for that opportunity. An enthusiastic group of fellow Brazilianists shared that year and experience with me. Teresa Cribelli, Jessica Graham, Ann Schneider, and Kari Zimmerman provided new perspectives for the development of my ideas. The National Endowment for the Humanities supported my postdoctoral reentry into the archives in 2012. This opportunity was a crucial turning point in the development of this book, and I am grateful to the readers and reviewers who identified its potential. I also thank Claudia Viscardi at Casa de Rui Barbosa, who gave me generous assistance at this time.

The work of dedicated archivists in Rio's city, state, and national archives allowed for my investigations to be fruitful and complete. Sátiro Nunes at the Arquivo Nacional led me to key collections. The digitization of Brazilian newspapers at the Biblioteca Nacional was an unanticipated game changer in my postdoctoral research. The work behind such a gigantic endeavor is a testament to how the improved accessibility of documents makes and remakes history. A book about Rio's street commerce would not be the same without the wonderful images that depict this long urban tradition. I am very grateful to all involved in preserving these images and public access to them, especially the team at G. Ermakoff Casa Editorial and the Arquivo Nacional, including Kátia Borges Oliveira. The Arquivo Edgard Leuenroth in Campinas revealed to me in 2008 a key source that changed everything about this story. The Centro de Pesquisa em História Social da Cultura proved to be another treasure chest for exploring Rio's past. Sidney Chalhoub introduced me to the center's rich repository and years later provided comments at a conference that helped refine the results of my investigations there.

I must confess that the best academic conferences I have had the pleasure of participating in took place in Rio and Niterói. Martha Abreu and Hebe Mattos co-organized an unforgettable international meeting to discuss the histories of the postabolition Atlantic world. I appreciate my participation in similar collaborations during the international symposium held at Casa de Rui Barbosa in 2013, organized by Isabel Lustosa and James Green. As a result of these international conferences, I learned much from a new generation of Brazilian historians, such as Giovana Xavier, Juliana Barreto Farias, Cristiane Miyasaka, Edinélia Oliveira Souza, Álvaro Pereira do Nascimento, Paulo Terra, and Carlos Eduardo Costa, who contributed to my work with their original scholarship.

At Russell Sage College, I am grateful for the research opportunities provided by the Schacht Faculty Research Grant, the Sage Research Institute, and the dean's office. I am especially grateful to Stephen Schechter, whose vast knowledge of everything showed me the way of a true scholar. Ekaterina Kagan and Manijeh Sabi became my dear friends and supported my growth as a junior faculty member. The motivated students I met at Sage inspired me to search deeper, teach better, and rethink the purpose of this book. Teresa Meade at Union College was a constant ally, and her contributions to my work run deep.

The superb team at the University of Texas Press has been this book's most crucial blessing in its final stage. My editor, Kerry Webb, valued from the beginning what I aimed to accomplish. I also thank my dear friends in Barcelona for their constant encouragement. It is with my sister, Elisabeth, that I share the profound experience of multiple journeys across the Atlantic. This book is especially for her. My mother's love and tireless support also fill me with gratitude. Finally, my husband, Jon Franklin, deserves my deepest gratitude. His heart walks with me and transforms everything I do, including this book, into something better.

INTRODUCTION

Chegando ao Rio de Janeiro foi trabalhar de ajudante de pedreiro numa obra mas pensava todo instante: quando eu tiver boa quantia vou comprar mercadoria pra trabalhar ambulante.
[After arriving in Rio de Janeiro he worked as a bricklayer, but he constantly thought: once I have saved up a good amount of money, I will buy goods to sell on the street.]
GONÇALO FERREIRA DA SILVA, *A BRIGA DO RAPA COM O CAMELÔ*
[THE FIGHT BETWEEN THE COP AND THE PEDDLER]

THE END OF SLAVERY might have been expected to usher in an era of liberty, but as a Brazilian abolitionist newspaper writer in 1883 observed, slavery's end was actually threatening laissez-faire freedom of commerce. In other words, free markets were not a natural consequence of the abolition of slavery because the Brazilian state remained punitive. The frequent arrest of street peddlers in Rio, he noted, demonstrated that "decidedly, the freedom of commerce has ended in this country!"[1] Brazil's final abolition of slavery in 1888 ended the horrific trade in persons but gave way to incomplete freedoms that reflected new forms of regulating and disciplining the public. In response, vendors in Rio de Janeiro sought to protect their freedom of commerce in a city that had a long and robust tradition of street selling. It seemed only natural that the economic freedom to sell on the street would go hand in hand with the political freedom of slave emancipation.

Between 1850 and 1925, the practice and regulation of street commerce in Rio de Janeiro (hereafter Rio) was central to the distribution and provisioning of basic goods and the state management of urban street labor. For vendors, who almost uniformly came from the ranks of slaves, former slaves, and poor immigrants, vending was also a site of newfound freedoms and restrictions. In their struggles to sell throughout the Brazilian capital, vendors engaged in citizenship building as participants with a right to the city and a right to free commerce. Their ubiquitousness throughout diverse neighborhoods of the capital reflected their practice of such rights and steady customer demand. Although free labor and republican ideology supported in theory the political and economic liberties that vendors sought, policing and state disciplinary measures during the Brazilian era of slave emancipation limited them. As practitioners of street commerce and residents of the city, vendors expected to benefit from the economic and political liberties of a postslave society. Urban authorities in Rio, however, generally did not share such a view.

Vending practices familiar to passersby of nineteenth-century Rio endure on Brazilian streets today. Sellers of fruits and sweets whom Christiano Junior (1832–1902) and Marc Ferrez (1843–1923) depicted in *cartes de visite*, small collectible photographs, in the mid- to late nineteenth century look a lot like the vendors who circulate through central and residential Rio today. Moreover, observers can note that earlier lithographs of peddlers and marketeers by Jean-Baptiste Debret (1768–1848), who lived in Rio 1816–1831, share a striking resemblance to some of Rio's street sellers today. Peddlers still travel significant distances to serve customers in a variety of urban neighborhoods, and the diversity of their offerings continues to reveal relations with suppliers, patrons, and official establishments. The peddlers whom residents and tourists may see today in affluent beach neighborhoods have often walked long distances from the city's peripheral neighborhoods. The extent of such vending practices is reminiscent of an earlier era that memorialist writers nostalgically refer to as "o Rio antigo," or "old Rio," and the persistence of vendors selling on city streets has influenced customary practice and regulations that recognize their formal status.[2]

A simple WorldCat library search for "Rio antigo" shows that this term becomes its own category worthy of encyclopedic description. Numerous books have been written on the history of its streets, neighborhoods, commerce, transportation, visual culture, political intrigues, social outcasts, social types, and urban legends. Today one can visit traditional street fairs, participate in walking and food tours, and buy from peddlers selling goods from the latest DVDs to sweets and patties. Efforts to revive old Rio through traditional street food and music may have the nostalgic effect on visitors that Brazilians term *saudade*. That street vendors may be a part of this nostalgic experience reveals their protagonism in an old Rio and continual presence in the modern city as well. However, coating with nostalgia the vestige of a slave or colonial past misrepresents vending's status as an informal, marginal, or exceptional occurrence in the city. Rio's street commerce is more than a traditional practice that survived the modern changes of the past century. Regulations toward street commerce and vendors' activities with patrons, other street sellers, and the customers they served reveal vending's informal-formal connections and its central role in urban distribution and provision. In Rio, as in other Latin American cities, street vending is a quintessential urban practice that resists official efforts to limit vendors' trade.[3] While tourists in Latin American cities may frequently buy goods from ubiquitous hawkers, street sellers are also circulating in less public areas to supply residents with everyday goods.

Laws and regulations tend to define economic practices as formal or informal, but the cultural normalization of Rio's street commerce shows an experience beyond a bipolar formality and informality. On the one hand, connections between the formal and informal are socioeconomic. On the other hand, they shape the everyday culture of food and household consumption. To this day, consumers in Rio can expect fresh and affordable fruits from street vendors who may readily slice a juicy pineapple or put a straw in a coconut for drinking water. Residents tend to know what street corners and areas certain vendors occupy, often neighborhood landmarks they customarily visit. Peddlers today will also work around store schedules to serve buyers after closing hours. Important neighborhood streets such as Rua do Catete thus remain animated with commercial hustle and bustle into the night. Beaches of the Zona Sul such as Copacabana and Ipanema have also extended the life of the street as peddlers haul heavy containers and walk long stretches of sand to offer sunbathers a variety of snacks and refreshments.

The popularity of street commerce in Brazilian cities inspired museum curators to prepare in 2006 the itinerant exhibit "Pelas ruas e calçadas" (Through streets and sidewalks), which was mainly composed of fifty-five images of street sellers from the early nineteenth century to the present.[4] Visitors may have recognized lithographs by Debret and photographs by Ferrez depicting Rio's various street-vending types (*tipos*). Enslaved workers hauling goods and immigrants selling foodstuffs illustrate in the traveling exhibit the long history of urban vending in Brazil. More recent images of individuals selling hot dogs, *cocada* (a coconut-based sweet), and goods from the hood of a car demonstrate the ongoing practice of urban vending. Furthermore, the museums that took in this exhibit provided visitors with the live experience of buying from street vendors. Museumgoers could purchase popcorn from a vendor in the same room where they looked at old images of street sellers. While the street sellers displayed in the exhibition's paintings and photographs could have been regular targets of policing, the museums' recognition of their importance illustrates a vending practice that is not merely informal or underground but essential to Brazilian urban life.

Toward the middle of the nineteenth century, the *sistema de ganho*, a system of earnings for urban slave masters and patrons, transformed street work in Rio into an official practice of urban slavery that was licensed and regulated. The current practice of street commerce in Rio has origins in urban slavery and the formal-informal relations that marked vending's turn to free labor. For most of the nineteenth century, masters who participated in the ganho system were accustomed to sending slaves to carry out street work for returned earnings. Free Brazilian workers and European immigrants sought to profit from similar arrangements with patrons later in the century. Masters and patrons were usually suppliers, thus creating the foundation for patron-client relations between free vendors and their employers. When vendors in the early twentieth century organized against policing by claiming the legitimacy of their work, they were appealing to the ganho system that had once protected them. Street sellers negotiated daily with patrons and suppliers, but their struggle for rights revealed a robust customary practice beyond patronage. Vendors' sense of urban belonging had been shaped by the patron-client relations that formed supply chains, but the practice of walking the city to meet diverse customers informed the political and economic value of their freedom.

During Brazil's period of gradual abolition from 1850 to 1888, the ganho system officially managed the free labor carried out on Rio's streets. At the same time, slaves, former slaves, and poor immigrants became increasingly vulnerable to policing and vagrancy charges. The nineteenth-century ideology of vagrancy (*ideologia da vadiagem*) contributed to the criminalizing of the urban poor, which assumed that centuries of slavery had incapacitated Brazilian free workers' ability to labor adequately.[5] Still, police officials tended to note in registry entries that arrested and detained street vendors had a formal occupation (*ocupação*) as street sellers. Police identification of vendors performing legitimate work was not enough, however, to drop vagrancy charges. Even if street commerce was a formal practice in the capital city, street sellers as free *ganhadores* (workers for earnings) did not enjoy the full benefits of free labor. Urban vending's association with slavery and the working poor cast a permanent shadow on Rio's street commerce.

The policing of street vendors as a result of the ideology of vagrancy had consequences for Rio's commercial establishments, especially those located in the center city. Under the ganho system, owners of food establishments hired slave and free ganhadores to transport goods and sell them on the street. In this way, owners of fixed commercial establishments hoped to reach consumers in distant locations and customers on the street. The formal request for licenses in the late 1870s often stated that owners of shops, bars, and small restaurants desired to hire free ganhadores to sell on the street. The connection between established petty commerce and street vending was formative. As Rio's population grew and vendors increasingly sold in the city's outskirts, businesses of central Rio adapted. By the early 1900s, patent requests for vehicles that could reach Rio's *subúrbios* (urban periphery) from the city center promised to easily deliver basic necessities to new residents. The connection between small businesses and street vending now extended around the Guanabara Bay.

As street commerce expanded with population growth, so did the vagrancy and public disorder charges against street sellers. Rio's urban slaveholding society had set a precedent for policing street workers, and the further empowerment of the police in regulating street commerce became a legacy of the gradual transition from enslaved to free labor in urban Brazil. While police officers attempted to discipline street vending that was dirty, noisy, and disorderly, the turn to free labor involved a municipal reordering that was meant to eliminate vendors and vending entirely from the city center. By the early twentieth century, urban reformers deemed street vending an obstacle to modernity and progress or, at best, an unfortunate aspect of city life. Policing thus intensified to remove unwanted vendors and vending from the street, a cleanup operation that would seem familiar to many peddlers in Brazilian cities today.

The administration of Mayor Francisco Pereira Passos (1903–1906) focused on removing vendors from central urban areas in Rio. An image captured by the municipally funded photographer Augusto Malta (1864–1957) in 1905 revealed the administration's position against street commerce. The image of an old storefront with several street vendors in front of it was marked with penciled diagonal lines that signaled their necessary removal.[6] Colonial and slave vestiges of street life and commerce were a blot on the modern city that Pereira Passos envisioned. Top-down elimination of vendors remained uneven, however, as officials tended to marginalize more than erase vending practices from the capital's streets. Vendors who worked without license may have been informal workers by choice, but they were also a consequence of repressive regulations of urban renewal and policing. The informality of street commerce further gained a spatial dimension when urban reforms pushed the poor to live in the city's marginalized areas, and vendors followed their neighbors and customers.

The measures that repressed vending during the Pereira Passos administration allowed street commerce to endure through the formal and informal relations that had sustained it all along. Prohibiting street selling in the city's center and regulating vendors and ganhadores with practices inherited from the ganho system reflected the administration's recognition that street commerce was a widespread if undesired practice of urban life. Supply lines involving producers and vendors continued to be organized around patron-client relations. Vendors' ties to suppliers demonstrated the long-standing connection between street commerce and established petty commerce. Formal and informal markets in Rio were thus interconnected, as they are in many other cities of the developing world today.[7] In Rio's street commerce, formal and informal selling practices were connected from their very foundation as shop owners supplied and relied on peddlers to sell their products since slave times. The proximity of these parallel and interconnected worlds explains the ambiguous municipal laws that have never fully banned street commerce from Rio to this day.

Repressive municipal measures likewise did not prevent street sellers from being active participants in the great debate over citizenship. On the contrary, vendors' resistance to policing framed their language of citizenship and urban belonging in the early postabolition period. Street sellers insisted on the legitimacy of their work as professions and rightful presence in the city, hence my use of the term "street occupations" to discuss their struggle for rights and recognition. The ganho system of slavery had established the laws and practices of street commerce in the nineteenth century on which people relied for access to basic goods. Street vendors further capitalized on the tradition to move throughout the city despite restrictions after slavery. As a result, a vendor's occupation acquired a double meaning: the right to inhabit urban space for street selling and the right to sell goods to expectant customers. Court records involving street vendors as well as their organizational activities in 1912–1914 reveal these spatial and professional dimensions of their street occupations. Afonso Henriques de Lima Barreto (1881–1922), a celebrated chronicler of early twentieth-century Rio, captured this in his writing about new immigrants taking up street selling and competing with veteran peddlers for space and customers.[8]

The practice and regulation of postabolition street commerce was shaped by the transitional decades of the latter half of the nineteenth century. After 1850, as slavery in Rio declined, the ganho system transformed into the urban institution that officially managed the transition to free labor for work performed on the street. By 1850, Brazilian slave society had developed in and beyond plantations with vast Atlantic and regional trade. The port city of Rio received around ten thousand enslaved men and women from west-central Africa each year at the height of the transatlantic slave trade. Slaves carried out most of the public street work in Rio such as lighting night lamps and collecting garbage. Selling goods on the street was central to provisioning this urban slave society, and slaves and free workers worked alongside and with each other.[9] In a capital city of about two hundred thousand residents in 1850, nearly 40 percent (eighty thousand) were enslaved blacks.[10] Urban vending brought together enslaved and free blacks since the early nineteenth century, as depicted in Jean-Baptiste Debret's paintings of Rio's port, plazas, and street corners. The mixed labor force of street work during slave times transformed the ganho system into an institution that could manage enslaved and free workers along patron-client lines.

The end of the transatlantic slave trade between Africa and Brazil in 1850 initiated the period when the ganho system came to administer the licensing of slave and free ganhadores. British opposition to the Atlantic slave trade had led to the earlier and never-implemented Brazilian law of 1831 *para o inglês ver* (for the English to see), claiming to end the slave trade between Africa and Brazil.[11] Britain had escorted the Portuguese royal court across the ocean to Brazil after the Napoleonic invasion of Portugal in 1807, and this led to the opening of Brazilian ports to British commerce. However, Brazil's rulers and planters still backed the slave trade against British abolitionist pressure. Despite the British blockade, ships with enslaved Africans continued to land in Brazil into the 1860s, and the enslaved men, women, and children were mostly sent to the coffee plantations of the southeast when they did not remain as slaves in the city. Meanwhile, cities witnessed the growth of the free black population, but men seeking ganhador licenses in Rio in the 1860s were still for the most part enslaved. This pattern changed in the late 1870s when free ganhadores with mostly European origins began applying for ganhador licenses in larger numbers. While ganho labor continued to be associated with slavery and black workers, the participation of poor whites introduced new dynamics and renewed patron-client relations beyond the institution of slavery.

The ganho system is thus a crucial starting point for understanding Rio's street commerce in the postabolition period. During the last decades of slavery in Brazil, the ganho system became an important part of urban slavery and the transition to free labor because of its ability to absorb the changing conditions of gradual abolition. It could systemically organize urban slave labor by managing master-slave relations while at the same time transferring the patron-client model to free ganhadores and their employers. Since poor immigrants and free blacks involved in Rio's petty commerce already worked along patron-client lines, the ganho system merely formalized those relations. The widespread practice of patronage in petty commerce thus helped urban authorities navigate the consequences of slavery's end. The ganho system's organization of patron-client relations positioned it as an adequate and available institution for authorities to manage a rising free labor force on city streets.

During the time of slavery, masters sent enslaved ganhadores to earn money on the street as sellers, porters, barbers, and healers. The ganho system allowed them to do so formally with the added benefit (or nuisance) of state supervision. A ganhador's license permitted *escravos ao ganho* (slaves selling goods for earnings) to work outside their masters' houses as long as they returned predetermined earnings to the slave owners. Once outside the master's house, the escravo ao ganho was also under the gaze of the state. As slavery declined, the ganho system eventually came to register employers hiring free ganhadores, accommodating the changing conditions of gradual slave emancipation. The 1870s and 1880s set a precedent for Rio's urban vending practices of the early postabolition period. The ganho system's model of patronage became the municipal instrument to which vendors then resorted in the early twentieth century to claim legitimacy.

While patrons and business owners used street vendors to market their goods, vendors relied on the protections their patronage offered. Maintaining dependency between workers and property owners was at the heart of Brazil's gradual approach to abolition.[12] After 1850, the next step in Brazil's gradual abolition of slavery was the freeing of the slave mother's womb to establish dependence between the children of slave mothers and the masters who ostensibly freed the children. The Lei do Ventre Livre (Free Womb Law) of 1871 permitted slave owners to use young non-enslaved workers and thus move toward a model of free labor that disrupted as little as possible the relations of slavery. In other words, the free children of enslaved mothers often ended up basically as slaves and indentured servants. After 1871, with the end of slavery in sight, southern European immigrants entered the world of Rio's street commerce in greater numbers. They peddled alongside slaves, adopting similar practices and becoming targets of the ganho system's increased regulation of free ganhadores. More than any other decade, the 1870s generated the practices of street commerce that shaped postabolition urban vending. The ganho system's reliance on patron-client relations to discipline a dependent workforce conditioned both black and white participants. Ex-masters and ex-slaves participating in street commerce often continued working together, and free immigrants entered similar arrangements, sometimes alongside free blacks. European immigrants usually took up patrons of the same national or ethnic background, and it was common for Italians, Spaniards, and Portuguese to work with each other as well. Syrio-Lebanese immigrants from the declining Ottoman Empire typically formed alliances with patrons and workers of their same background.

While the ganho system of the 1870s secured urban labor along patron-client lines, the next decade saw the formal introduction of the police as the main regulators of ganho labor and, consequently, street commerce. Detention records reveal that by the mid-1880s, as the city population neared a half-million inhabitants, more street sellers were jailed on vagrancy and public disorder charges than for unlicensed vending. The licensing process for free and enslaved ganhadores changed in 1886 when the municipality required registration with the police. A police-issued permit number now sufficed to license a ganhador without the need for an employer or guarantor to sponsor him or her. This increased the regulatory role of the police and lessened the influence of patrons, substituting patronage with police supervision. Patron-client relations with private business had given vendors some safety from policing, but the decline of the ganho system weakened such protections, which vendors tried to recuperate in the early twentieth century.

The ganho system's administration of urban street labor during the gradual abolition of slavery resulted in a shared experience for European immigrants, slaves, former slaves, and descendants of slaves who participated in street commerce. Vendors at the turn of the twentieth century experienced street commerce as a slave legacy with experiential and structural dimensions shaped by the continuity of patronage, policing, and state discipline. The ganho system's structural ability to manage enslaved and free labor particularly contributed to this shared history between urban slaves and free workers. Immigrants engaging in licensed street commerce entered an old institution of urban slave society, the ganho system, and even if they chose to remain unlicensed, street vending was still created by the buying and selling practices of that society.

While the ganho system's management of slave and free labor optimized it as an institution of gradual abolitionism that helped authorities discipline the street, the increasing number of free people working on the streets of Rio demanded more than the discipline of patronage could offer. By the late 1870s, poor European immigrants were present everywhere on Rio's streets, intensifying authorities' preoccupation with how to deal with this perceived disorder. Rio's police hence gained power to regulate street selling activities and discipline unwanted behavior. The 1886 ganho law required police registration; two decades later, in 1903, Mayor Pereira Passos reinforced the role of police in disciplining the street. That same year he expelled street commerce from the city's central neighborhoods. African and non-African street vendors thus became easier targets for charges of vagrancy and public disorder. Racial and ethnic difference, however, still made this shared history uneven, as Afro-descendant vendors had a greater disadvantage than European whites against policing.

As Rio's population grew and its urban periphery expanded, especially after the final abolition of slavery in 1888, a specialized suburban group of vendors developed among some who lived there and others who traveled there. Vending methods were adapted too. Patent seekers invented new kinds of animal-driven carts and carriages to supply this growing area of the city with goods from downtown businesses. Small farmers in rural areas also hired vendors or peddled their wares themselves to their new neighbors. The city's post-abolition geographical changes along with policies of urban renewal notably resulted in the dislocation of a mostly Afro-Brazilian population to growing shantytowns and suburban areas. Street vendors followed their customer bases, while the police tracked these migrations for the cause of establishing public order. The emergence of a regular newspaper column titled "Nos suburbios" (In the suburbs) in the Rio daily *A Época* reflected these new policing concerns.

While innovation in transportation and vending technologies allowed businesses to reach new suburban customers, the policing of street vendors in these areas increased. Pereira Passos's strengthening of the police resulted in the systemic persecution of peddlers, as alleged in complaints. In a city where street vending was a formal part of small commerce, the policing of vendors contributed to the expansion of informal practices, especially in the newly settled urban periphery. Concerns about the overwhelming number of informal and unlicensed street peddlers and policing them were frequent topics of newspaper discussions. Vendors asserted that police were targeting them, most of all in new suburban areas, and resisted policing with claims to their right to public urban spaces for selling without abusive tactics or regulation.

Street vendors' notions of urban citizenship developed in their collective organizing. Street commerce to this day has been a continuous yet contested source of economic and civic activity; vendor associations were an important bridge from the mutual aid societies of slaves and immigrants to the postabolition associations formed to secure economic liberty and claim citizenship. The cooperation and conflict between former slaves, African descendants, and mostly European immigrants is central to understanding street commerce in the early postabolition period. Vendors negotiated the conditions of economic liberty and political freedom in courts and labor associations according to vendor-supplier and patron-client relations, peddlers' appeals to honorable work and citizenship in courts, and the civic and labor associations they formed to secure citizenship and their right to the city.

Detention records demonstrate that vendors were targets of vagrancy and public disorder laws regardless of having licenses. Attaining a license, therefore, not only was costly but also guaranteed little protection from police. In efforts to protect themselves from excessive policing, street vendors, particularly those who sold sweet baked goods, sought to organize with patrons and suppliers. The association they subsequently formed, the União Protetora de Comércio Volante (UPCV), lasted two years, 1912–1914. Rio's sweets peddlers, who were mostly Afro-descendant, were at the center of this organization. Calling upon patrons for protection was a legacy of the ganho system that they hoped to revive against a disciplinary state. Creating an alliance with the people who supplied them failed, however, which led to the dissolution of the association and vendors' deeper distrust of patrons.

The periodization I follow in the book from 1850 to 1925 starts with the end of the transatlantic slave trade to Brazil and ends with Rio's street-commerce regulation of 1924. This seventy-five-year span had four distinct periods in the practice and regulation of street vending in Rio. The end of the Brazilian transatlantic slave trade marks the first period, 1850–1871. At this time the ganho system came to manage enslaved and free labor, which included the licensing of street sellers. The end of slavery became inevitable with the passing of the 1871 Free Womb Law, pulling a greater number of Europeans to migrate to Brazil. The European and immigrant backgrounds of peddlers still did not absolve them from the rules of the ganho system. During the second period I trace, 1871–1888, a shared history developed between enslaved blacks and free European immigrants who were ganhadores, transforming the process of gradual abolition into a shared experience of slavery's legacy.

In order to place police control over free street sellers in the capital city, the ganho law of 1886 required all ganhadores to register first with the police and then with the municipality. The insignificance of a patron or master's influence over the procedure of ganhador licensing revealed the state's repositioning as the main manager of street labor. Shortly afterward, the Penal Code of 1890, enacted months after the military intervention that inaugurated the First Republic, further empowered the police and redefined inappropriate street behaviors such as vagrancy and public disorder. Mayor Pereira Passos strengthened street policing in 1903. Further, the 1903 prohibition of street commerce under his administration, reinforcing a 1901 law, was tied to his larger plans for a Europeanized capital city. This third period, 1889–1906, brought changing official attitudes toward street commerce and the modern city as well as criminal charges that led vendors to defend their work in court. The early postabolition years were also a time when engineers, inventors, and other men of science proposed new technologies for street commerce—projects that some of them had started in the 1870s and 1880s. What modern streets and peddlers looked like for them stood in contrast to the removal strategies of the Pereira Passos urban reforms of the early twentieth century.

In the final period I examine, 1907–1925, the consequences of Rio's penal and urban reforms marked a new beginning for organized street commerce. The population of Rio exceeded one million by 1920, city streets were widened, markets expanded, workers unionized, and urban vending persisted. Vendors formed the UPCV in 1912 as a trade union and civic association to resist abusive policing and increasing licensing costs by renewing the patron-client relations that had formed street commerce. Seeking to recuperate the protections that patronage from suppliers had offered vendors in the nineteenth century, the UPCV engaged street sellers in issues of postabolition citizenship. The group insisted on vendors' right to exercise free commerce on

Rio's streets, the legitimacy of their occupations, and their rightful presence in the city.[13] Meanwhile, the regulation of street commerce vacillated between toleration and prohibition. Adding some relief, the passing of regulation in 1924 reinforced the former. The 1924 measures reflected the persistence of customary practice and vendors' tireless and tolerated activities in the city, rationalizing the space that they regularly used for working and accommodating to their daily practices.

Part 1, "Transition," frames urban vending in Rio according to the conditions of gradual abolitionism. Chapter 1, "Between Slavery and Freedom," introduces urban vending in Rio as a practice rooted in slavery while adapting to free labor. The ganho system organized the licensing of slave and free street workers, requiring the masters of enslaved vendors and the patrons of free vendors to become guarantors. Quantitative and qualitative analysis of more than eight hundred licenses focuses on these patron-client relations as well as the demographics shaping Rio's street commerce between 1850 and 1888. The businesses of masters and patrons that appeared in license requests illustrate vendor-supplier relations and the connections between street vending and fixed commerce such as stores, warehouses, and restaurants, that is, formal-informal links.

Chapter 2, "A Policed Workplace," is a social history of criminality that focuses on the policing of free street peddlers and ganhadores during the last two decades of slavery (1870–1888). Registry entries list hundreds of street sellers who were held at Rio's municipal jail as police authorities had become more concerned with repressing vagrancy and public disorder than with regulating the transactions of buying and selling on the street. This shift was evident after officials of the ganho system increased the regulatory role of the police over licensing in 1886. Responding to a notable increase in street arrests, the press in the capital city commented on the limits of vendors' economic and political liberties that the abolition of slavery had not secured. Reporting vendors' arrests gave the press an opportunity to shed light on the limited freedoms that followed the end of slavery.

Chapter 3, "Inventing a New Street Commerce," presents the technical discourse that envisioned a modern era for urban vending at the turn of the twentieth century. If the policing of Rio's streets was intended to eliminate inappropriate aspects of vending, the rationalization of street commerce reflected its industrial potential. Between 1885 and 1909, men of science, mostly engineers, requested patents for inventions they had created to transform food provisioning and selling methods in the capital. Vending practices inherited from the slave period were deemed filthy and backward, while investing in new vending technologies, they argued, would modernize and sanitize street buying and selling. Furthermore, an improved and modern street commerce would humanize conditions for vendors after centuries of brutalizing slavery.

Part 2, "Endurance," explains vendors' ongoing selling and civic participation despite restrictive measures. Chapter 4, "A Detriment to the Law," is based on the quantitative and qualitative analysis of detention and court records of vendors' arrests between 1890 and 1902. The founding of the first Brazilian republic in 1889 and the passing of the 1890 Penal Code strengthened laws against public disorder and vagrancy that targeted vendors as a nuisance in the modern city. Analysis of nearly one hundred court records reveals how liberal ideology and court processes shaped the meaning and experience of citizenship and free labor. Court records also illustrate that judges were often more accommodating to the realities of street commerce than were Rio's police, as judges did not uniformly consider vending an illegitimate or inappropriate line of work.

In chapter 5, "An Honest Occupation," I examine assertions by street sellers, patrons, and their defenders in court as they claimed citizenship and honor against criminal charges. Likewise relevant here are Pereira Passos's urban reforms of 1903–1906 and a collection of court records extending into the 1920s. Vendors and their legal representatives resisted official attitudes that street commerce was an unwanted legacy of slavery. Defendants argued that although selling on the street was a practice of the poor, it was nevertheless legitimate and honorable. Courts that exonerated vendors underscored the practice of vending as an individual's political and economic right in the postabolition city.

Chapter 6, "Vendors and the City Associate," adds another dimension to the discussion of citizenship. The purpose, membership, and activities of the UPCV reveal that it operated as both a mutual aid society and a trade union. In this final chapter I evaluate the successes and failures of vendor organizing in 1912–1914 as larger political and economic circumstances influenced other workers in Rio to organize. The fate of the UPCV was tied to the changing relations between street sellers, suppliers, patrons, and government. Newspapers in the capital also were part of the civic culture surrounding worker organizing at this time, supporting street vendors' right to the city and claim to free labor.

The book's conclusion is focused on the ruptures and continuities that made Rio's street commerce as slavery declined and vending became more informal in the postabolition years. Between 1850 and 1925, the practice of street selling in the Brazilian capital reflected the experience of the gradual transition from slavery to freedom and revealed the significance of patronage and policing. A brief discussion of two vendor associations, registered in

1936 and 1938, further demonstrates the diversity of street-selling participants still influenced by the dynamics of diaspora and patronage. The similarity to earlier forms of civic and labor organizing sheds light on the ruptures and continuities that shaped vending in Rio from the mid-nineteenth century to the early twentieth century. Vendor organizing captures street sellers' persistence and endurance in Rio as well as the links between formal and informal commerce in ways that police and court records only partially reveal.

PART I

TRANSITION

CHAPTER 1

BETWEEN SLAVERY AND FREEDOM

IN THE NINETEENTH CENTURY, street commerce was an indispensable aspect of Brazilian urban slave society and a logical site for regulating the transition from slavery to free labor. In the city of Rio, slaves, free Africans, Brazilian-born free men and women, and free immigrants sold goods and services to urban residents. The women and men plying their skills and wares on the street captured the attention of passersby and travelers, many of whom noted the peculiarities of Brazilian slave society.[1] Street selling, however, was not merely an ad hoc arrangement for provisioning the city. Rather, the ganho system organized enslaved and free street vendors in the city, establishing a formal structure to street selling's myriad informal practices. Vendors and other street workers licensed under the ganho system most markedly lived between slavery and freedom in the decades leading to abolition. The ganho system and ganhadores reflected the uneven transition from enslaved to free labor, beginning with the final prohibition of the transatlantic slave trade between Africa and Brazil in 1850 and ending 13 May 1888 with the final and summary emancipation of all slaves.

The ganho system's ability to adapt to the conditions of free labor allowed it to hold the attribute of free labor and individual mobility. As ganhadores seemingly moved freely throughout the city working in transportation, commerce, and manufacturing, and as the slave "left the slave barracks and enter[ed] the streets," he or she became "feared and despised."[2] Despite the ganho system's nominal legitimacy, the relative freedom of movement it gave black ganhadores in the city threatened the slave system. Licensed ganhadores may have been allowed to walk the city and bargain for wages, increasing their chances for socioeconomic mobility, but their status as workers or vagrants was usually a matter of interpretation for city police and judges.

Ganhadores' ambiguous position between slavery and freedom eventually came to shape the social relations of street vendors in freedom. The presence of free African and African Brazilian ganhadores revealed that "the kind of free [black] . . . that a slave society produces directly reflects the state of slavery within that society and tells much about the other groups as well."[3] In Rio, those other groups included free immigrants born in Europe, Asia, and elsewhere in the Americas. These nonblack ganhadores still did not escape the racialization that resulted from centuries of slavery in Brazil as the ganho system was adapted to the conditions of free labor.

The perpetuation of patron-client dependency, a holdover from slavery, was central to the ganho system during the gradual abolition of slavery in Brazil. Proponents believed a patron-client system was necessary to formally regulate the increasing numbers of free workers in the city who might otherwise turn to vagrancy. The system of patronage and the policing of poor workers thus came to shape laws governing the ganho system. The organization of slave and free labor under one system developed from criminal law. The licensing of enslaved ganhadores started after the passing of the 1830 Criminal Code, which was intended to subject urban free workers to supervision by private patrons and public agents. After the final prohibition of the transatlantic slave trade in 1850 and the subsequent growth of the free black population, the municipality of Rio began to process licenses for free ganhadores too. At this point, free ganhadores were mostly freed men and women born in Africa (*libertos*), while in the 1870s Europeans and other foreign immigrants entered the world of street commerce in larger numbers.[4]

After 1850, licensing measures for free and slave ganhadores were parallel procedures, with the difference that masters sponsored slaves and patrons sponsored free ganhadores. The ganho system's elasticity hence allowed it to become an institution that facilitated the gradual transition to free labor. In this respect it was similar to the hireling slave system in New Orleans that made it "possible for urban economies to maintain a flexible [slave and free] colored labor force without disturbing, legally at least, the institution of slavery."[5] Gradual slave emancipation in Brazil inevitably disturbed the institution of slavery, but its proponents aimed for a smooth and measured shift that would upset as little as possible the interests of slave holders. In Rio, the ganho system unsettled slavery to the extent that everyday struggles and gradual abolitionist laws transformed the experiences of ganhadores and pressured the structures underpinning it. Yet the culture of patronage that the ganho system supported remained virtually unchanged.

As the nineteenth century advanced, individuals of African descent carried into freedom the skills they had learned in bondage. European, Asian, and South American immigrants entered a practice of street commerce that was associated with slavery. Municipal licenses to sell goods on the street were commonly known as "black ganhador licenses" (*licenças de negro de ganho*), a term that nonblack immigrants learned to use when seeking vending licenses from municipal authorities.[6] Histories of the Brazilian ganho system have tended to overlook the considerable proportion of ganhadores who were not slaves or of African descent at this time but instead were free foreign immigrants mainly from southern Europe.[7] Free and poor nonblack immigrants were therefore participants in Rio's structural and experiential turn to free labor, further transforming urban vending into an Atlantic diasporic practice shaped by both the slave trade and migration.

VENDING AND MARKETEERING IN AN URBAN SLAVE SOCIETY

The world of street commerce that developed in nineteenth-century Rio was in large part a consequence of the transfer of the Portuguese royal court to Brazil in 1807–1808. The prince regent João and approximately fifteen thousand Portuguese women and men took up residence in the colonial port city where more than a third of the population was enslaved. Subsequently, the city and its colonial slave society were transformed. The conversion of the colonial city into an imperial center, along with the opening of Brazilian ports to British trade, increased the demand for slave labor. As a result, close to ten thousand enslaved men and women hailing mainly from west-central Africa were brought to Rio every year during the first decades of the nineteenth century.[8] Most African arrivals were sold to plantation owners, but many remained in Rio as gardeners, hunters, porters, muleteers, boatmen, sailors, factory workers, quarrymen, lamplighters, street cleaners, craftsmen, artisans, musicians, artists, and peddlers.[9] Urban slaves who worked outside masters' homes generally had greater autonomy and freedom of movement than their rural counterparts. Slave owners who lived on small landholdings on the city's periphery employed slaves who were generally rural workers. While district boundaries changed throughout the turn of the century, street ganhadores and vendors mostly worked in the central districts of Santana, Sacramento, Candelária, and São José, all of which were near the Guanabara Bay. Map 1.1 illustrates this area of downtown Rio, which remained similar during the nineteenth century's slave period. Map 1.2 names the district divisions of the Brazilian capital city.

The Portuguese royal court's settlement in the Brazilian capital eventually contributed to the greater autonomy of street peddlers. The 1810 decree loosened trade barriers in Rio's port and suspended the earlier law that pro-

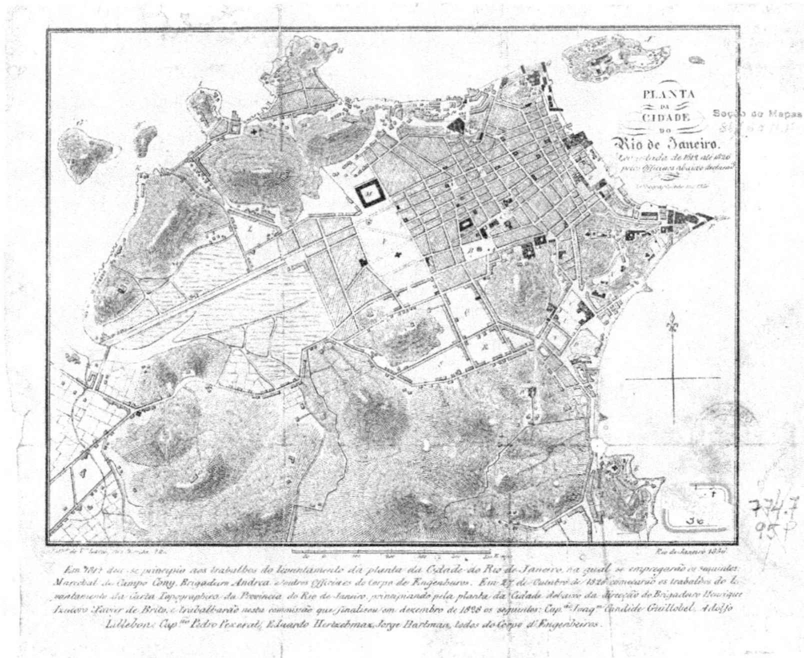

MAP 1.1. Plat of the city of Rio de Janeiro, mapped 1812–1826. Lithograph by V. Larée, 1836. Courtesy of Coordenação de Atendimento a Distância, Arquivo Nacional, Rio de Janeiro.

hibited small commerce in private homes and on the streets.[10] Unhampered by the previous colonial code, an increasing number of peddlers—slave and free—now took up the sale of grains, fowl, vegetables, sweets, and other basic goods. In colonial times, Portuguese sellers primarily known as *mascates* dominated door-to-door vending as slaves carried their goods for them. By the nineteenth century, slave owners preferred to instruct their slaves in the business of peddling, and door-to-door selling became a task performed by male and female slaves of all ages and physical abilities. Under this new arrangement, many enslaved vendors distributed goods produced in their master's households such as wax candles and food, whereas more valuable items such as silk and silver continued to be sold by non-Africans. Eventually, African and slave labor became the principal means to supply basic goods to the growing urban population in Rio. Slaves expanded these practices, working on the streets on Sundays, holidays, and nights to sell products that they had made, bought, or even stolen. Some successful vendors worked all day with their masters' permission, which allowed them to save earnings toward purchasing their own freedom.[11]

Slaves for hire (*escravos de alugel*) were enslaved men and women whom masters rented out to individuals who generally could not afford to own slaves or were temporary residents in the city. Under this hireling system, the municipality of Rio also rented slave labor for urban public works such as the construction of roads and buildings. In 1831 the slave owner Guilherme de Castro was still awaiting payment for the two months his slave was employed as a mason in the urban square Largo da Carioca. In 1852 Theotônio José Dantas submitted a letter requesting that he be compensated for the death of his slave Daniel, whom the military had contracted as a builder and who had died while putting out a fire.[12] In contrast to escravos de alugel, escravos ao ganho were wage-earning slaves who were not on loan. Instead, ganhadores could hire themselves out and bargain for wages with third parties if they returned agreed-upon amounts to their masters. Slaves for hire, ganhadores, and domestic slaves made up most of Rio's slave population Slaves being hired out by themselves or masters was not exclusively a Brazilian practice; Richard Wade notes that in several Atlantic cities it evolved from slave owners and officials' needs to reshape the institution of slavery according to urban life.[13] Rio's ganho system was adapting slavery to the demands of the city and also to the changing conditions of gradual abolition and free labor.

The growing demand for urban slave labor and the dramatic population increase by the mid-nineteenth century raised official concerns about policing

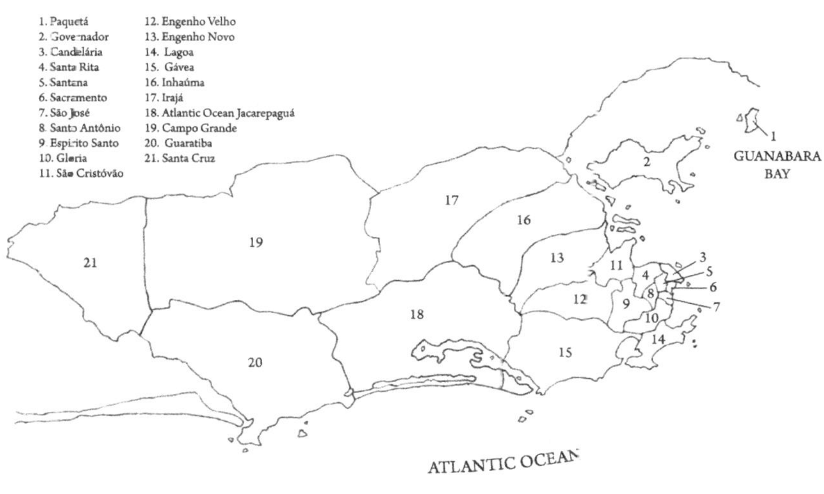

MAP 1.2. Districts of Rio de Janeiro, ca. 1870. Adapted from Nogueira da Silva, *Negro na rua*, 43. Map updated by University of Texas Press.

the streets. As a result, enslaved ganhadores dealt with an intensified regime of surveillance shaped by the 1830 Criminal Code and the municipal ordinances (*posturas*) of 1838, 1854, 1860, and 1870. The municipal government took on a greater responsibility for policing urban slaves and repressing potential resistance, as cities lacked the private supervision that plantations enforced.[14] The era's posturas brought little change in the methods of regulation toward slave and free ganhadores, but fines and time spent in prison increased. While the 1830 Criminal Code outlined for the nation the types of behavior deemed criminal, municipal ordinances focused on the regulation of street work and commerce. Eventually, ideologies of work and public behavior coalesced with official attitudes about vagrancy, which authorities defined as an absence of work and therefore subject to criminalization. Responding to the higher number of blacks on Rio's streets, the municipality introduced in 1838 an amendment to the 1830 Criminal Code to repress vagrancy more effectively by requiring work permits from all ganhadores. The amendment "regarding the fraudulent behavior of vagrants, beggars, lottery vendors, slaves, and ganhadores" also limited street sellers to working during daylight hours.[15]

While the regulation of Rio's street commerce continued to be connected to the dynamics of urban slavery, other laws emerged reflecting municipal concern over appropriate street work and behavior. Title 4 of the 1830 Criminal Code addressed noise pollution and moral offenses by prohibiting loud speech on the street. This particularly limited peddlers' ability to promote their goods by a practice popularly known as the *canto do trabalhador* (worker's song). Their *cantos* as soundscapes of vending endured nonetheless. Competition among street hawkers in the Brazilian capital was stiff, and therefore they created vibrant cries and catchy lines that residents either relished or abhorred. Title 4 still permitted the canto do trabalhador for commercial ends during official work hours, from seven o'clock in the morning until six o'clock in the evening, but, as arrest records reveal, vendors' cries during normal work hours still could lead to public disorder charges.

Legal risks aside, vendors' musical announcements were a memorable aspect of Rio's street commerce well into the twentieth century, and memoirs and chronicles celebrated such soundscapes. Writer Adelino Magalhães (1887–1969) nostalgically recalled the festive singing of peddlers outside his grandmother's house on Rua Marquês de Abrantes. The ice cream vendor sang, "Sorvete, ioiô, sorvete, iaiá" (Ice cream, "massa," ice cream, "missus"), reflecting the creolization of slave language. Vendors also appeared after dinner, he recalls, announcing knick-knacks, sweets, and other goods: "Miúdos! Olha os bons miúdos!—Baleiro! Balas de coco, de ovo, altéia, hortelã-pimenta!—Biscoitos, sinhá!" (Meat! Look at the good cuts of meat! — Candyman! Candies of coconut, egg, marshmallow, mint! — Cookies, ma'am!).[16] The six o'clock and later seven o'clock curfew was seldom observed as nighttime offered street vendors more freedom of movement and opportunities to escape slavery. Shops and market stalls were allowed to stay open until ten o'clock at night, but slaves were not allowed to hang around those premises.

Soon after the abolition of the transatlantic slave trade in 1850, municipal laws concerning street work shifted. The end of slave trade between Africa and Brazil, which the British had been advocating since 1830, motivated property owners to tighten labor management and maintain the market relations of slave society. A new set of municipal laws in 1854 listed the conditions under which enslaved and free ganhadores could work in Rio.[17] Male and female vagrants of all ages and skin color without proof of occupation would be fined ten milréis and incarcerated for eight days.[18] Title 7 stated that individuals selling stolen or counterfeit goods would be penalized with the higher fine of thirty milréis and eight days of jail time. Individuals unable to work because of physical disabilities were allowed to beg on the street with the appropriate municipal license. The 1854 regulations reinforced the 1838 municipal code, which stated that slave owners were not allowed to use escravos ao ganho without first registering and licensing them. In doing so, a master became the slave's guarantor (*fiador*) and responsible for any fines incurred by the ganhador. A free ganhador needed the sponsorship of a fiador as well to work on the street.

After 1854, all ganhadores were required to wear a visible metal pin (*chapa*) and have their license with them at all times. The fiador usually paid the two hundred milréis for the license in the process of registering the enslaved or free ganhador. Slaves working without the required chapa and license ran the risk of spending eight days in the *calabouço* (jail for slaves); free ganhadores faced the same penalty in the city jail. Ganhadores wearing false chapas could be fined thirty milréis and eight days in the calabouço or city jail. If slaves worked after seven o'clock in the evening they needed to carry same-day written permissions from their masters.[19]

A law enacted in 1851 required mascates, who were mostly free door-to-door sellers, to pay for licenses that had to be renewed annually. In the second half of the nineteenth century *mascataria* became a common vending practice among Syrio-Lebanese immigrants. Mascataria by then usually involved peddling valuable goods that enslaved ganhadores were not allowed to sell. Free mascates who sold jewelry, gold, and silver paid one hundred milréis for an annual license; those who sold porcelain, glass, ceramic, and wooden goods paid fifty milréis; knick-knacks, iron, aluminum, and other metallic goods required a license of twenty milréis. According to newspapers that reported street arrests, slaves peddling such valuables soon became suspects and were arrested for selling stolen goods.

The policing of street commerce made the master-slave relations that shaped vending more vulnerable to state intervention. The private world of the master's house was permeable to the public and policed world of the street.[20] On 14 June 1850, José Maria Ribeiro registered one of his slaves as a ganhador and paid for a license that would allow his slave to *mascatear fazendas* (sell fabric goods) throughout the city and its outskirts. Two months later, the enslaved ganhador was arrested because he was found peddling in the suburban district of Campo Grande without a license, which he claimed he had forgotten and left at home.[21] The ganhador was held in custody for a day, and even though his master turned in the original license, he still had to pay a fine of ten milréis. The established amount to release the enslaved ganhador from jail was thirty milréis, but since Campo Grande was a rural area with few ganhadores and Ribeiro's slave had been selling the goods of a mascate, he was not arrested for violating a law of the ganho system.[22] Instead the slave was arrested for violating a law that required all mascates to sell under a particular license that listed merchandise weights and measurements.

Ribeiro and the enslaved ganhador were thus held accountable for regulations that applied to mascates and not ganhadores. In the ganhador's run-in with the law it made little difference that he was a slave, revealing vendors' status between slavery and freedom as slaves took up the vending occupations of their masters. Ribeiro had been a mascate who passed on the skills of mascataria to his slave, technically an enslaved ganhador and not a free mascate. Hence the master formally appealed to authorities for reimbursement of the fine based on proof of the ganhador's license. Ribeiro apparently assumed that it did make a difference that his peddler was a slave and as such not trained in the measurements and weights associated with mascataria. Law enforcement officials held otherwise, contending that a slave could be charged with violating the laws of mascataria if he had been selling goods as a mascate. Vending practice more than slave status took precedence in this case.

In other instances, wearing the required metal pin or having the license at hand did not result in a ganhador's protection from public or private policing. The incident involving Estevão Benguela exemplifies the vulnerability of street ganhadores.[23] An enslaved man shipped from the African port of Benguela, Estevão was one of the many African-born ganhadores working in Rio's street commerce. As he was returning to his master's house on 5 September 1850 an hour after the six o'clock curfew, a pedestrian accosted Estevão and beat him.[24] Eyewitnesses recounted how Estevão defended himself by showing his ganhador's license, but his attacker took it from him and then tied him up. A neighbor who knew Estevão and his master confronted the attacker, who responded that he had been privately hired to capture a fugitive slave who looked just like Estevão. The victim was eventually released from jail, but the assailant kept the ganhador's license and metal pin. Five days later, Estevão's master submitted an official complaint to the municipality because of the inappropriate trespassing of fugitive slave policing; he also requested replacements of his slave's license and metal pin and stated that he did not intend to pay for them. Whether he received them is unknown, but Estevão would have probably still felt unprotected or vulnerable with them.

Licensed street sellers could fall victim to the abusive policing of ranked police officers, as an incident that occurred 15 March 1872 demonstrates. On that day a group of licensed *quitandeiros* (produce vendors) set up their post to sell vegetables in the Praça das Marinhas, one of Rio's main food markets in Candelária. The local inspector soon approached them claiming that their licenses were invalid and "confiscating all vegetables and immediately auctioning them off to passersby." Later in the day, infuriated by this abuse of power, the quitandeiros walked to the inspector's office in Candélaria to protest the unjust confiscation of their licenses. The inspector dismissed their complaint by responding, "Take it to the newspaper!" Peddlers sometimes found support in the capital city's liberal press, but this time the offended quitandeiros did not go to a newspaper office. They instead filed a complaint with the city council and wanted their licenses returned immediately, with payment for the confiscated vegetables. In their complaint they accused the inspector of unfair treatment, arguing that many other quitandeiros of the Praça das Marinhas were selling without licenses because they were the inspector's "protected ones."[25]

At the beginning of the nineteenth century the term *mercado* (street market) generally defined any agglomeration of people who regularly sold goods in a specific open-air location.[26] Since colonial times, authorities had regulated vending practices by designating specific locations for the sale of certain items. In 1637, officials allowed slaves to sell fruits and vegetables only outside the perimeter of the city. The previous year, municipal law established that fish could only be sold at Praia de Nossa Senhora do Carmo, a central port area between the Largo do Paço and Rua da Alfândega. This spot became commonly known as Praia do Peixe (Fish Beach), where in the nineteenth century wooden stalls for selling fish still stood near the main food market in Candelária. In 1830 the municipality established that only the owners of market stalls and cosignatories were allowed to sell fish to the public and would be fined for rancid goods.[27] Peddlers of fish, who were primarily enslaved and free men born in Africa, frequented Rio's commercial center as vendors. During the first half of the nineteenth century, slave owners commonly requested ganhador licenses for their slaves to sell fish. By the middle of the century, the number of nonslaves taking out licenses to sell fish on the street increased considerably. Fish vending had not become an exclusive domain even though the 1830 posturas aimed to protect suppliers. Small fish markets sprang up throughout the city, especially near central beach areas, as population increase led to new centers of food distribution. In 1859 Antônio Pereira da Silva requested a license to establish a small fish market at Praça da Igrejinha to address residents' needs in the growing suburban district of São Cristovão.[28]

Praça do Mercado, also known as the Mercado da Candelária, was the primary market square in nineteenth-century Rio. Around 1830 the traveler Robert Walsh observed market stalls that exposed "piteous" fruits, fish, and meat, as slaves sold sweets, refreshments, coffee, and food in nearby streets and plazas.[29] The space in the Mercado da Candelária was organized to improve the conditions for selling clean foods such as meat and fish that had been sold in the nearby Praia do Peixe. Candelária's new marketplace was divided into three main parts: the center offered the sale of fruits, vegetables, fowl, and eggs; the side facing Guanabara Bay was for fresh and salted fish; and the area facing the Largo do Paço, near the imperial palace, was meant for dried goods, cereals, and flour. A total of 111 *barracas* (wooden stalls) composed the Praça do Mercado; in 1853 all were occupied, with 29 for selling fish, 48 for dry goods, and 34 for vegetables and fowl. At least 31 barracas were run by municipal officers and accountants, and the rest were reserved for private sellers who would acquire the necessary city license.[30]

With this concentration of trade in central Rio, the working poor regularly came together to socialize around food. Port workers habitually stopped by the market in Candelária to grab a bite after a day's work. In 1864, owners of barracas applied for a special license to remain open until 4:30 rather than 2:30 in the afternoon in order to serve the stevedores who finished work after 2 p.m.[31] Vendors regularly walked onto piers selling fruit and other refreshments to workers, a practice that reformers targeted at the end of the nineteenth century.[32]

The regulation of vending practices in Candelária reflected the rationalization of space and commerce and its ties with the outer reaches of the city. The Praia do Peixe was renamed Praça das Marinhas (Marina Plaza) in the nineteenth century. Meat was typically sold in Candelária's main market and fish at the Marina Plaza. Goods sold there could not be resold by others if exposed to the public for more than six hours. The town council established the regulation of prices and measurements and outlawed *atravessadores* (resellers) from

FIGURE 1.1. Rio de Janeiro's center and port area, ca. 1880. Photograph by Marc Ferrez. Courtesy of G. Ermakoff Casa Editorial, Arquivo Images2You.

the city who traditionally purchased goods in the city to sell at higher prices in rural or semirural areas.[33] Vendors who sold vegetables from their boats along the city's bayfront, many of them near the main market square, were required to be licensed the same as those on shore. It was common for *lavradores* (small-scale growers) to bring their produce in boats and offer cheaper prices to disadvantaged buyers or to middlemen.[34] In 1850, lavradores who transported food by boat or foot into the city did not have formal vending locations. In 1850, lavradores requested that the city council grant them a space for selling goods near the Marina Plaza, but it was not until 1874 that they gained a vending location near that spot.[35]

Throughout the course of the nineteenth century, the municipality formalized small open-air markets in the city since the Mercado da Candelária alone could not supply the entire population of the Brazilian capital city. The Mercado da Glória appeared in 1840, as did other small marketplaces around the same time that were similar in size to the small mercados of the colonial era.[36] In the district of Santa Rita, the Mercado da Harmonia was created in 1853 and was as sophisticated as the marketplace in Candelária. The proximity of these new marketplaces to *cortiços* ("beehives," urban tenements) further enhanced consumption and socializing around street vending activities. And markets changed as Rio's population grew (figure 1.1). In 1872 the municipality transformed street barracas into *chalets*, embellished and sanitized stalls with sun umbrellas, to "better serve the less fortunate people of Rio and their basic needs."[37] By the 1890s, however, small market centers near cortiços were shut down in the interest of public health and urban renewal.

While ganhador licenses reflect a male-dominated street commerce, sources from police records to travelers' accounts agree that many talented street sellers in Brazil were African-born women.[38] Slave owners considered African-born Mina women to be very skilled in the art of marketeering.[39] Many sold fish on the street, while women known as *ganhadeiras peixeiras* were also common in port areas. Slave owners seeking to profit from urban vending specifically desired to purchase "strong and corpulent" black women "of the [African] coast" to sell goods on the street. Urban residents knew well, according to British traveler Daniel Kidder, that African women had "great commercial wisdom."[40] For that reason, Mina women who had honed their marketeering skills in African urban centers sold as quitandeiras on Brazilian urban streets.[41] Street commerce carried out by West African women was a transatlantic experience that encompassed Brazil and the Caribbean.[42] In several West African societies, women were pillars of commercial activity, circulating basic goods for family sustenance. As a result, Nagô, Jeje, Mina, and Bantu-speaking women came to dominate street commerce in Brazilian Atlantic cities such as Rio, Recife, Salvador, and São Paulo. Brazilian-born female slaves (*crioulas*) were not as involved in street commerce since slave owners preferred them for domestic work, a pattern that changed only slightly in the latter half of the nineteenth century.[43] In 1849 in Rio, 66.4 percent of the slave population was born in Africa and 33.5 percent in Brazil, a ratio reflected in the ganho system and the practices of urban vending.[44] Fluency in the Portuguese language was thus not a necessary condition for street work in the ganho system.

Urban quitandeiras occupied several corners and squares where they sold fruits, vegetables, and herbs from barracas and small wooden tables known as *tabuleiros*. Spaces near churches and religious brotherhoods serving the city's black population were the most common. The chronicler and Rio resident Joaquim Manuel de Macedo (1820–1882) described the market by the church Nossa Senhora do Rosário, which also housed the Afro-Brazilian brotherhood Irmandade de Nossa Senhora do Rosário dos Homens Pretos, as an area that quitandeiras dominated. Macedo notes the shameful "decaying, pestilent, and unhygienic" state of the church, which he describes as in "ruins" in the middle of the nineteenth century. "The streets that surround the church complete the sad picture," he laments.[45] On one side of the church, barracas and tabuleiros occupied Largo da Sé, where African-born quitandeiras offered daily spectacles of inappropriate behavior, insulting outcries, and gales of laughter that offended passersby "who were not habituated to such dialects of indecency and immorality." Although Macedo recalls the church's "glorious era" and religious festivities, its time had passed. Now in the 1850s–1860s, the city council was putting an end to such "primitive" behavior.[46] Quitandeiras selling throughout the city thus became the targets of increased policing and public scorn.[47]

Around the time that Macedo expressed his indignation about the quitandeiras in Largo da Sé, the city council passed measures to improve the conditions of street marketeering in wealthier neighborhoods. In 1860 officials besieged the quitandeiras in the district of Lagoa, specifically the barracas near Botafogo's beach and São Clemente Street. The 1844 law established the need for licenses and protection of food from the sun when sold in market stalls, and in 1860 the municipality agreed to supply barracas with *chapéus de sol* (sun umbrellas) with license registrations. Quitandeiras were given up to eight days to pay in full for the licenses for their barracas.[48] The issue that most concerned authorities, more than having the appropriate chapéu de sol, was the disorderly manner in which quitandeiras occupied a marketplace and offended respectable residents. In 1870 residents of the district of Sacramento complained that quitandeiras selling sweets off tabuleiros in the Largo da Carioca and Rua Gonçalves Dias "obstructed public transit."[49] They noted that although the inspector already had arrested some quitandeiras, the problem persisted. Neighbors objected that even if arrested, quitandeiras "did not leave silently, but insulting officials" and causing great disarray. Since colonial times, enslaved and free quitandeiras had asserted their right to public space for selling food throughout the city (figure 1.2). Regular clashes with the police demonstrated quitandeiras' resistance, organizational skills, and role in supplying goods to other urban residents.[50]

Ganhador licenses permitted immigrant vendors to move throughout the city peddling a range of goods from fruits and vegetables to metal spoons and glass bottles. Portuguese vendors as well as enslaved ganhadores commonly sold fish up to the middle of the nineteenth century.[51] Other foreign-born residents also made a living as ganhadores. On 14 June 1862 the Frenchman Henry Jannit, who owned an ice storeroom on Rua Praia do Sacco, requested a license to sell ice on the street. Peddlers typically sold ice from handcarts that had to display the name of the seller in wax. Ice was commonly used to preserve fruits in the market stalls of Candelária's main square.[52] Wood for cooking was similarly sold at markets and from carts that ganhadores typically pushed.[53] Owners of taverns, coffee warehouses, and *botequins* (small bars or coffee shops) solicited licenses to sell ground, roasted coffee from streetside tables. Some Portuguese and Spanish shop owners licensed their *caixeiros* (clerks) to work as ganhadores selling coffee and other goods from their taverns and botequins. The Spanish immigrant Francisco Paz requested a ganhador's license to sell coffee on the street that was brewed in a tavern on Rua das Marrecas. The owner of the tavern was his fiador.[54]

Ganhador licenses from the latter half of the century illustrate that shops, warehouses, and small factories were centers of distribution where patrons supplied vendors with goods to sell throughout the city. Although vending practices were shifting with European immigration, shopkeepers still employed ganhadores of African descent and remained close to the Afro-Brazilian client base. In 1874 José Pinto Moreira, whose ethnic background remains unknown, requested a license "to continue selling coffee in front of the church Nossa Senhora da Candelária." The religious brotherhood Irmandade da Nossa Senhora da Candelária had given José permission to sell in an area that would not disturb passersby.[55] This brotherhood provided protection and mutual aid to Afro-descendant residents who were not enslaved.[56] Owners of cigar and cigarette factories likewise requested licenses to have street sellers in transited areas such as the city's main train station.[57] The ganho system was a means to distribute goods to passersby, and the items that peddlers sold mostly came from suppliers with shops, according to license registrations.

Vendedor de tabaco, Jean-Baptiste Debret's 1825 painting of a tobacco seller and enslaved ganhadores, illustrates a shopkeeper supplying tobacco to a slave who is shackled to five others (figure 1.3). The slaves depicted may

FIGURE 1.2. Quitandeiras, 1875. Photograph by Marc Ferrez. Courtesy of G. Ermakoff Casa Editorial, Arquivo Images2You.

FIGURE 1.3. Tobacco seller and enslaved ganhadores, 1825. Lithograph by Jean-Baptiste Debret. Courtesy of G. Ermakoff Casa Editorial, Arquivo mages2You.

have belonged to the shop owner, and the tobacco may have been destined for street selling or carrying to another destination. The shopkeeper may have hired these enslaved men from someone else, or the enslaved men depicted could be picking up their earnings as ganhadores. Street vending persisted as a branch of fixed commerce into the twentieth century. By supplying vendors, shopkeepers facilitated the link between formal and informal selling practices through patronage. While street commerce was a formal economic activity that was licensed and regulated, it still could operate informally with connections to well-established suppliers. The officer depicted on the right reflects the regulatory role of the police in overseeing vending.

LICENSING FREE GANHADORES

The licensing of free ganhadores took place in 1858–1867, 1879, and 1880–1886, three periods that reflect different moments in the gradual turn from enslaved to free labor. Prior to 1858, few free ganhadores requested licenses, and in the 1860s the licensing of enslaved ganhadores virtually disappeared.

After the midcentury halt in slave importation and turn toward free labor, authorities started to reveal the consequences of the turn to free labor in the area of street commerce as they became more concerned with the regulation of free ganhadores. After the passing of the 1871 Free Womb Law, the city council was increasingly preoccupied with disciplining the activities of free ganhadores since immigrants were entering the city in higher numbers. The new regulation regarding free ganhadores protected the relations between patrons and clients often forged in slavery.[58] Guarantors became as important as slave masters in acquiring licenses for ganhadores, and patronage continued to shape the horizontal and vertical relations that made up the world of street commerce and allowed for the social mobility.[59]

Consequently, the licensing procedures for enslaved and free ganhadores remained similar between 1850 and 1888. Throughout the 1850s and 1860s, the municipality licensed twenty-six free ganhadores of Portuguese, Spanish, Brazilian, and African descent.[60] By 1878 the number exceeded that of those two decades combined but was considered low at the time and a signal to officials that most free street workers preferred to remain unlicensed. Policing therefore intensified efforts to punish unlicensed ganhadores and discipline the street. As a result, more vendors took out licenses after 1878, as arresting unlicensed street sellers was a recurrent issue into the twentieth century.

Ganhadores generally took out licenses from the municipality in the presence of a scribe and treasurer. If literate, the free ganhador tended to sign the license registration himself; usually a scribe or guarantor signed for an illiterate ganhador. In some instances, self-employed free ganhadores represented themselves and paid for their own licenses and registration. Still, most free ganhadores were illiterate and poor and had to rely on the resources of patrons. By 1886 a guarantor was no longer required for ganhadores to attain licenses, and regulatory responsibility over ganhadores fell more heavily on the police.

The fiador was legally responsible for the ganhador's behavior. The ganho system thus reproduced the dependency between patrons and clients, analogous to the relations between urban slaves and masters. One fiador could sponsor several ganhadores at a time, which was the case in 1867 when the *negociante* (businessman) Manuel José da Silva sponsored four Portuguese men sharing the same residence in the São José district.[61] Between 1858 and 1867 several fiadores from Candelária sponsored African-born ganhadores who were former slaves. They were men described as Mina, Cassangê, and Congo who shared the same residences with their fiadores (and probable ex-masters). In 1855 João Pinheiro sponsored Anastásio of the Cabinda nation to work as a messenger for the royal court, as it was also common for the government to employ African ganhadores as builders, cooks, messengers, and drivers.[62]

FIGURE 1.4. Fowl vendors, 1825. Lithograph by Jean-Baptiste Debret. Courtesy of G. Ermakoff Casa Editorial, Arquivo Images2You.

Immigrant participation in street commerce incorporated and changed existing vending practices during the latter half of the nineteenth century. African-born men and women tended not to be involved in the street selling of red meat because of its higher market value. Peddlers of this type tended to be Portuguese and free Brazilian-born men of light skin color who sold meat they got from traditional *açougues* (butcher shops) mostly located on the Catete neighborhood's main street.[63] Earlier in the century Debret painted the enslaved men who sold chickens (*galinhas*) that they carried in big straw baskets over their heads (figure 1.4). Debret shows fowl placed in baskets—usually destined for more formal marketplaces—and poultry with feet tied and carried on sticks by *pombeiros* (fowl vendors) who tended to sell on the street. European immigrants later adopted these techniques and peddled on the street barefoot like slaves, encountering conditions analogous to slavery not only in the ganho system but in the shared material conditions of poverty. In 1895 Marc Ferrez photographed barefoot European immigrant vendors carrying birds in big baskets on their heads like the black peddlers Debret painted in 1825.[64]

In January 1879 municipal officials remarked that the previous year they had only licensed thirty-nine ganhadores, although immigrant participation on the street had visibly increased. The low number shed light on the decrease in slaves working on the street. The passing of the 1871 Free Womb Law and subsequent migrations pushed the free population in Rio from 185,000 in 1870 to 220,088 in 1872, while the slave population decreased from 50,092 to 48,939.[65] Municipal officials claimed that the absence of ganhador license requests in 1878 was largely a result of this shift since immigrants had "invaded" the city and "deliberately neglected to obtain licenses as ordered by Title 5, Section 2, and Paragraph 5 of the Municipal Code."[66] Immigrants who became ganhadores preferred to remain unlicensed and unmarked by an institution associated with slavery, as had African-born free ganhadores in the Northeastern coastal city Salvador da Bahia in 1857.[67] These free black ganhadores, many of whom were former slaves, formally resisted the municipal ordinance that obligated them to wear a chapa, claiming that such a mark forced on them was like being identified as a slave. The stricter policing of free ganhadores seemed to follow the frequent police observation that "indigent immigrants were causing much more than their share of trouble on the streets" of Rio.[68]

Given authorities' apprehension about the large number of unlicensed ganhadores on Rio's streets, more street policing led to the licensing of 757 ganhadores during July and August 1879.[69] From July 25 to July 30 alone, more than 100 ganhadores took out licenses, an unprecedented number that reflected the stricter enforcement of ganho laws. One of the first men to be licensed was the former slave Domingos Bernadino, who had been a "vendor with a basket" (*empregado com cesto*) since 1877. He had started to work as a ganhador while enslaved, which was the case of most free blacks who roamed the streets of Rio carrying baskets. In his request Bernadino stated that he was unable to continue working unless licensed. He had been arrested and then compelled to take out a ganhador's license. The metal pin he had to wear was a probable reminder of a slave past that he preferred to forget but could not escape as a free man.

Europeans engaged in street commerce throughout the colonial period, making African slaves carry their items. In the second half of the nineteenth century, Europeans returned to the streets in greater numbers and applied for "black ganhador licenses," the term street vendors commonly used whether enslaved or free. Immigrants thus entered one municipal system that organized free and enslaved street labor.[70] The ganho system's licensing process racialized Europeans in an Atlantic setting where slavery's violent uprooting of men and women born in Africa influenced the migration of poor, free Europeans to the Americas and the population of ganhadores in the Brazilian capital.[71]

Although the vending landscape in Rio was rapidly changing as a result of immigrant participation, half of the licensed ganhadores in 1879 were still

Brazilian-born. This group took out approximately 47 percent of the ganhador licenses that year; Portuguese ganhadores took out 24 percent, Africans 18 percent, and Italians and Spaniards less than 5 percent each. A small number of slaves appeared in the municipal record books of free ganhadores, indicative of how slaves and free workers applied for licenses side by side. Enslaved and free ganhadores did not share the same guarantors. Most license registrations did not list fiadores' professions, but the ones that did show that guarantors were mostly negociantes (39 percent). A smaller number of registrations indicate that some fiadores were proprietors, government employees, carpenters, and construction workers. Those who declared themselves to be government employees were civil servants, policemen, military officials, and judges who hired ganhadores for official or personal use.

Business owners' home addresses and those where ganhadores lived illustrate the concentration of petty commerce in Rio. Patrons who were negociantes lived for the most part in the more affluent Candelária district, whereas few free ganhadores resided there although they worked there. Other areas with significant concentrations of fiadores were Sacramento and São José. Fewer patrons and ganhadores took out licenses the farther away the former resided from central Rio. The peripheral district of Engenho Novo at this time was not home to any patrons of street commerce, but several ganhadores lived there, according to license requests. Fiadores tended to live in townhomes that had shops on the ground floor where some ganhadores lived and worked. Downtown shopkeepers also rented market stalls in nearby plazas, and from these they supplied ganhadores.

The São José district housed the highest number of free ganhadores after 1850, as immigrants from southern Europe tended to settle there. São José was one of Rio's oldest neighborhoods and known for being crowded, poor, and unclean. Urban renewal in the early twentieth century addressed its perceived squalor by flattening the Morro do Castelo, the hill with a cortiço that mainly characterized this district.[72] A significant number of free ganhadores also inhabited Sacramento and Santana. African Mina workers tended to live in Santana, which the historians Flávio dos Santos Gomes and Carlos Eugênio Líbano Soares have described as Rio's "true African citadel of the second half of the nineteenth century."[73] Among Rio's districts, Santana had the lowest number of slaves in the first half nineteenth century and, after Sacramento, the largest free population.[74] The African citadel was mostly composed of free black workers, many with ties to the ganho system.

White immigrants who became ganhadores entered an urban system that developed out of slavery, while free black ganhadores represented the slave past. License registrations tended not to state the ages of the ganhadores, but older African-born ganhadores had been working on the city's streets for decades. Such was the case of the sixty-year-old Mina liberto named David Cabello de Goma. David's last name, which translates as "hair of rubber," centered on a physical feature and reveals his previous status as a slave. David continued to work for his former master, the owner of a wet and dry goods shop in today's neighborhood Bairro da Saúde. The former master turned guarantor of a free ganhador may have freed David to ensure years of servitude and a lasting patron-client relationship.

Many free Africans, like their slave counterparts, worked for suppliers who produced certain goods such as beer or bread that ganhadores then sold on the street or delivered to households and small businesses. Africans soliciting licenses were mostly Mina, and although scribes were not consistent about noting African nations in free ganhador licenses of the 1870s and 1880s, their nations usually appeared as last names. Accordingly, sixty-two were Mina, six Cabinda, five Congo, two Mozambique, two Benguela, one Angola, one Mangue, and one Cassangê. If the registry noted that a ganhador required a license to work as a *carregador* (porter), an occupation usually associated with slave labor, applicants tended to be African-born men. However, some Portuguese ganhadores were also porters, as it was a common and respectable line of work for underprivileged Europeans living in port cities.

According to the 1879 registry, of the 187 free Africans licensed as ganhadores, 20 percent were ex-slaves who continued to maintain labor arrangements and shared residences with their ex-masters. Africans whose last names were the same as the corresponding fiadores are a strong indicator that they had been the guarantors' slaves, even if living in separate locations.[75] The African ganhador Caetano de Mendonça lived on Rua Princesa dos Cajueiros in Santana, and his fiador, Marques de Mendonça, lived on Rua da Alfândega in Candelária. One license registration did specify the fiador as being the ganhador's former master: Sebastião Martins de Azevedo was a businessman on Rua Visconde de Itauá in Candelária who sponsored the Brazilian-born Martins de Azevedo. The ganhador carried his ex-master's last name but lived on his own on Rua São Pedro in Sacramento. Of the African ganhadores who were possibly the ex-slaves of guarantors, 23 percent lived in the same residences as their fiadores. José Gomes of the Congo nation was a porter and the ex-slave of Augustinho Leopoldo de Sousa Guimarães; both fiador and ganhador lived in the same house on Rua do Rezende in Santo Antônio. Three African Mina men, João, Pedro, and Júlio Felix, shared a residence with the same fiador and ex-master on Rua Lourenço in Santana. Groups of African ganhadores who acquired licenses together usually lived in the same places and shared the same guarantors.

Only one woman registered in 1879 as the guarantor of an African ganhador. Leoparda, a midwife (*parteira*), sponsored Manuel Feliz Veloso, whom she described as "very loyal" (*muito fiel*). They lived in separate residences, but this may also be an example of a former master-slave relationship. It was common for the license registrations of Africans who had been slaves to include statements like this from their fiadores; another such description was "well accustomed and vouched for his good behavior" (*pessoa de bons costumes e de conduta afiancada*). Some documents even state that the fiador "is responsible for the behavior of this free black man" (*responsabiliza-se pela conduta do preto livre*) to appease anxieties generated by the growth of the free population of color. The emphasis on proper behavior echoed the language of newspaper ads announcing the sale of slaves as being "very loyal" and "well behaved." Although all free ganhadores required official guardianship, the legacy of slavery pushed some fiadores to distinguish free African ganhadores as trustworthy—a descriptor that never appeared in the license registrations of free European immigrant men.

Portuguese men were the largest immigrant group to take out licenses in 1879. Some fiadores who backed Portuguese men also sponsored free African ganhadores. In July 1879 Domingos Machado, a negociante on Rua do Rosário in Candelária, sponsored both Ernesto Federico do Nascimento, a forty-year-old Portuguese immigrant, and a free African Mina named Luis. The absence of a last name reveals that Luis had been a slave. Portuguese immigrants regularly stated that they were requesting licenses as a means for earning a living and supporting their families. This was the case of Manuel de Oliveira Cardoso, who worked for a shopkeeper of wet and dry goods (*secos e molhados*). Several free descendants of Africans stated that they were soliciting ganhador licenses to continue working on the street. A third of all Portuguese men requested ganhador licenses in groups with individuals who were related and/or resided in the same places, often in the cortiços of São José.

The number of Italian and Spanish ganhadores in license requests combined was less than half the proportion of Portuguese applicants in 1879. This suggests that most Spaniards and Italians performing ganho work were on the street without licenses, especially considering the numerous arrests and detentions of Italians at the turn of the century. A small number of Italians did take out licenses with compatriots; that rate was considerably higher among Spanish ganhadores. According to the residences listed in license requests, Italians preferred to settle in Santana, the African citadel, and in Santo Antônio, while Spaniards tended to reside in São José, which was heavily populated by their fellow Iberians from Portugal.

Most of the small-business owners who sponsored ganhadores resided in the affluent central district Candelária. Owners of secos e molhados tended to live in the Portuguese-dominated São José district, the Portuguese stronghold of petty commerce in the Brazilian capital. Other fiadores were bakery proprietors (*donos de padaria*) and owners of warehouses of some sort, such as coffee, cloth, wood, and maintenance gear. Some ran *casas de pasto* (small restaurants), botequins, and kiosks, selling prepared foods and items like lottery tickets, cigarettes, and coffee. Smaller numbers of fiadores were pharmacists, beer brewers (*fabricantes de cerveja*), tavern owners (*taverneiros*), and owners of small stores that sold cheese, ham, tobacco, perfume, and knick-knacks.

Most fiadores were Brazilian and Portuguese negociantes, the latter known for monopolizing Rio's petty commerce and the former for inspiring violent anti-Portuguese sentiment among Brazilians earlier in the century.[76] Foreign-born fiadores in the ganho system came from other countries in smaller numbers. One was the Englishman John Crashley, who lived on Travessa do Ouvidor and had good Portuguese writing skills when he sponsored the ganhador Manuel de Almeida. License requests do not list any Italian-born fiadores, as Italian immigrants in these years tended to be poor and underprivileged, experiencing little social mobility. Some Spaniards were fiadores and even became successful negociantes, having settled in Rio earlier in the century. The Spaniard Vicente González Pinto sponsored four Spanish ganhadores in July 1879. All four workers shared the same residence with each other and with their fiador on Rua do Lavradio in Santo Antônio. They all worked at this location, which was also a casa de pasto that González Pinto managed with a Portuguese co-owner.

Bartolomeu Peres, a Spanish shopkeeper of dry and wet goods, sponsored two Spanish immigrants in August 1879, one of them specifically to work as a porter. Other license requests from 1879 indicate that Peres also sponsored one ganhador from Mozambique and four Brazilian-born workers. Peres's name reappeared in four license requests of 1886, when he sponsored more Brazilian-born ganhadores. Three of these ganhadores shared the same residence as Peres, which was also where his store was located. The ganhadores likely lived in a room behind the shop, as was common for many caixeiros. Peres enjoyed a prosperous life as his business grew during a time of political and social upheaval. He sponsored several ganhadores throughout a decade in the same shop location. A Spanish shopkeeper thus had been able to consistently employ ganhadores of various origins during a transitional era when patron-client relations strongly influenced urban free labor. His license applications shed a different light than the traditional Portuguese monopoly on Rio's petty commerce.

João da Cunha was a classic example of a Portuguese shopkeeper in central

Rio. He owned an established charcuterie in 1879 that sold cheese, pork, and tobacco and was likely connected to the Atlantic trade that supplied him with Iberian goods.[77] João da Cunha sponsored four Portuguese and three Spanish ganhadores. Two of the Spanish ganhadores lived in the same hostel on Rua da Ajuda. All seven ganhadores were hired as the shopkeeper's *caixeiros à venda*, delivering goods and selling them on the street. Da Cunha hired the Spaniard José Ramos Sanchez to work as a ganhador with a cart (*carreta*). The fiador had no history of sponsoring African- or Brazilian-born ganhadores, indicating the strong Iberian presence in Rio's petty commerce.

Unlike European-born shopkeepers, bakery owners employed more Brazilian than immigrant ganhadores. The city's bread industry was rooted in urban slave society and became an important site for the employment of free men of African descent. In 1861 bakery proprietors submitted a complaint to municipal authorities showing that by then they hired free rather than enslaved men to deliver and sell bread. Since deliverymen were not selling goods on the street, owners of bakeries contended that the license requirement should be waived for their deliverymen. These owners could not afford to purchase slaves, so they employed free men. They argued that they could not afford the additional costs of licensing. The distinction they made between hiring free men who delivered bread (*entregadores*) and free men who sold bread on the streets (*ambulantes*) intended to shed light on their choice not to use slaves, for which they believed they should be compensated by not having to take on the cost of licensing free vendors.[78] The bread industry's participation in the abolitionist movement revealed owners' economic as well as humanitarian concerns.[79]

Negociantes who ran botequins, kiosks, taverns, and casas de pasto relied on ganho labor and street vending to extend commerce and reach distant urban consumers. Rodrigo de Sousa Ribeiro managed a botequim on Praça das Marinhas and sponsored one Portuguese and two Brazilian-born ganhadores to sell goods throughout the city. The Portuguese ganhador lived in the immigrant enclave of São José and the Brazilians in the parish of Sacramento. Domingos de Sousa ran a kiosk on Largo da Carioca and hired one Portuguese and two Spanish ganhadores. The fiador José Joaquim owned a kiosk in Candelária and sponsored the ganhador Francisco Coelho da Motta to "make baskets throughout the city" and "earn a living by carrying goods in open baskets over his head." A kiosk owner on Praça Dom Pedro II employed two Portuguese ganhadores for similar activities. The fiadores assisted customers from inside the kiosks and other business sites, and street ganhadores walked streets near and far selling and carrying goods for their guarantors.

Owners of small restaurants and taverns also employed street ganhadores who tended to be Portuguese or Brazilian-born men. One tavern owner sponsored three Portuguese men who all lived on the same street in São José. A few fiadores brewed beer and employed Brazilian ganhadores who mostly lived in Santa Rita. One brewer sponsored an African Mina to carry and sell beer on the street and shared a residence with him in Santo Antônio.

The city council continued to issue ganhador licenses throughout the 1880s, as the policing of ganhadores increased. From 1880 through 1886, fifty-six licenses were registered. By the mid-1880s, Italians comprised the largest ethnic or national group of licensed free ganhadores. More Italian immigrants landed in Rio at this time, and they subsequently took out ganhador licenses in larger numbers. In general, more European- than Brazilian- or African-born workers requested licenses now. Italian ganhadores tended to live in Santana, the so-called African citadel of the nineteenth century. By the 1880s, however, Afro-Brazilians were moving to other areas of the capital city such as Praça Onze and Gamboa. At the same time, European immigrants rapidly settled in central Rio as employer preference for European immigrants in the city center further displaced Afro-descendants to the city's outer neighborhoods. In the 1880s, as opposed to the 1870s, tavern owners were the most common type of guarantors, sponsoring several Italian ganhadores. Most negociantes still lived in Candelária, but only one who applied for a license in the 1880s traded from that area's old commercial hub in the Marina Plaza. Several fiadores and their ganhadores continued to share residences on the eve of abolition, reflecting ongoing patron-client relations that endured into the twentieth century.[80]

Changes in the regulation of the ganho system by the mid-1880s anticipated the imminent end of slavery and the transition from private to public or individual to state supervision of street workers. The one African-born man who requested a ganhador's license in 1886 did not have or need the guardianship of a fiador that year. Instead, before soliciting a license from the municipality, ganhadores registered first with the police. Upon registration, ganhadores received matriculation numbers that substituted the need for guarantors when they retrieved licenses from the municipality. Police registration replaced the fiador, a pattern that was present in other regulatory changes that placed Rio's police as administrators of street activities such as religious festivals. The city council ceased to directly oversee such events in the 1880s, passing on that responsibility to the police.[81] The ganhador licenses registered in 1886 and 1887 reveal this shift from municipal to police administration, foreshadowing a legal culture that positioned the police as street commerce's main regulators during the early postabolition period.

THE GANHO SYSTEM AS AN URBAN INSTITUTION OF TRANSITION

Street vending and the ganho system, both vital institutions for the maintenance of Brazilian urban slave society, remained crucial to Rio in the latter half of the nineteenth century and the transition to freedom and free labor. Ganho labor shifted from a slaveholding arrangement to a structure that organized slave and free labor under one municipal system. The licensing requirements for free ganhadores established in 1838 were influenced by the emerging populations of free and freed workers of African descent. The subsequent passing of gradual abolitionist laws starting in 1850 and especially after the 1871 Free Womb Law created pull factors for Europeans, especially from the southern peninsulas, to migrate to Brazil. The influx of poor Europeans who typically regarded street vending as a basic opportunity to earn a living in the city entered the world of urban trade and pressured the ganho system to manage immigrant labor. The substantial licensing of free ganhadores that took place in July and August 1879 demonstrates that the policing of street labor was as much influenced by the growing numbers of European immigrant street workers as it was by the increasing presence of free people of color in the city.

Municipal regulation of street labor responded to a particular Atlantic experience of freedom that in Rio was conditioned by the legacies of slavery and the migrations stimulated by the transition to free labor. In having to solicit black ganhador licenses and follow municipal procedures that submitted Europeans to dependent relations with patrons and government, white immigrant workers participated in an Atlantic experience of freedom that was linked not only to the political economy of free labor but to the local practices of urban slave society. The ganho system was adapted to the conditions of free labor by organizing both free and slave street vendors.

By 1882, municipal authorities had eliminated distinctions between the fines incurred by slave and free ganhadores, reflecting how slave and free street labor could be managed with one system. The ganho system thus was transformed into an instrument for the gradual transition to free labor, and new laws reflected such adjustments.[82] Consequently, enslaved and free street vendors of African and European descent were structurally and experientially working between slavery and freedom. They negotiated the terms of their work with patrons, suppliers, customers, and municipal and police authorities habituated to the African slave origins of Rio's street commerce.

CHAPTER 2

A POLICED WORKPLACE

THE 1868 INAUGURAL EDITION of the Rio newspaper *O Trabalho* (Labor) opened with a mission statement that promised to speak in the name of all Brazilian workers. The newspaper was "filling this lacuna," which the authors identified as the absence of the working class in Brazilian nation building and industrial development. Moreover, the paper's founders sought to shed a "fraternal light on free labor obscured by centuries of slavery," hoping that "unoccupied field hands, so many uncultivated skills, [and] so many unhappy [workers] . . . [could] be free of the ignorance and vagrancy that steal from [free] labor to increase with lamentable permanence the growing statistics of crime." Free labor ideology here was inclusive of workers as artists, artisans, merchants, factory workers, and "laborers of all types from the rudest to the most delicate and complicated thinker, all producers, and finally and especially exploited agricultural workers." Unused labor, the editorial board argued, not only resulted in "ignorance and vagrancy" but in criminal activity; idleness was a threat to public order.[1] The policing of Rio's streets made manifest a sweeping view of vagrancy in punishing vendors as vagrants and therefore criminals. Writers who reported street policing in newspaper columns defended vendors as natural participants of free commerce and compatible with the era's liberal and free labor ideologies.

Anxieties about the transition from enslaved to free labor and the loss of property began to transform types of work performed by the poor into manifestations of pathological behavior. Free labor may have had the potential to liberate the individual's soul, according to Christian abolitionist thinking, but what qualified as legitimate labor generally excluded marginal lines of work performed by the urban poor. The legacy of slavery shaped impressions of free labor, and street vending carried out by free workers was not a desirable alternative for local officials in Rio wishing to erase the slave mark from the Brazilian capital.

In the late nineteenth century, Rio's main newspapers engaged in the debate over the future of free workers and discussions about urban crime. The press displayed the changing landscape of the city's streets that ganhador licenses also confirmed. Police arrests of petty thieves, interventions in illegal gambling, and restrictions on illegitimate street commerce appeared daily in newspaper columns that reported the events of street life. In their observations of peddlers and the law, news stories of the 1880s illustrated street vending at a crossroads between ganho regulation and criminal law, a lens also supported by the licensing system of the era. Police arrest and detention records further demonstrate this. While police authorities approached street behavior related to slavery and street commerce as criminal, liberal newspapers were less intransigent. For them, street vending, rather than a pathology or backwardness of slavery, was in effect a natural practice of free labor and commerce.

Changing perceptions of street commerce were hardly immediate or total, reflective of the general unevenness in the gradual shift to free labor. Newspaper writers expressed ambivalent attitudes toward the issue of social control, often depicting Rio's police force as ineffective or irrational but still necessary. The newspaper column Occorrencias das ruas (Street occurrences), published weekly in the prominent *Gazeta de Notícias* discussed everyday incidents involving police and the urban poor in Rio. The public's fascination with the city's underbelly led editors to publish the column on the paper's front page. Street vendors were frequent protagonists in the sardonic scenarios that writers re-created in favor of arrestees and mocking police officials.[2] An incident reported on 4 March 1883 between the Portuguese Antônio José da Fonseca and an unnamed ironsmith portrays the police unfavorably. Fonseca's attempt to sell a horse to an ironsmith for a modest price prompted the column's writer to mock the "idiot" ironsmith for not accepting such a bargain. According to the weekly observer, the situation worsened when the candid ironsmith notified the police of the stolen horse, unnecessarily involving officials and leading to the arrest of all involved—the Portuguese seller, the horse, and the ironsmith. "Well done, Mr. Ironsmith!" the article concludes.[3] Another column in 1883 describes two Englishmen selling cigarettes in the city's port area at night when they were arrested for selling stolen goods.[4] The writer remarks, "Decidedly, the freedom of commerce has ended in this country!" and denounces the overregulation of street commerce and police obstruction of free trade and individual freedom that also limited Brazilian peddlers.

While front-page columns like Street Occurrences portray the landscape of a declining urban slave society, the classified section at the end of the paper illustrates the needs of proprietors inclined to hire free workers for street work. Slave-for-hire advertisements that previously dominated classifieds were practically nonexistent by the 1880s. Instead, employers wanted free workers. Throughout the nineteenth century newspapers supported slavery by serving men and women who wished to buy, sell, or hire slaves. With the gradual abolition of slavery, newspapers became a site for the hiring of free labor, including street vendors. Classified help-wanted ads for free male peddlers—"white or of color"—to sell food and other goods on the street still used old descriptions from the slave period, such as requiring workers to be "loyal," and exposed other legacies of slavery. An employer looking for a "boy (*menino*) or an old black woman to sell sweets in the neighborhood of Botafogo" revealed—in the juxtaposition of these two types of street sellers—the endurance of slave practices and the higher number of young free workers.[5] The term "menino" rather than *moleque* reflects an increase in the number of free immigrant and Brazilian children selling on the street. The term "old black woman" points at the slave practice of having aging women who were good sellers work on the street. The employer thus targeted different candidates of the transitional era. In newspaper classifieds and front-page columns, Rio's press participated in and reflected this changing landscape.

The enslaved and free workers who engaged in street commercial activities came into contact with the police in a variety of settings. The registry entries of the municipal House of Detention show that arrests of street peddlers resulted more in criminal charges than commercial or municipal infractions related to the system of ganho or their street trade. Registry books recorded the daily movement of enslaved and free detainees in and out of the detention center, noting the accused person's place of residence, nationality, age, civil status, occupation, skin color, literacy, and physical traits along with the date, place, and charge of the arrest. When analyzing the variables of gender, skin color, nationality, age, occupation, and reason for arrest, cross-referenced with the enslaved and free status of detainees, the policing of street vendors in the 1870s and 1880s appears to be more informed by the 1830 Criminal Code than by later municipal regulation of ganhadores or street commerce.

Although the ganho system regulated street selling through the use of licenses, criminal law increasingly was applied to street vendors regardless of licenses. In arresting and detaining black ganhadores at the turn of the century, the police treated them as suspected criminals committing acts of vagrancy and public disorder first and as workers earning a living through ganho work second.[6] Municipal officials attempted to regulate street commerce by formalizing the patron-client relations of the ganho system through licensing, while increasing policing as a form of regulation transformed vendors' workplace—the street—into a space of criminality. The detentions of street sellers between 1868 and 1888 reveal these structural and experiential dimensions of the transition to free labor. One the one hand, the laws of the ganho system such as licensing informed regulation and policing. On the other hand, antivagrancy laws increasingly dominated policing practices over license regulation.

Enslaved and free workers had traditionally shared similar lines of work in the Brazilian capital. Slaves, former slaves, European immigrants, and racially mixed Brazilians worked together in some of the city's factories, lived together in crowded cortiços, and peddled side by side on the street.[7] After the importation of slaves born in Africa ended, slaves in Brazil were largely sent to coffee plantations in the southeast. Urban slave labor was directed more toward transportation and freight services than to the ganho system, resulting in the greater presence of immigrant and other free laborers on city streets.[8] Although the argument of substitution has explained the presence of free immigrants in work practices that had been relegated to the enslaved, the supposed replacement of one group for another obscures the diversity of urban life. As in other Atlantic port cities, slave and free workers in Rio—African, black, mulatto, white, immigrant—composed the diverse working poor who shared struggles of poverty throughout the transition to free labor.

In Rio as in other Atlantic port cities, the free toiled alongside the enslaved. The history of Brazilian slavery and freedom is inaccurate when defined by the misperception that free labor—often considered synonymous with white immigrant workers—replaced black slave labor. The model of substitution has led to bipolar historical analyses of the late slave and early postabolition period, separating the labor history of the twentieth century from the history of nineteenth-century slavery. In a 2006 Brazilian social history, Flávio dos Santos Gomes and Antônio Luigi Negro discuss the experience of slavery alongside other forms of compulsory work based in free labor.[9] Africans, Brazilians, indigenous people of the Americas, and foreign immigrants often worked together in places other than plantations and factories. As a result, the more recent approach Seth Rockman describes toward the history of slavery and free labor has put "diverse workers into the same story," showing that class is a shared material condition more than a shared consciousness or identity.[10] Urban vendors came from a diverse population of African slaves and their descendants, immigrants from Europe and the declining Ottoman Empire, and indigenous Americans. They shared not only the same historical stage but also the poverty and informal networks that characterized street commerce in Rio.

As the state became increasingly involved in matters that had traditionally concerned the private authority of masters over slaves, urban slaves resorted to using the law against their masters in efforts to free themselves.[11] Slaves influenced Brazilian civil legislation and played a fundamental role in the legal process of dismantling slavery.[12] Still, state intervention in master-slave relations placed vendors under the gaze of the police. The arrest and incarceration of slave and free vendors in the Casa de Detenção reflected, Thomas Holloway notes, the persisting "attitudes and practices of the system of repression [that] were transferred smoothly to the nonslave lower classes."[13] The notion that the enslaved and free poor merited punishment and not a chance for rehabilitation was crucial to the maintenance of slave society. Alexandra Brown asserts, "Jails were intended to serve as repositories of detention rather than places where prisoners would be adequately punished or reformed. . . . The framers of the [1830] Criminal Code did not seek to transform free prisoners through the penitentiary model that focused on reflection and moral re-education."[14] The 1890 Penal Code was similar in this regard.

Punishing alleged criminal behavior rather than enforcing street commerce regulations was in line with the (un)official attitude toward freedom as slavery declined—that free labor and commerce were not to be enjoyed by all Brazilians. Policing measures revealed that street selling was not a practice of free commerce according to urban officials. The writer or writers of Street Occurrences argued otherwise. They defended peddlers as victims of excessive policing and advocated for vendors' right to earn a living. By the 1880s street commerce was on the edges of Rio's underground economy, the criminalized world, and entailed practices of subsistence and survival central to distributing goods in the city. Views in Street Occurrences were empathetic toward vendors and condemning toward police. Freedom would only be complete if all commerce and labor were entirely free, but freedom in Brazil's post-slave society would remain conditional and incomplete. Where writers may have seen the essence of free commerce in street selling, most urban officials saw an unwanted slave legacy that had to be at the very least restricted.

STREET PEDDLER DEMAND AND REGULATION IN A RIO NEWSPAPER

Newspaper advertisements exposed change in urban slave labor. In the early 1880s the *Gazeta de Notícias* classifieds regularly advertised employers' need for free street peddlers. Ads seeking to purchase or hire slave labor had decreased by the 1880s as the end of slavery became certain after passage of the 1871 Free Womb Law. Patron-client relations continued to shape street commerce, but now employers and suppliers promised good pay. They also requested that vendors be sponsored (*afiançado*) by guarantors, loyal (*fiel*), and of good conduct (*boa conduta*). The latter descriptors had characterized dependable workers in slave-for-sale and slave-for-hire advertisements and now persisted for free workers.[15]

Newspaper ads of the early 1880s were often searches for free street vendors to sell sweets, pastries, fruits, vegetables, ice cream, and cigars and cigarettes. The papers and gazettes themselves published announcements to hire street peddlers to sell the periodicals.[16] The widespread use of child *jornaleiros* (newspaper vendors) brings to light the demand for child labor that was also significant in the sale of sweets, cigarettes, and flowers. The slave period had defined certain street occupations for poor children and influenced employer preferences for young boys of "good conduct" (menino/*pequeno de boa conduta*). Since the passing of the 1871 Free Womb Law, however, the term moleque (indicating the slave status of a child) rarely appeared in newspaper ads for street vendors who were not adult men or women.

Formal relations among employers, suppliers, newspaper publishers, and peddlers shaped the world of street commerce as much as informal arrangements created the terms of employment. A classified ad from 19 January 1880 exposes the links between production, supply, and distribution in street vending. The employer in this case sought a free white or colored male to farm a small plot of land (*chácara*) and then sell fruits on the street.[17] Those interested in the work could inquire at a shop on Rua Visconde de Itaúna in the heart of the commercial Candelária; job ads for free laborers usually listed addresses where candidates could apply. The store sold goods that the chácara produced and peddlers then distributed throughout the city, expanding the owner's profits. This form of community outreach was typical of the ganho system. The goal was to reach a wide variety of buyers and consumers beyond the storefront. Vendors and their suppliers connected rural and suburban areas with the city center, expanding petty commerce and provisioning distant neighborhoods that downtown establishments could not reach otherwise.

Newspaper classifieds of the 1880s reflected other attributes of the ganho system that accommodated the new conditions of free labor and reproduced old practices of slavery. In particular, the language of patronage continued to appear in ads. An ad published on 6 April 1883 seeking a peddler of candy (*baleiro*) describes the job as paying well (*paga-se bem*) and the employer as "not seeing [skin] color" (*não se olhando a côr*). The inevitable end of slavery was pushing patrons to overlook skin color in a work that slaves had traditionally performed. The shifting cityscape, now including more European immigrants, transformed street commerce previously associated with Africans. In not seeing color the employer welcomed African descendants and white immigrants, opening the peddling of *balas* (candy)—traditionally associated with enslaved vendors—to new types of free workers. The ad also seems to indicate equal treatment toward free blacks and whites by claiming not to see color. The employer also promises that the seller would be "treated like a family member" (*trata-se como pessoa de família*), taking in the peddler as a worker whom the patron would house.[18] Advertisements like this one did not use the term *ganhador* in seeking free street vendors and thus avoided slavery-related terminology even if patronage was alive and well.

While newspaper classifieds portrayed the formal side of street commerce, the weekly Street Occurrences column in the *Gazeta de Notícias* reported events that situated peddling between formal and informal practices. Acts of thievery, public disorder, homicide, suicide, transportation accidents, gambling, and contraband were ill-fated events that merited nearly daily reporting. Contributors to Street Occurrences particularly addressed the detention of street vendors for allegedly breaking a law of the ganho system such as selling without a license. Reporters also noted several occasions when peddlers were arrested for violating acts of the 1830 Criminal Code. Discussion in this news section displayed a policing of street commerce that was influenced by municipal ordinance and criminal law yet leaning toward the latter.

The most frequently reported street occurrence was theft (*furto*), whether police arrested individuals for allegedly stealing or for selling stolen goods. Rockman describes similar conditions in the Atlantic port city of Baltimore during the early American republican years, when "officials knew that the underground economy in clothing, household goods, and even foodstuffs provided every incentive for needy people to engage in theft."[19] In addition to stolen goods often resold in stores and pawnshops, items that police suspected to be stolen were marketed on the street. Vendors who were enslaved tended to be usual suspects, as was the case of João, who in 1883 was arrested on Rua do Cotovelo for selling a piece of cashmere fabric, a parasol, and eight metal spoons. Since João was unable to give the policeman an explanation of the origin of such objects, he was arrested. The officer confiscated the goods, and hours later the owner of a store appeared at the precinct headquarters to recover his stolen possessions. The arrest of Inocêncio Cândido de Oliveira on 12 February 1883 also exemplifies the theft and informal selling of goods. The property owner Antônio Madeira accused Oliveira of stealing a pair of earrings. Upon arrest, the suspect confessed that he was guilty and no longer possessed the earrings, which he had sold to a tavern owner.[20]

Police and columnists alike identified several arrestees as thieves and *gatunos conhecidos* (known pickpockets) in their reports. Felisberto Antônio de Lemos Castro was reported as a "known thief, drunkard, and vagrant" who was arrested for selling stolen chairs on the street.[21] Newspaper writers frequently reported the occurrence of selling stolen poultry. Male street vendors of Portuguese, Chinese, and African descent were often arrested for selling fowl taken from backyards. Stealing fruits and vegetables from greengrocers to later sell on the street was another way for slaves and free people to get by. Police officers working a night shift in May 1883 caught a couple of men crawling into one of Rio's distinctive kiosks "to leave it empty."[22] In these cases, being a thief was also associated with being a vagrant (*vadio*).

Survival could be a legitimate reason for thievery, according to some newspaper reporting, but the press coverage of petty crimes was also indicative of public interest in the urban underworld. Newspaper writers showed, nevertheless, that there was nothing mythical in the crude reality of poverty and survival. Slaves attempting suicide, homeless people living in carts, and poor immigrants newly arriving and disoriented, as well as interracial violence and transportation accidents such as being run over by a tram car and hospitalized in the Santa Casa da Misericórdia were all too common and lamented in the columns of Street Occurrences.

This type of reporting also reflected the larger political climate of the turn from slave to free labor. Throughout 1883 the *subdelegado* (police officer in charge) of the Second Precinct in Santana became a recurring character in the *Gazeta de Notícias* column. Writers noted that he was either one of the few enforcing municipal law on street sellers or taking matters too far and policing beyond the law. Santana included the streets surrounding the Campo de Santana (later named Praça da República), a landscaped square with a fountain that served as a hangout for capoeira, a workplace for laundresses and kiosk owners, a site for street vending, a space for social and romantic encounters, and a place of popular resistance.[23] Santana, also known as Little Africa, was a densely populated and bustling neighborhood of central Rio and a microcosm of the challenges facing a city in transition. Not surprisingly, newspaper reporters took an interest in everyday events that took place there, among them the regular interactions between street vendors and the police.

Street Occurrences in the 4 March 1883 edition of *Gazeta de Notícias* was entirely dedicated to law enforcement in Santana. Municipal law ordered that workers transporting goods were not allowed to walk on sidewalks (*passeios*). They had to use the middle of the street instead in order not to disturb pedestrians on passeios. The column's writer mocked the ordinance by pointing out that in all neighborhoods and even in some areas of Santana individuals could carry whatever they wished "on their heads, backs, in bags, trunks, tables," even their mothers-in-law if they wished. Upon entering the Second Precinct of Santana, where the notorious police officer worked, it was "the law to carry one's mother-in-law—sorry, the cargo—in the middle of the street." Highlighting the uneven application of municipal ordinances in different parts of the city, the writer condemns its inconsistent application with allusion to a popular assumption about mothers-in-law: "May either other subdelegados follow the law or the subdelegado of the Second Precinct of Santana allow, as in all other areas [of the city], each person to bear his [own] cross, not his mother-in-law, which is not for him to carry on his back."[24]

Street workers having the universal right to earn a living and bear their crosses in all places (and not the weight of the law or a mother-in-law) reflected the era's free labor ideology. In making this statement, the newspaper's position was in line with the several abolitionist spokesmen it employed and published. Shifting the transport of goods from sidewalks to the center of streets rationalized urban space, an urban reform that Rio newspapers generally supported. But there were limits to state intervention and policing. The abuse of law enforcement in the second district of Santana became an official burden that interfered with legitimate work practices and people's efforts to get by.

Furthermore, reporters observed that the accumulation of fines imposed on an individual upon arrest in the second district of Santana was quickly enriching municipal coffers. Santana's Second Precinct subdelegado was notorious for fining several tavern, grocery, and botequim owners as well as illegal gambling in urban tenements "of low reputation" and a number of unlicensed peddlers. Altogether, such fines "glorified the treasury of the municipality."[25] On 6 March 1883 the subdelegado arrested João da Rosa, Maria Benedita, and Maria da Conceição for selling rotten meat from a street table. He also detained several men who were carrying goods on sidewalks rather than in the middle of the street, as the law dictated. Dues from fines went to the municipal treasury, which a columnist called a "millionaire" thanks to the subdelegado's diligence.[26] In fact, the news writer argues, this police officer "was doing more for the municipal government than the councilors themselves!"[27]

The influence police had on the practice of street commerce went beyond law enforcement. A 12 February 1883 newspaper column reflects the culture of self-discipline that the policing of vendors helped create.[28] In this case, the ganhador carregador André Joaquim Fernandes turned in to a police officer of the Second Precinct of Santana a basket full of vegetables that did not belong to him. An individual had hired Fernandes to transport the goods from a downtown market to the market area in Largo de São Domingo. Once he reached his destination, Fernandes did not find his employer or patron, so he decided to take the basket to the police and avoid any suspicions of thievery. Such exemplary behavior, however, was not what some newspaper readers sought.

Reporters apparently thought they were meeting readers' interest in the urban underworld by describing unlawful street behaviors such as peddling without a license, selling watered-down milk, walking the streets with an unlicensed milk cow, and selling rotten meat. The confiscation of spoiled meat was habitual and revealed the poor conditions of Rio's main slaughterhouse (*matadouro*), a problem that was widely debated in town council meetings throughout the nineteenth century. The fine for selling substandard meat was considerably higher than those for other vending-related infractions; defiant vendors claimed that their meat was "perfect."[29] Newspapers mostly focused on the policing of sellers who violated municipal and commercial regulations, and incarceration records from the Casa de Detenção substantiate peddlers' greater vulnerability to being criminalized as vagrants despite having ganhador licenses.

ENSLAVED AND FREE VENDORS IN THE CASA DE DETENÇÃO

The same subdelegado of Santana's Second Precinct who captured attention in the paper's reporting of Street Occurrences arrested five individuals on 26 February 1883 for transporting heavy loads on the city's sidewalks.[30] The arrest of the Italian Francisco Capero, the Portuguese José Francisco, the free black woman Januária, and two enslaved men named Silvestre and João resulted in fines totaling twenty milréis. The diversity among incarcerated individuals demonstrates that slaves, free blacks, and European immigrants were similarly vulnerable to street policing. In particular, the registry of the Casa de Detenção lists these regulatory infractions in the diverse profiles of enslaved and free street sellers and ganhadores.

Before the Casa de Detenção became Rio's main jail, a section of the Casa de Correção (corrections center) opened on the same site in 1834, becoming the first institution of confinement in Latin America. Its panoptical model aimed to correct "unruly slaves" and convicted criminals with corporal punishment rather than reform and rehabilitation.[31] Construction of the penitentiary center took place in the peripheral Cidade Nova district and was never fully completed as envisioned. The first full wing, inaugurated in 1850, became the Casa de Correção; the second wing, built some years later, became the Casa de Detenção.[32] Holloway notes that after the prohibition of slave trade between Brazil and Africa in 1850, the corrections center "gave traditional elites new mechanisms for coping with the pressures from below."[33] He argues that "the establishment and development of the urban police system were a necessary precondition for the transition from slavery to the free labor regime."[34]

Announcing abolitionist sympathies on its front page, the weekly Rio newspaper *O Artista* published a chronicle on 21 April 1883 depicting the living conditions at the Casa de Detenção. Naming the detention center on Rua do Conde d'Eu a "holy house" (*santa casa*) for criminals, the chronicle's author describes it as a source of "satisfaction and contentment" for the chief of police and the country's ministers of justice. The author's comparison of the detention center to a santa casa for the infirmed poor run by a religious order only emphasized that the detention center was not a place for healing and rehabilitation. Instead, it was a "lugubrious living space, ruled by arbitrariness and despotism, where victims had no recourse to appeal to higher authorities." Hygienic "comforts" were rights "not observed": "For example, . . . nutrition was appropriate for a leprous dog." Between ten and twenty men shared small cubicles where they slept like "sardines in a can." They were "crammed in a sea of granite with a simple blanket that served as both mattress and cover." This blanket, the writer notes, was "an enigma for the detainee," since as a floor mattress it was as cold as stone, but as a cover it was hot as hell. According to the author, this enigma revealed the despotic nature of "power, [which] had such bizarreness." Another incongruity was that "novices of vice" were intermixed in the same cells with the more experienced "masters of vice and crime." The author points at this condition as nonsense, given that the latter lured the former deeper into a world of crime and thus obstructed their chances for rehabilitation.

Even if full rehabilitation was doubtful, the abolitionist newspaper writer concludes that detainees including slaves were still citizens. The state was hence responsible for feeding and housing them if it expected a detainee to rejoin society as a "useful citizen for the nation." The author does not make distinctions between free and enslaved detainees, as in the detention center free and enslaved detainees shared close spaces of incarceration. Reminding the state of its duty toward citizenship building—even in detention centers—reflects not only concerns with penitentiary reform but also the discursive connection between marginality and citizenship as not mutually exclusive. Like this writer, detainees also considered themselves persons with rights.[35] The criminalization of vagrancy and public disorder such as quarrels, drunkenness, and homelessness influenced policing to approach street vending as an activity associated with these conditions and behaviors. As described decades later by the chronicler João do Rio, the prison in Rio was "where the streets sometimes end." Peddlers, he notes, even entered and exited the detention center with considerable freedom to supply inmates with goods, transforming the prison into an extension of the street in matters of commerce and not just criminality.[36]

The registry entries of the municipal detention center illustrate the criminal extension of street commerce, making them a unique historical site for examining the shared history of the diverse working population on the Brazilian capital's streets. In the decades preceding abolition, detained vendors were usually charged with public disorder, vagrancy, and the suspicion of being runaway slaves. Public disorder was by far the main reason for street sellers' arrests and detention. Few detainees, in general, were later processed in court.[37] Moreover, public disorder and vagrancy charges overrode the protection that a ganhador license could offer street vendors.

The arrest and detention records of 523 street sellers between 1868 and 1883 shed light on the vulnerabilities of the vending population against the policing practices of the late slave period.[38] The Casa de Correção was the usual destination for detained slaves, but due to overcrowding and its closing in 1874, many were sent to the Casa de Detenção.[39] Still, most inmates in the Casa de Detenção were free individuals and not enslaved. Almost all who identified as street vendors were illiterate. Table 1 in the appendix displays the variety of specializations associated with street commerce that detention center officials wrote under "occupation" (*ocupação*) in registry entries. These are organized according to gender and slave and free status.

More than 20 percent of the street vendors incarcerated in the Casa de Detencão were enslaved, and several were suspected slaves even if they claimed to be free. Women made up 37 percent of all the enslaved vendors detained, a proportion that stands in contrast to the absence of women seeking ganhador licenses at the time. Most enslaved female vendors were listed as being between forty and fifty-nine years old and "natural subjects" of African nations. Imperial authorities used the term "natural subject" (*súbdito natural*) to define origin according to the monarchical notion of homeland, even if African nations were a European construct. Women of the Mina nation comprised 74 percent of the incarcerated female slaves who were vendors; authorities identified fewer as Congo, Angola, and Benguela in origin. Enslaved African female vendors tended to be quitandeiras; one woman claimed to be a ganhadora and another a vendor of sweets (*doceira*). These vending practices were traditionally associated with female slave work, as travelers observed throughout the nineteenth century and earlier.

Younger female vendors who were enslaved tended to be Brazilian-born from outside the state of Rio, in Bahia, Pernambuco, or Ceará. These were common origins for Northeastern slaves who were forced to move to the Southeast after transatlantic slave trade ended. Scribes at the detention center described most enslaved women as black (*pretas*); racially mixed women made up 38 percent of the enslaved group of female street sellers. Like their African counterparts, *pardas* (mixed-race women with lighter brown skin) selling on the street worked for the most part as quitandeiras, who were heavily policed in the markets and squares they regularly occupied.[40] Enslaved street quitandeiras were mostly African-born, but detention records reveal that Brazilian-born women were still a significant presence.

Men were 63 percent of the enslaved vendors in the Casa de Detenção in 1868–1883, which was 13 percent of the total free and slave-vending population sample. Their ages ranged between twelve and eighty-one years, and the majority were listed as between forty and sixty-nine years of age. About half of the men were born in Africa, and most of those were Mina. A smaller number were listed as belonging to the Benguela, Mozambique, Congo, Angola, and Cabinda nations. Authorities also noted skin color; nearly all enslaved men were listed as pretos and a few were racially mixed *pardos*, *cabras* (light-skinned mulattos), and *fulas* (dark-skinned mulattos). More than half of the enslaved men participating in street commerce were ganhadores, while only 22 percent were quitandeiros. Vending practices carried out by slaves were thus gendered, as males often walked the city as ganhadores and females worked in fixed locations as quitandeiras. Police records generally did not list quitandeiros as ganhadores, but quitandeiros could have arrangements with patrons that were organized within the ganho system. So, quitandeiros could be ganhadores and vice versa.

Upon arrest, all but three slaves gave authorities the names of their owners. It was protocol for the police to contact masters, who were then responsible for paying incurred fines. Having a ganhador license could entail protection, but it was not a guarantee against unpredictable street policing. Most slave owners were men, although women owned 30 percent of the detained vending population that was enslaved. Female slave owners tended to own more female than male slaves and employed both in the occupations of street commerce as quitandeiras, ganhadores, and shoe shiners. Male slave owners placed enslaved men in a variety of vending activities, whereas female slaves working on the street were almost exclusively quitandeiras. Slaveholders who were men owned a higher percentage of African-born men and women; female slave owners tended to have Brazilian-born slaves. The ganho system in which urban slave owners formally participated thus was predominantly male and mostly enlisted enslaved men born in Africa. Mistresses tended to belong to lower-middling classes that could afford to purchase the cheaper Brazilian slaves.[41]

A total of eleven men and one woman whom the police suspected to be enslaved claimed to be free. They did not have their freedom papers with them, and some had been arrested for violating curfew hours. None declared to have masters, and most had places of residence they used as proof of freedom. Urban slaves sometimes lived outside their masters' houses, so a document proving freedom rather than residence was the decisive piece of evidence for authorities. Most vendors suspected to be slaves resided in Santana and Santo Antônio, and those born in Africa tended to be middle-age ganhadores. One forty-year-old Mina ganhador was married but did not list a place of residence. The only woman in this group, a fifty-year-old unmarried Mina quitandeira, did not have a home address either. Perhaps both were withholding information that would reveal slave status, but the inability to provide proof of residence also reflected the social insecurity of being poor, free, and African.

The Casa de Detenção was built to hold nonslaves in order not to mix them with the enslaved detainees in the corrections center. Of the 523 detainees involved in street commerce in the sample between 1868 and 1883, 380 were free men and 10 were free women. Most were illiterate. Married men made up 14 percent of the sample; these were engaged in a variety of street selling activities and typically around thirty years old. Italians from Naples and Concezo between the ages of twenty-two and sixty were prominent, working as mascates, shoe shiners, quitandeiros, and sellers of tin goods (*funileiros*). Many lived in Santana, which had been predominantly inhabited by Afro-descendants throughout the century. The sample reveals that only four married men between the ages of thirty and sixty-five were born in Africa and resided in São José, an area of the city commonly populated by European immigrants. Two of them were ganhadores, another was a quitandeiro, and a fourth man was a mascate. In other words, all were participants in Rio's street occupations; while quitandeiros and mascates could technically be ganhadores as well, their vending practices were specific enough to have developed into particular names and forms. The mascate was a younger man who may have identified himself to authorities as such rather than as a ganhador to imply higher status. The Brazilian married men were either born in Rio or Northeastern states such as Bahia and Pernambuco. Two were labeled "white," a newspaper vendor and a knife sharpener, and three were mulatto ganhadores. Another Brazilian-born man was a black shoe shiner from Rio. African and non-African street vendors were, therefore, still neighbors in most areas, further indicating that street commerce was a shared and contested space.

A majority of the detained men who were participants in Rio's street commerce were unmarried, and only a few were widows. The profile of male widows was significantly more diverse than that of married men and representative of street commerce as a survival strategy for older and more vulnerable men of all backgrounds. Male widows were mostly between fifty and sixty years of age and came from Africa, Brazil, Spain, Italy, and Portugal.

Other, younger male street sellers originated from France, China, Uruguay, Paraguay, Peru, and Belgium, indicating street commerce's position as an economic practice of survival and subsistence among new immigrants in the city. Ganhadores tended to be poor Africans, Brazilians, and European immigrants, while mascates generally claimed higher status and European heritage.

Unmarried vendors born in the city of Rio were mostly young men who were racially mixed or black. Although some were listed as quitandeiros, street sellers, and ganhadores, almost half were shoe shiners. These detained Brazilian-born vendors mostly resided in Santana and Sacramento neighborhoods. Most Brazilians born outside the city of Rio de Janeiro were young men engaged in vending occupations rather than shining shoes. More than one-third of Brazilian vendors from outside Rio were racially mixed ganhadores, and another third were vendors of sweets, vegetables, and newspapers. Shining shoes was thus an occupation that outsiders seldom practiced and blacks born in Rio dominated.

Unmarried southern European immigrants were the next significant group that appeared in the sample of detainees. In the middle of the nineteenth century, most were Portuguese immigrants, followed by a considerable number of Italians, whose numbers would increase at the turn of the century, and a smaller number of Spaniards. Single Portuguese males tended to be young, below the age of twenty, and to have migrated from different regions in Portugal. In Rio they mostly resided in São José, Sacramento, and Santa Rita and engaged in a variety of vending activities including ganho work. Portuguese-born ganhadores in the sample were mostly young men in their twenties and thirties, an age group that frequently migrated from the Iberian Peninsula and the Portuguese Atlantic islands. Unmarried Italian men were mostly young immigrants from the southern province of Cocenza. They engaged in a variety of street selling practices and settled for the most part in Santana. A few Italians were ganhadores and shoe shiners, but most were peddlers of lottery tickets and vegetables. Some were also mascates, according to authorities' entries. Unmarried Spanish immigrants were a minority in the sample; a few migrated from the northwestern Atlantic coast of the peninsula and the Canary Islands. Spanish vendors were usually more than thirty years old and carried out assorted street selling activities including ganho work. One was the lone Spanish shoe shiner among Rio natives and a few Portuguese men.

Unmarried men born in Africa made up 11 percent of the sample. While the presence of Minas is not as notable in this group as among enslaved detainees, their number among free men was still higher than from other African nations and indicative of the type of work former and freed slaves performed. Carrying out some form of street selling for ex-masters who were patrons established continuity between vendors and suppliers. Incarcerated free African vendors were between forty and seventy years of age and lived throughout the city, with the highest concentration in Sacramento and not Santana's Little Africa. About half of African-born male free vendors were ganhadores who, like quitandeiros, tended to belong to the Mina nation. Their work had likely started in slavery, and as the ganho system accommodated free labor, former slaves continued working ao ganho.

Unmarried immigrants from China, France, Belgium, and South America also participated in Rio's street commerce. Authorities identified young French peddlers among the detainees as mascates. They usually described Chinese immigrants as having dark skin, and most were listed as vendors of fish. A handful of non-Brazilian South American peddlers appeared as ganhadores in detention entries, which further demonstrates the ganho system's importance in organizing immigrant nonslave labor on the eve of abolition.

Free white immigrant street peddlers, African and racially mixed ganhadores (slave and free), and Brazilian black shoe shiners largely formed the ethnic landscape of street commerce in Rio at the time. Ganhadores of African origin or descent were arrested for alleged violations of the 1830 Criminal Code rather than for being unlicensed workers. Municipal authorities had become increasingly concerned with the licensing of free immigrants in 1878–1879, but many vendors in this group were also jailed on charges of vagrancy and public disorder rather than for lacking licenses. If the detainees had ganhador licenses, they seemed to offer little protection from street policing, regardless of the ethnicity of the ganhador.

In addition to providing a demographic lens on the enslaved and free detainees who were participants in Rio's street commerce, detention records list the reasons for their arrests as well as their street selling activities and vending locations. Vendors were arrested for violations of the 1830 Criminal Code or for violating municipal ordinances regarding ganho work. While most detainees were held for violations of the Criminal Code, instances when peddlers were detained for lacking ganho licenses speak of the particular vulnerabilities in the vending population. Table 2 in the appendix lists the types and frequency of arrests according to slave and free and male and female vendors in the sample. The majority of these sellers were arrested in Santana, where policing was perhaps the heaviest, followed by Sacramento, São José, and Espírito Santo.

Most street vendors who were incarcerated sold food and other consumer goods like household items and lottery tickets. A slight majority were arrested for vagrancy, followed by disorder, capoeira, and drunkenness. Detained food vendors commonly specialized in the selling of sweets, which reveals the vulnerability of Afro-descendant street workers who dominated this practice. Male and female sweets vendors were, as a group, 50 percent black and 50 percent white, and only a few were slaves. Disorder and vagrancy were the most common charges for their arrest. Peddlers of leafy greens (*vendedores de folhas*) were also numerous. Vendedores de folhas tended to be white, male, and immigrant.

Disorder was a common charge against detained Africans and Brazilians. Theft charges were more frequent among European immigrants. All groups were equally vulnerable to vagrancy charges, demonstrating that policing against vendors could be influenced by race or skin color, but more so by the impulse to remove vendors in general from the street.

It was common for vendedores de folhas to be arrested with others as a group. In general, group arrests involved individuals of the same skin color and who, if white, were immigrants. People who sold lottery tickets on the street, which was an illegal practice, were also arrested with other sellers of the same type. These peddlers were usually immigrants from Portugal, Italy, or Spain, but the detention center did list one fula from the Brazilian state of Minas Gerais. Although most lottery games were outlawed during the slave period, most vendors of *bilhetes* (lottery tickets) were arrested for vagrancy, disorder, drunkenness, and capoeira—not for promoting illegal gambling.[42] Newspaper sellers were also frequently arrested in groups usually of boys of diverse backgrounds working in Sacramento.

License requests in the 1860s as well as travelers' accounts earlier in the century show that many enslaved ganhadores sold fish in Rio. However, fish vendors held at the detention center were mostly free men, indicating how immigration was changing and the ganho system accommodated an urban slave society in transition. Europeans, Chinese, and racially mixed Brazilians participated in greater numbers in this line of work that former slaves seemed to drop. Street fights rather than vagrancy led to the arrests of many of these non-African street sellers, perhaps reflecting ethnic tensions in this line of work. Although detention records do not explain the details of such quarrels, and even if street commerce's shared spaces could lead to cooperation, conflict and resistance due to ethnic and racial difference were to be expected.

Enslaved vendors frequently sold birds on the street, and some free immigrants adopted this vending practice when they entered the city in greater numbers at the turn of the century. The 1868–1883 sample of detention records shows that chicken vendors were mostly European immigrants along with a few free blacks arrested on disorder and vagrancy charges. The frequent mention in Street Occurrences of the arrests of individuals selling stolen fowl is not replicated in the detention records. The penalties for selling stolen birds may have been resolved before suspects were taken to jail, perhaps a regular practice between this type of street sellers and police officers. Similarly, vendors and carriers of coffee who traditionally were enslaved and a common sight on Rio's streets were by 1879 mostly immigrant and Portuguese.

Vendors selling tin household items, funileiros, were usually European immigrants working along patron-client relations with Portuguese suppliers. In Rio, men who worked with tinplate tended to be of Portuguese origin.[43] Disorderly behavior was the most common cause for the arrests of funileiros, followed by vagrancy, drunkenness, and theft. In one case, five Italian funileiros were arrested in Santana for stealing. Most of the men in this group were from Naples, Italy, and resided together in a house on Rua São Pedro in Sacramento. A smaller yet still noteworthy number of funileiros were free men born in the city of Rio and racially mixed. Both immigrant and Brazilian-born funileiros thus had access to local suppliers and participated in a street occupation that was mostly carried out by free and not enslaved workers.

Mascates were almost exclusively immigrants from Italy, Spain, Portugal, and France. Syrio-Lebanese participation in this area of street vending significantly rose at the turn of the nineteenth century. European mascates peddled fabrics, silver, gold, and porcelain, but their higher position in the vending community did not protect them from frequent vagrancy and theft charges. Several vendors listed as mascates in Rio's detention center were second-time offenders for not having met the "term for official employment" (*termo de tomar ocupação*), which forced first-time detainees charged with vagrancy to be formally employed or tied to a patron within fifteen days of their release from jail. Through their attachment to patrons, mascates, regardless of their higher status for selling costly goods, were like other street commerce participants who depended on suppliers. Mascates' contribution to the development of petty commerce in Rio is today memorialized in the statue of a mascate located in downtown Rio in a highly frequented commercial area known as SAARA (Sociedade de Amigos das Adjacências da Rua da Alfândega). This statue of a white immigrant mascate silences or replaces black vendors' important contributions to commercial growth in Rio.

Detainees who were listed as ganhadores were African, European, and Brazilian. Most ganhadores held in detention were free workers, but more than half of the enslaved detainees were ganhadores. Still, free ganhadores in the sample were largely white and in this case Portuguese. Work "ao ganho" was nonetheless the form of street work with the closest ties to slavery, and most ganhadores were jailed on vagrancy and public disorder charges. It was common for ganhadores to be arrested on two charges—vagrancy or public disorder along with inebriation or physical offense. Ganhadores, unlike other street sellers, were arrested individually rather than in groups. Free ganhadores detained for vagrancy came from diverse areas of the city such as Santana, Sacramento, São José, Santo Antônio, and Espírito Santo. While ganhadores arrested for vagrancy were usually white, those arrested for disorder and/or inebriation were more likely born in Africa. A number of ganhadores were held as suspected escaped slaves. These men were mostly born in Africa and arrested in Santana. Only one ganhador was detained for the practice of capoeira, and he was Portuguese. By the late nineteenth century, the African Brazilian martial art of capoeira had incorporated into its ranks many European immigrants.[44]

Shoe shining was the fourth most frequent street occupation in the sample from the detention records and a particularly common line of work among male blacks and mulattos born in Rio. The arrests of these individuals occurred throughout the city but especially in its central districts. Disorder, which many times included disobedience toward police officers and inebriation, was the most common charge in the arrests of *lustradores* (shoe shiners), followed by vagrancy. The practice of capoeira was another activity leading to the detention of several lustradores who were Brazilian blacks and had records of recidivism. Knife sharpening was another common street occupation for free Brazilian blacks and mulattos as well as European immigrants. The knife sharpener regularly traveled city streets in European and American urban capitals at the time. In Rio, policing for vagrancy and public disorder made them vulnerable to criminal charges.

In detention records, female vendors were considerably outnumbered by men working on the street. Still, enslaved and free African women who sold on the street were regular targets of policing. Among the ganhador licenses registered between 1879 and 1887, only one record lists a woman, of Brazilian origin, whereas detention records frequently list women who were ganhadoras. The registry entries from the detention center therefore provide a more complete profile for female street vendors at this time rather than licenses.

Of the forty-one enslaved female street sellers in the sample, thirty-seven were quitandeiras, two sold sweets, and two were identified as peddlers of unspecified goods. Authorities noted that more than 80 percent of the detained slave quitandeiras were black, and of these 50 percent were Mina. Several quitandeiras were slaves from the state of Bahia, reflecting the internal slave trade between Bahia and southern Brazil. A considerable number of women in the sample had migrated from Bahia and worked as vendors, domestic servants, and laundresses in the Brazilian capital. Most enslaved female vendors were arrested as suspected *fugidas* (escaped slaves). Authorities alleged that certain women had escaped because their physical appearance corresponded to descriptions in newspaper ads. Female vendors who worked alone or did not carry the appropriate license or permission were also usual suspects. Other reasons for their arrests were alleged disobedience, inebriation, public display of improper behavior, and vagrancy, all of which could lead authorities to suspect that they had escaped slavery.

The most frequent incident that caused free black female street sellers to be arrested—vagrancy charges being low—was what authorities considered to be disorderly behavior. These women were mostly quitandeiras between twenty-eight and forty-eight years of age. About half of them were Mina and the other half Brazilian women born in Rio or the state of Bahia. Some slave and free women who were street sellers were arrested for prostitution, which authorities officially noted as participation in obscene, sexual, or immoral acts. Behavior that the police treated as disorderly could be quitandeiras' assertion of their right to sell freely on the street.[45] Female street sellers defied not only police but also local residents and business owners who regularly complained about them to municipal officials.[46] Protests about unhygienic and rowdy conditions that quitandeiras generated on the street sought to establish greater social order in urban slave society.

During the slave period, some female African vendors specialized in making *angu*, a mixture of manioc flour and meat that was fried and typically sold to workers in Rio's port area. The painter Jean-Baptiste Debret depicted makers and vendors of angu as African women who would set up their stands from six o'clock in the morning to two o'clock in the afternoon (figure 2.1). They were usually surrounded by vendors of fish and vegetables. These open spaces became popular spots of African socialization that developed later in the century into *casas de zungú*, homes associated with Afro-Brazilian gatherings and informal selling and gambling.[47] Fearing slave rebellion, authorities criminalized casas de zungú, and detention records show that Brazilian-born nonblack participants were arrested on related charges. Regardless of race or gender, people arrested in casas de zungú were usually workers involved in some aspect of street commerce, as the shared spaces of vending extended into other areas of sellers' lives.

The sample of detainees shows that five out of seven arrested for being in casas de zungú were slaves, the other two being quitandeiras born outside of Rio. The men found in casas de zungú were shoe shiners, quitandeiros, and ganhadores of African descent. Those taken to jail had mostly been arrested in Sacramento, but Street Occurrences reports reveal that the subdelegado of Santana's Second Precinct was quite involved in policing casas de zungú. He arrested "eleven individuals of suspicious reputation" in a house on Rua do General Pedra where "they customarily spent the night for 200 réis a bed."[48]

FIGURE 2.1. Vendors of angu, 1825. Lithograph by Jean-Baptiste Debret. Courtesy of G. Ermakoff Casa Editorial, Arquivo Images2You.

The owners of the house were also fined for not having the proper rental license. That same week, the subdelegado and several inspectors made arrests in other casas de zungú and informal gambling centers. The black couple Lázaro and Luzia was arrested for having a *casa de dar fortuna* (fortune-telling house) where the police confiscated "silver, three blades, and a tin box with several knick-knacks."[49]

A few registry entries from the detention center reveal the arrest of individuals for working on the street without ganho licenses. Vagrancy or public disorder were the charges commonly applied if a vendor lacked a license, indicating the policing more than the regulation of street commercial practices. Although lacking a ganho license was seldom reason for arrest, this was not case on 23, 24, and 28 August 1883 in Santana. The arrests of street workers specifically for violating ganho licensing ordinances were made in response to municipal pressures to enforce street commerce regulations.[50] On another level, these detention records illustrate how the infamous subdelegado from Santana policed street vending with the use of vagrancy laws. Sidewalks, streets, and casas de zungú were everyday spaces within his surveillance, as seen in Street Occurrences reports describing his arrests of street sellers and subsequent fines. Registry entries from the detention center show that individuals were arrested and then held for periods that spanned one day to three weeks. According to these entries, the ganhadores arrested in Santana in August 1883 were detained for vagrancy and lacking ganho licenses.

The application of both ganho ordinances and criminal law points to the gradual shift in the regulation of street commerce away from municipal law and toward criminal law. A precedent took place with the creation in 1866 of the Urban Guard, which was abolished in 1885 because of its agents' excessive use of violence. The primary focus of the Urban Guard was the threat of public disorder, Holloway notes, "whether real or potential." People were therefore arrested, he finds, "for behavior that was neither a crime nor an infraction of ordinances, such as individuals found carrying objects or packages, which by reason of quality or condition of such individuals . . . [made] them suspect. It was not a crime to carry a package in public, but if it appeared to a patrolling guard that a certain type of person should not be carrying a certain package, the culprit would be subject to arrest."[51] In 1883 ganhadores were still detained for being unlicensed, but they were not fined and punished for a municipal violation. They were now arrested and held for days at the detention center on charges of criminal violations associated with vagrancy or public disorder.

New approaches in how authorities at the Casa de Detenção noted violations involving unlicensed ganhadores begin to reveal the shift toward criminalization, which was more pronounced by the early postabolition period. On 23 August 1883 street ganhadores were detained for "not having a license." On 24 and 28 August ganhadores were detained for both "vagrancy and not having a license." Adding vagrancy to the reason for their arrests transformed these unlicensed ganhadores into offenders of criminal and not just municipal law. Vagrancy laws could aim to redirect free workers to employers or patrons more effectively than licensing, as upon release from jail those who had been detained on vagrancy charges commonly agreed, officially, to find employment. Consequently, lacking official proof of employment such as a ganhador license was a criminal violation that could be interpreted as vagrancy. Criminal violation became a more applicable law for policing slave and free workers who earned a living on the street despite the established regulations of ganho work. Vagrancy laws could impose criminalization and patron-client relations, whereas official ganho law could only address the latter.

The detention of unlicensed ganhadores who had become vagrants in the eyes of the law was not an occurrence particular to a specific ethnic or racial group at the time. Detention entries and Street Occurrences reports depict the diverse types of individuals whom the Second Precinct subdelegado of Santana arrested. Newspaper writers did not have the space to fully describe individuals, but the registry entries of the Casa de Detenção reveal that thirty-three free men were arrested in Santana between August 23 and 28 and give a social profile of each. The detained unlicensed male ganhadores included twenty-four whites, eight blacks, and one mulatto, a composition that reflected the observation made by municipal officials in 1878 when they complained that immigrants had invaded the streets of Rio. Most whites in the group were southern European immigrants, sixteen from Italy. Six ganhadores were Portuguese, unmarried, and twenty-something except one who was sixty years old. There was one young Spaniard from the Galician city of Pontevedra. There were five Brazilians—four pretos and one pardo—born outside of Rio except for one. Four ganhadores were born in Africa, and two of these were Mina. Men born in Africa, in this group, were considerably older than their Brazilian and European counterparts, pointing to their longer participation in ganho work.

CRIMINAL LAW AS A REPLACEMENT OF THE GANHO SYSTEM

The street policing of ganhadores in the decades preceding final abolition influenced the regulation of urban vending in the early twentieth century. Enslaved and free peddlers, ganhadores, porters, shoe shiners, and knife sharpeners were among those most vulnerable to police enforcement of the 1830 Criminal Code. Increasingly, the policing of criminalized street behavior was taking precedence over municipal ordinances governing the system of ganho and regulating street commerce since the early nineteenth century. Some unlicensed street vendors were charged with violating both criminal and municipal laws, as exemplified in the group of free ganhadores who were arrested in Santana in August 1883.

The merging of urban vending and criminality pushed street commerce practices to become more informal with the end of slavery. Street policing responded to official concerns about the transition to free labor regardless of abolitionist ideas about liberty and free commerce. As one newspaper columnist described, the high number of arrests involving street peddlers was violating the very principles of free commerce. While many abolitionist liberals would have agreed with this statement in 1883, the increasing number of arrests and detentions of peddlers for vagrancy and public disorder show an experience of freedom that was uneven. Policing established the contours of liberty for street vendors, which more than economic regulations limiting their freedom.

The rise in police arrests sheds light on a state limiting the freedom of peddlers to engage in free commerce on city streets. The precedent established by the ganho system lost importance as licensing and street commerce regulation were gradually replaced by the application of criminal law. A newspaper columnist argued that each person who worked on the street had the right to bear his own cross, that is, the right to work freely and earn a living. But policing became an infringement on free individuals' work such as street vending. Consequently, the decades leading to the abolition of slavery positioned street commerce between criminal law and municipal ordinance, while the police as overseers of street discipline set a strong precedent that pushed urban vending toward a path of informality.

CHAPTER 3

INVENTING A NEW STREET COMMERCE

A DIVERSE ARRAY of street vendors populated the city's corners, alleys, and market squares, altering not only public space but vending styles as well. Selling practices from the mid-nineteenth century persisted as new immigrants adopted existing customs. Despite the free status of many sellers, slavery still influenced the practice of vending and shaped the distribution of basic goods to urban residents of all classes. Free peddlers plied their wares much like enslaved vendors did throughout the 1800s, that is, in ways urban reformers thought to be a drag on progress and an undesirable legacy of slavery. Meanwhile, scientists and entrepreneurial men sought to modernize urban vending by introducing technologies that reformed rather than eliminated existing practices. The rationalization of vending through technological innovation reflected street commerce's formal place in the city and its potential, while policing continued to limit its activities by enforcing vagrancy and public disorder laws. The proposed patents and their authors reveal the transnational nature of street commerce as well. Not only were Rio's street vendors hailing from a diverse Atlantic world, but inventors in Brazil were themselves of varied international backgrounds and aware of street commerce practices in major European and American capitals. These inventors defended street selling as fundamental to urban public health, proposing an alternative development to overcome the legacies of slavery and benefit the growing population of the Brazilian capital. In doing so, they attempted to formalize street vending in the postslave city.

Inventors and patent seekers envisioned a new world for street commerce during a time of transition from slavery to freedom and monarchy to republic. Innovative vending technologies became the "catalyst of modernity" that was to liberate street commerce from its slave past.[1] Ideologies of free labor, public health, and urban reform found expression in the patents that inventors of vending vehicles and accessories solicited from the state. Their proposals for an improved street commerce modernized food distribution according to the promise of free labor and free commerce. New technologies intended to support humanitarian working conditions for street sellers were central to this reinvention. Further, hygienic devices were meant to sanitize street selling for consumers. Innovation in street cart designs promised advances in marketeering practices. Patent seekers aimed to transform street commerce into a modern industry that erased the slave past and served modern consumers. The drawings that accompanied their patent requests depict the average peddler as young, male, and white. The proposed rationalization of street commerce was explicit in technological innovation and implicit in racial and gender bias. By the twentieth century's first decade, propositions for new inventions incorporated advertising and eye-catching displays of images that reflected a new type of consumer capitalism in street commerce.

In the late nineteenth century, Brazil's landed elite still had a strong hold on national politics, but a new generation of *bacharéis* (university graduates) defended the development of urban industries to lessen the country's economic dependence on agricultural exports. In the patent office, inventors proposed ideas for an improved and rationalized urban street commerce that promised modernity, humanitarianism, and hygiene. Patent requests for vending technologies remained consistent throughout the period 1885–1909 despite the ruptures marked by the end of slavery in 1888, the birth of the First Republic in 1889, and the 1901 and 1903 official prohibitions of street commerce in Rio's city center. The lobbying for such patents over decades demonstrated street vending's importance in the city's supply and distribution chains. The daily transactions carried out by street peddlers added up to a significant market that inventors and patent seekers pressured the municipal government to reform. The main idea running through the proposals was erasing the slave past through technological innovation, a theme consistent with the abolitionist influence on urban reform. The end of slave work, proponents argued, could only improve the conditions for street selling, while specific vending practices needed to be reformed. The rationalization of street selling, furthermore, promised to improve the appearance and uses of urban public space. Not all urban officials shared this belief, but that did not disqualify street commerce, at least not yet, from being compatible with the modern city.

Between 1885 and 1909, engineers, physicists, industrialists, and military officials sought to patent inventions with an aim to transform vending methods deemed filthy and backward. Their proposals were filed in the repository of Rio's Arquivo Público (Public Archive) from which the state granted patents.[2] In the area of street commerce, new vending instruments anticipated sanitized transactions between sellers and consumers as well as improved conditions for vendors. An 1889 design by Paulo Vieira de Sousa is exemplary for being, in his words, a "humanitarian and hygienic" addition to street commerce. Concern for a humanitarian street commerce reflected a Brazilian free labor ideology that sought to dignify manual labor. Sousa aimed to protect food from dust, heat, and disease while the peddler transported heavy loads without being overburdened.[3] Overexposure to sun and heat spoiled foods and caused disease, resulting in "tropical" approaches to miasma and germ theory.[4]

Abolitionists argued that slavery also dehumanized nonslave workers by depriving them of the full fruits of free labor. The discursive use of the term "humanitarian" had origins in nineteenth-century Brazilian abolitionist discourse.[5] Brazilian abolitionist Joaquim Nabuco portrayed the relationship between free labor and human subjectivity as spiritual, dignifying, and liberating.[6] During his self-imposed exile in London in 1863, he wrote the treatise *O abolicionismo* (published in Brazil in 1883), in which he uses the term *humanitário* to link Christian political ethos with Brazilian patriotism.[7] Six years later, in 1869, the Humanitarian Society for Abolition was established in Rio, modeled after British antislavery societies that called their members "humanitarians." An article in the Brazilian press about the abolitionist Luiz Gama (1830–1882) points out that "no one could have equally borne his humanitarian burden."[8] Gama was a descendant of Africans in Brazil and his humanitarian burden spoke to the mark of slavery he sought to overcome as an abolitionist and a man of color.

Campaigning in Recife for a parliamentary seat in 1884, Nabuco used antislavery rhetoric to appeal to the free urban electorate by exalting the transformative and dignifying power of free labor.[9] He used the word humanitário in his speeches to call for the end of slavery and the long-awaited emancipation of all free urban workers limited by slavery. In a similar vein, patent applicants deemed Rio's traditional vending practices backward and oppressive for all by using the term "humanitarian" to argue for reform with slavery's end. Meanwhile, the whitening of street vendors in the drawings annexed to written requests reflect the abolitionist preference for white immigrant labor over black national workers in Brazil.[10] It seemed that a street vendor's humanness could be enhanced in the eyes of officials reviewing patent requests by minimizing the presence of black workers in street commerce.

Although patented, the inventions did not transform most vending practices on the ground. Nevertheless, they provide an opportunity to examine discourses of modernity, technology, and free labor ideology from the perspective of a scientific and entrepreneurial community of the period in Rio. Investing in patent applications demonstrated that street commerce was not antithetical to industry or the modern city. Patent requests revealed expanding economic and social sectors during a period of intense urban transformation. Rapid population growth and the gradual end of slavery increased the need for street commerce in distributing basic goods to urban residents. New technologies were developed to facilitate this as an increasing number of residents populated the urban outskirts. New migrations to the city were transforming the spaces of street commerce, even if petty commerce was still concentrated in central Rio. The proposed vehicles for street selling were designed for traveling rough roads between the city's center and periphery to serve new residents.

One inventor in particular was at the forefront of this technological innovation. A foreigner in Brazil, US-born Morris N. Kohn engaged in a variety of endeavors, from proposing water pumps that transported bathing water from the ocean to the city's *morros* (hills) to carrying out an unyielding campaign to gain a monopoly over all street commerce in Rio.[11] The strategies that Kohn and other inventors proposed also were meant to prevent the spread of disease through food. Public health was at stake, and they claimed their creations could protect consumables from dirt and miasmic contamination. Many sought to patent hygienic houses, beds, cigarettes, liquid pumps, pillows, and coffins and even hygienic ships that cleansed passengers before they descended into port. Such hygienic and humanitarian concerns reflected an Atlantic and local free labor ideology that considered street vending modern, civilized, and racialized. This stood in contrast to municipal political interests that desired to eradicate street commerce from the Brazilian capital.

MORRIS KOHN AND THE CHANGING WORLD OF STREET COMMERCE

Kohn, a mechanical engineer from Hartford, Connecticut, and a resident of Rio since the 1870s, formally entered the world of Brazilian street commerce by founding a company that specialized in crafting vending instruments such as handcarts, portable tables, and shoeshine chairs.[12] He was one of several foreigners who had responded to royal patronage aiming to modernize Brazil. Aside from introducing a variety of inventions, Kohn also promoted hygienic vending technology in a tenacious campaign for monopoly over all street commerce in Rio. Between 1870 and 1900 he pressured municipal officials to exclusively adopt his handcarts and portable tables and compel all vendors to abandon their old ways. Both imperial and republican administrations, however, rejected Kohn's plan, arguing that any form of monopoly contradicted the principles of liberal, free commerce. Kohn was not able to realize his dream of monopoly but nevertheless pursued an urban landscape remade by technological innovation and free labor.

The engineer from Connecticut migrated to Brazil at a time when Emperor Dom Pedro II recruited foreign intellectuals to help modernize the country.[13] Kohn created electric and telephone systems in different regions of Brazil and designed modernized beds for workers. He was a versatile inventor and solicited patents for a variety of innovations unrelated to street commerce. Kohn and a business partner, the US citizen James Walter Graham, soon obtained a royal patent for the introduction of chemical-based fire extinguishers in 1875.[14] The catalog for the 1875 National Exhibition in Brazil notes that "in the short span of time that [Kohn] has been residing [in Brazil], he has worked incessantly to endow the country with new and beneficial industrial utilities. An inventive mind and already a holder of three patents, all a result of his fertile imagination and genius, Kohn will briefly introduce to Rio de Janeiro an improvement of the utmost importance."[15] Four years later, Kohn was living in the heart of Rio's commercial district with a house on the prestigious Rua da Alfândega. As a resident of this area, Kohn soon became acquainted with the importance of street commerce in distributing basic goods to people. But before fully committing to the reformation of urban vending, he partnered in 1879 with Carlos Martins da Silva, a resident of the city of Nitéroi across the bay. Together they established a business of renting out and selling shoeshine chairs, cases, and accessories.[16] The Empresa de Engraxadores was Kohn's first attempt at reforming street commerce in the Brazilian capital. Kohn's ambitions further consolidated in the street vending company Empresa Ambulante Doméstica (EAD), which he established in 1887 for the technical and hygienic improvement of all street commerce in Rio and used to apply for patents in São Paulo as well.

In 1887, from the EAD's headquarters on Rua Sete de Setembro, Kohn wrote a letter to the city council explaining the objectives of his enterprise. Primarily, the EAD was committed to "the industrial improvement and perfection" of street vending, which Kohn asserted could not be done without government support.[17] He described street vending as an industrial practice that largely characterized Rio's commerce, and he proposed modernizing it through a monopoly, which in fact contradicted the very principles of free commerce. "Filthy tables, market stalls, and other frightening sights" posed a risk to public health, and Kohn argued that he had the solution—an offer that would "greatly benefit the capital city" and that the municipal government could not ignore. Kohn first requested permission to station approximately twenty "hygienic handcarts" from which vendors would sell fruits, sweets, vegetables, coffee, and refreshments throughout the bustling streets of Candelária and São José. He contended that his handcarts would improve and sanitize vending practices to the extent of ensuring public order and proper nutrition. He specifically chose locations for stationing handcarts that would not disturb passersby or police officers. Kohn assured officials that his vehicles would be immediately removed from the street once a product was sold out or at least by two o'clock in the afternoon, since most foods were perishable and a threat to public health if overexposed to the elements.

Arguing that public and private partnership was crucial for the harmonious operation of a modernized street commerce, Kohn proposed that all peddlers in Rio be required to sell goods by using handcarts and tables manufactured by the EAD. Rio's municipal leaders, however, remained skeptical about Kohn's intentions. Four months before the final abolition of slavery in 1888, imperial officials interested in sanitizing street commerce approved Kohn's request for allowing hygienic handcarts to operate in the proposed locations "but never to the exclusion of other vendors, as that would constitute favor toward one company, or a hateful monopoly."[18] In a frustrated response, Kohn wrote that it was the "hygienic obligation" of municipal authorities to substitute the old system of "filthy vending tables" with the EAD's new models. He insisted that by not fully supporting his proposal, the municipality would suffer great economic losses due to the deterioration of public health caused by a backward street commerce. City officials, however, ignored his appeal but proceeded to change some aspects of street selling to support public health.[19]

Perhaps motivated by Kohn's ambition, municipal officials and the Comissão de Saúde e Praças (Commission on Health and Public Spaces) "urgently" addressed the sanitation of street commerce and approved "efficient measures that guaranteed the healthy condition of food that street vendors sold to the public."[20] Drawing on miasma and germ theories of contagion, the commission argued that "vendors travel the streets and roads of the municipality, stationing themselves in public squares, street corners, etc., without protecting their products from sun rays, rain, dust, insects, disease, poison, and infectious animals, while commercial transactions take place with such defects visible to buyers." In a meeting of the city council in the Imperial Palace on 28 July 1887, the city councilor Cândido Alves Pereira de Carvalho successfully proposed an ordinance establishing that starting in September all street vendors would sell meat, vegetables, fish, and perishable goods using new handcarts, not exclusively made by Kohn, that substituted old vending tables and baskets. Infractions would result in a fine equal to that for lacking a vending license, thirty milréis.[21] In addition, city councilors established a new regulation for vending on Sundays and holidays. While the rule required most businesses to close on Sunday, food markets, bakeries, and street peddlers were allowed to sell their goods until one o'clock in the afternoon.[22]

The proclamation of the First Republic on 15 November 1889 did not disrupt Kohn's campaign for monopoly. As the new republic institutionalized more economic liberties, Kohn viewed the transition as an opportunity rather than an obstacle for monopoly. On 29 December 1889 Kohn approached the Department of Hygiene with all the documentation he had collected over the previous years to continue advocating for monopoly and the superior quality of his vending apparatuses. Although republican officials stated that Kohn's "hygienic handcarts seemed not much different from those currently in use," they recognized the need for sanitation. This time Kohn compared his handcarts to "those used in the United States, Belgium, Holland, France, and other European countries preoccupied with public health."[23] Making reference to street commerce in European and North American centers reflected a transnational circulation of technical knowledge cast for local purpose. It also reminded officials that Rio was lagging behind its more heavily industrialized peers.

On 21 May 1890 Kohn transferred complete ownership of the EAD to a new business partner, Jerônimo Máximo Romano—a move that may have been motivated by the belief that a Brazilian would have a better chance at negotiating with officials in the new republic. Kohn remained a partner in the company, but he now centered on technical rather than business matters. Romano picked up where Kohn left off, seeking a state license that would grant the company a twenty-five-year monopoly over all vending apparatuses in Rio. The EAD proposed to pay the municipality 3,600 milréis annually for being the main outfit that regulated street commerce. The term "hygienic" continued to emphasize the unique handcarts, tables, and shoeshine chairs that Kohn designed. In 1890 republican officials reinstated the 1887 municipal law that declared that "meat, vegetables, fish, poultry, and other goods sold by street vendors would cease to be transported in baskets or tables, now having to be transported by push carts, which municipal officials would have to approve first according to quality and adequacy." In 1890 officials also renewed EAD's business license but like their imperial predecessors rejected the "hateful" twenty-five-year monopoly that Kohn and his partner sought.[24]

In addition to pressuring the municipality for a monopoly over vending technology, Kohn pursued individual patents for technologies that promised to modernize urban vending. In 1885 he submitted his first patent request for hygienic handcarts, claiming that they guaranteed the "comfortable, dynamic, and easy transportation" of goods such as fish, meat, milk, fruit, and vegetables.[25] Beyond promoting hygiene, the vehicle included an umbrella, a foldable table, scales for weighing, and an icebox to preserve food. Kohn understood the importance of an alluring presence for commercial success and suggested that his handcarts be painted with advertisements. Two years later Kohn sought to patent a "simple, clean, and elegant" model for shoeshine chairs (*cadeiras de engraxate*) that would "greatly improve the current system." The chair had drawers for brushes, rags, and polish and additional features such as a pillow for the shoe shiner to sit on, an umbrella to protect the customer, a niche for newspapers, and other compartments "destined for the sale of objects."[26]

An incident on a busy commercial street in central Rio illustrates the tenuous coexistence between peddlers and shoe shiners that Kohn's multipurpose chair was intended to mitigate. On 16 May 1885 thirteen residents of Candelária came out in defense of the Italian *engraxate* (shoe shiner) João Lucas, who worked on the busy street Rua Primeiro de Março and was often pestered by Agostinho Carmo, a vendor of refreshments who always positioned himself right next to Lucas. Lucas's customers were victims of Carmo's irritating behavior, and a number of them submitted a complaint to municipal authorities. All thirteen men who signed the complaint had witnessed Carmo "get too close with his handcart to the chair, throw water in their direction while he cleaned out drinking glasses, and use obscene language."[27] The competition for space between peddlers and shoe shiners could disturb customers, and Kohn's multipurpose chair aimed to substitute unnecessary peddling and conflict.

In 1887 Kohn requested patents for his shoeshine chair and for "portable and hygienic containers and tables." The containers and tables would be built specifically for the sale of meat, fish, vegetables, and sweets, and the models differed in design according to the product for sale. Emphasizing that there was "nothing more important for the hygienist than the clean distribution of food," Kohn argued that his invention "eliminated all the grave inconveniences" of traditional urban vending, which exposed food to "decay, decomposition, and corrosion." The tables and containers were made of zinc and had openings for ventilation, a sun umbrella, and "comfortable" accessories such as a head piece "to facilitate transportation when carried on the vendor's head."[28] Altogether, Kohn's hygienic handcarts, tables, containers, and shoeshine chairs highlight his knowledge of vending practices on the ground. Having an office in central Rio certainly facilitated such awareness.

In December 1887 Kohn solicited another patent, this time for "fire-resistant kiosks." Rio's kiosks were then a prominent aspect of street commerce and largely made of wood. Kohn proposed instead a model made of zinc to resist fire. It was common for kiosks to remain open at night, functioning as street cafés and snack bars where the working poor socialized. But poor electrical wiring or candlelight made kiosks unsafe and easily combustible. Kiosks were also vulnerable to street rioting. The 1880 Vintém riot, during which Rio's residents protested the fare increase for riding *bondes* (tram cars), resulted in the deliberate damage of public and private property, and kiosks were targeted by protesters.[29] These picturesque booths were the victims of innocent pranks as well. The writer Luís Gastão Escragnolle Dória (1869–1948) noted how in 1925 a group of university students decided to move a kiosk at night as a joke. The following morning the owner was shocked to find his kiosk standing across the street.[30] As kiosks were popular sites of leisure and sometimes of social unrest, they were the targets of urban reformers. For Kohn, upgrading them required sturdier materials and less vulnerability to everyday problems. This approach challenged municipal interests that aimed to eliminate kiosks altogether.

Scientific, creative, and entrepreneurial, Kohn was undoubtedly one of Rio's most prolific inventors at the turn of the twentieth century. He was also one of the first inventors to apply for government patents to improve vending methods, and his tenacious campaign to gain a monopoly reflected his ambition to outdo competitors. An examination of the vending vehicles and devices that other inventors sought to patent at the time affirms a flourishing street commerce.

HUMANITARIAN AND HYGIENIC VENDING TECHNOLOGY

A few inventors who submitted patent requests for new vending technologies between 1890 and 1909 stated in their reports that they had been in the application process for at least fifteen years, some since the 1870s. Because of the similarities between inventions, it is useful to examine vending technologies according to common themes rather than chronological order. Even though some requests appeared during the late slave period, they reentered the patenting process in the early 1900s, revealing that the ideology of free labor remained consistent. By the first decade of the twentieth century, Parisian-influenced designs appeared, but despite the attempt to reconcile vending with urban renewal, new regulations restricted street selling practices. Soon after the 1903 municipal ban on street commerce in the city center, inventors ceased to solicit patents for vending equipment.

The variety of vending vehicles, accessories, and improvements that inventors designed spoke to the socioeconomic needs of a growing urban population, public health concerns, and the supply and distribution of basic goods. In patent applications, street vending was modern, humane, and clean, conducted from kiosks that were fire-resistant and diverse models of hygienic handcarts and tables designed to comfortably transport poultry, eggs, meat, fruits, vegetables, sweets, refreshments, and baked goods to urban and suburban populations. Inventors provided solutions in a time of food shortages and price inflation.[31] By the twentieth century, however, technological innovation had not been the expected catalyst for modern vending in Rio.[32]

As previously noted, the term "hygienic" regularly appeared in patent requests to legitimize the uses of vending technologies, and technical sophistication varied according to invention. The word "hygienic" could describe simple trays that attached to windows and doors for people to sell goods on the street from the comfort of their homes.[33] The term could also apply to meticulously engineered vending apparatuses and vehicles. Concern for the physical comfort of the peddler followed the preoccupation with hygiene. In 1889 the Brazilian Paulo Vieira Sousa, a resident of Rio, requested a patent for his "auxiliary handcart." Unlike others of its kind, Sousa's handcart was capable of transporting heavy materials. A hand-drawn design accompanying the patent request lists the cart's capabilities. An advanced suspension system would cushion the handcart from jolts and collisions, as it was "endowed with handles and legs connected to a mobile axis that adjusts the center of gravity to facilitate the transportation of any weight with proper equilibrium and without tiring the vendor."[34] So, the handcart was "humanitarian and hygienic" and facilitated the work of peddlers, who were now no longer confined by the legacy of slavery in street vending.

In 1891, Manuel Moreira Dias submitted a patent request that was based on a similar idea. The accessory named "Illapso" could be added to any handcart as a supplemental device that adjusted the center of gravity to ensure equilibrium and physical comfort. Dias emphasized that the accessory allowed for the faster transportation of heavy weights and therefore fostered the prevention of accidents. Peddlers and carts often collided on crowded streets, "not only damaging produce, but oftentimes the street vendor as well."[35] In a postslave city, the protection of personhood was as important as the protection of property.

Quitandeiros and other vendors who used their shoulders to balance large baskets or carry heavy goods walked city streets seemingly unburdened (figure 3.1). Anyone who looked twice could appreciate the heavy loads they carried. In 1897 Artur Augusto Azevedo introduced a neck apparatus for vending that he said would distribute weight on a peddler's shoulders.[36] Azevedo's model preceded Manuel Antônio Guimarães's 1902 "Hygienic Street Peddler." Gui-

FIGURE 3.1. Quitandeiro and broom vendor, 1895. *Carte de visite* with photographs by Marc Ferrez. Courtesy of G. Ermakoff Casa Editorial, Arquivo Images2You.

marães, like Azevedo, wanted to improve the "inconvenient system of baskets" that vendors traditionally used to transport fresh produce. The Hygienic Street Peddler was specifically "designed to substitute the traditional system of baskets that vegetable and fish vendors use," a system that "left much to be desired for in terms of hygiene since goods were easily bruised and spoiled" as well as damaging vendors' necks and shoulders. Guimarães added a pillow to the wooden bar from which baskets hung to pad peddlers' shoulders. This piece, which seemed to choke the neck, ensured comfort nonetheless, Guimarães promised. The Hygienic Street Peddler was so effective, he asserted, that it could withstand the weight of three or more baskets (figure 3.2).[37]

Some inventors created vending vehicles to market goods that were particularly Brazilian, such as coconut sweets, sugarcane juice, and other products that residents of the capital city enjoyed. Fresh sugarcane juice was one of Rio's most popular refreshments, and people of diverse social backgrounds enjoyed it during the hot summer months. In 1825 Debret depicted a manual sugar mill (*engenhoca*) that made sugarcane juice in urban households.[38] Debret's painting shows slaves at work in a Rio household, but this type of manual sugar mill could also be found on plantations and in small towns.

Debret also painted city street peddlers selling cane juice already poured into glasses on trays.[39] In 1888, the year slavery was finally abolished in Brazil, the French citizen and Rio resident Antônio Jacques Junot identified the

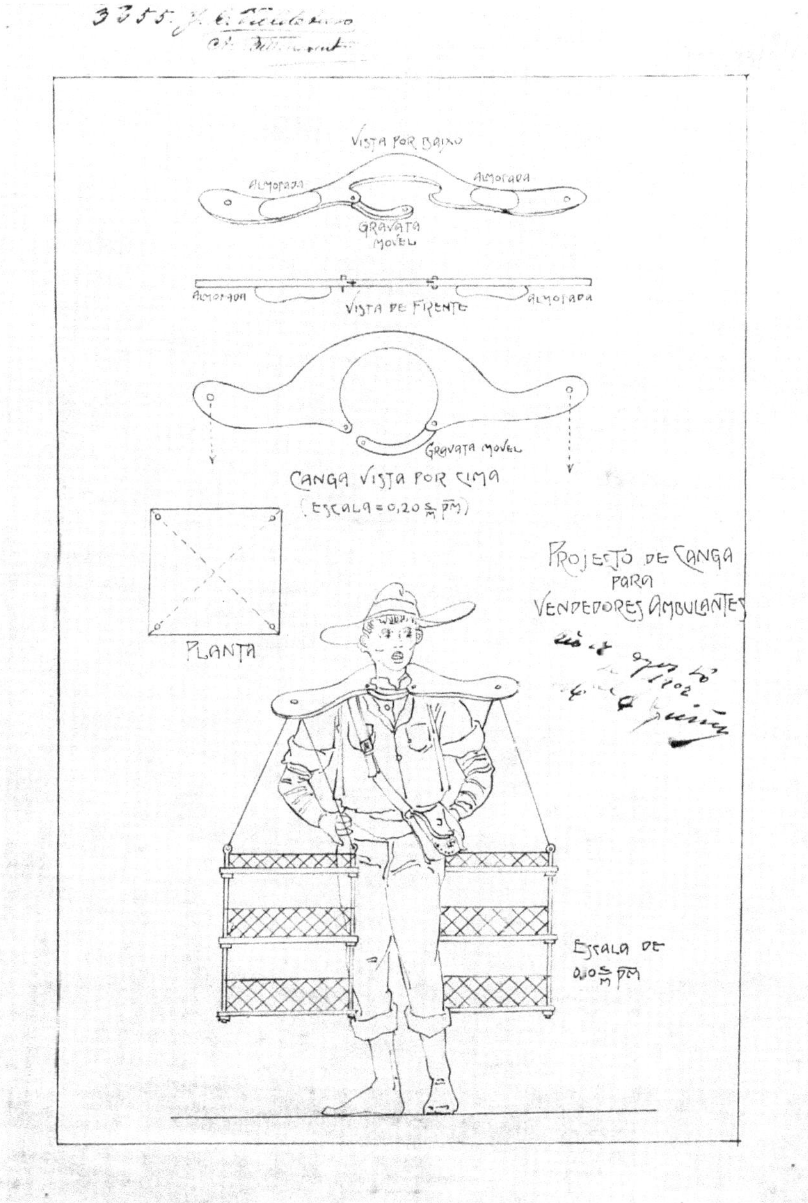

FIGURE 3.2. Hygienic street vendor yoke, 1902. Manuel Antônio Guimarães, patent request 3312. Courtesy of Coordenação de Atendimento a Distância, Arquivo Nacional, Rio de Janeiro.

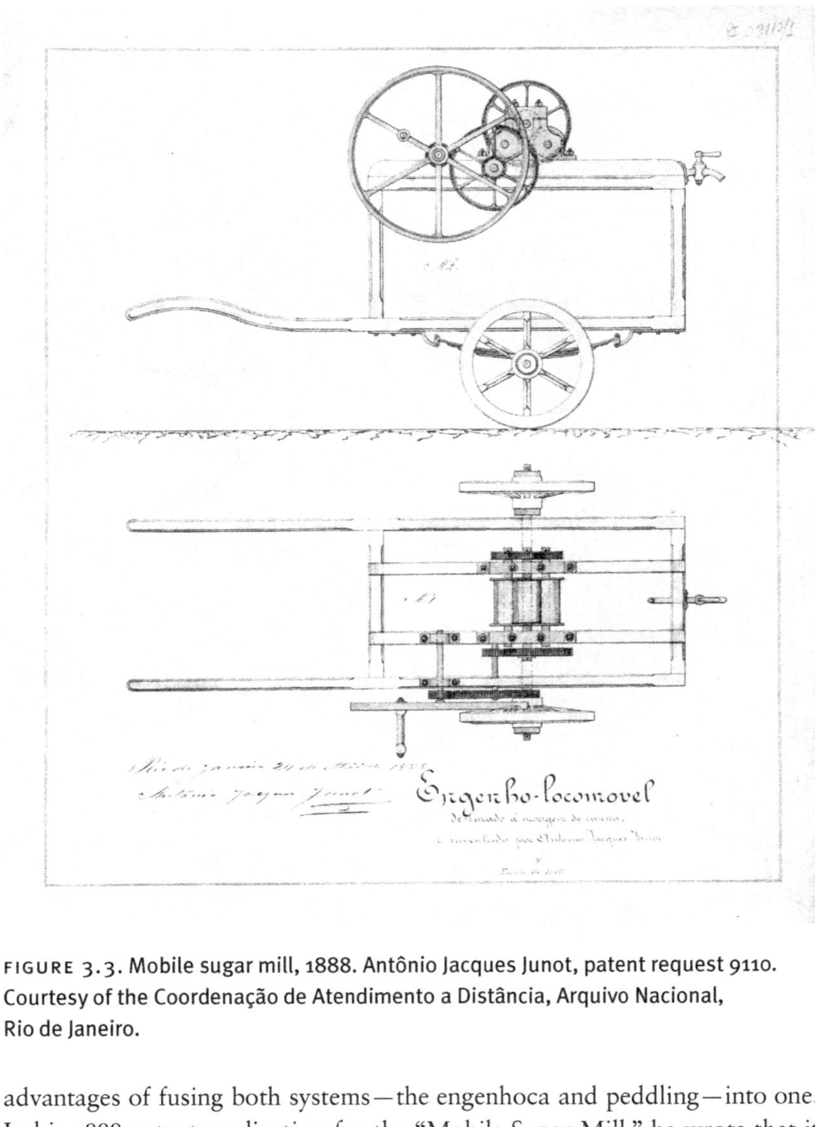

FIGURE 3.3. Mobile sugar mill, 1888. Antônio Jacques Junot, patent request 9110. Courtesy of the Coordenação de Atendimento a Distância, Arquivo Nacional, Rio de Janeiro.

advantages of fusing both systems—the engenhoca and peddling—into one. In his 1888 patent application for the "Mobile Sugar Mill," he wrote that it was "made to mill sugar anywhere in the city and to sell juice to people on streets, plazas, and in residential and suburban areas."[40] The vendor could now crush sugarcane as he walked with the help of the rotation of wooden wheels mounted on the handcart (figure 3.3). Junot explained that since cane juice fermented rapidly, his invention could freshly squeeze juice on the spot. As a result, juice "always reached the hands of the consumer before fermentation occurred . . . always fresh." A patent request in 1893 by Carlos Augusto de Castro e Silva proposed a similar idea. He named his mobile engenhoca the "Ambulatory Sugar Mill"; it was designed to be animal-driven and made of wood. As opposed to milling the cane manually, Castro e Silva's vehicle would systematically connect the mill's rotation with the carriage's wheels. Consequently, carriage movement and cane squeezing occurred simultaneously. The inventor contended that street vendors "could now take advantage of the warm season, when consumers sought cheap refreshments."[41]

Candy and baked goods were other popular items peddled on the streets of Rio, most often by slaves and free Afro-descendants. Owners of bakeries relied on male workers who delivered fresh bread to private households and businesses, a practice that created tension between police and bakery owners.[42] Rio's bread industry experienced great transformation during the urban and public health reforms that Mayor Pereira Passos initiated. The year after the end of the Pereira Passos administration, the municipality ordered the immediate adoption of closed baskets and special vehicles imported from France for the "hygienic distribution of bread." Bakery owners responded with complaints, asserting that such a law was a great imposition on their economic liberty and they needed at least sixty more days to purchase the French-made carriages. Their grievances revealed anxiety surrounding an accelerated modernity that overlooked the realities of daily food distribution. Bakers protested that they could not meet the "time exigencies" that the municipality was imposing on them and requested patience and "tolerance." Although there were numerous alternatives to imported European vehicles for bread delivery, as evidenced in the many Brazilian patent requests that displayed a local understanding of innovation, urban officials in 1908 still favored an imported European modernity. Bakery owners noted how the municipality "did not find the means to obtain such a vehicle [in Brazil] and thus had to order it from a French factory, which was not able to deliver the vehicle immediately, as it was necessary to create a model that was elegant, portable, and suitable for the distribution of bread in Rio."[43] This was testament to the disconnection between officials and local patent seekers who could have easily created such a vehicle.

Patent applicants also created different types of boxes and containers that promised to improve the sale of sweets that to this day are a popular Brazilian street food.[44] Starting in 1892 and for the next fifteen years, Odilo Lorenzo sought to patent the "Perfected Box for the Sale of Sweets," which was made out of glass, wood, and metal—an "invention destined for the street peddler of sweets." It was "a light, elegant, and hygienic apparatus with fitting compartments and good ventilation that protected [goods] from dust and other unsanitary things."[45] Enslaved and free peddlers in the city had sold sweets

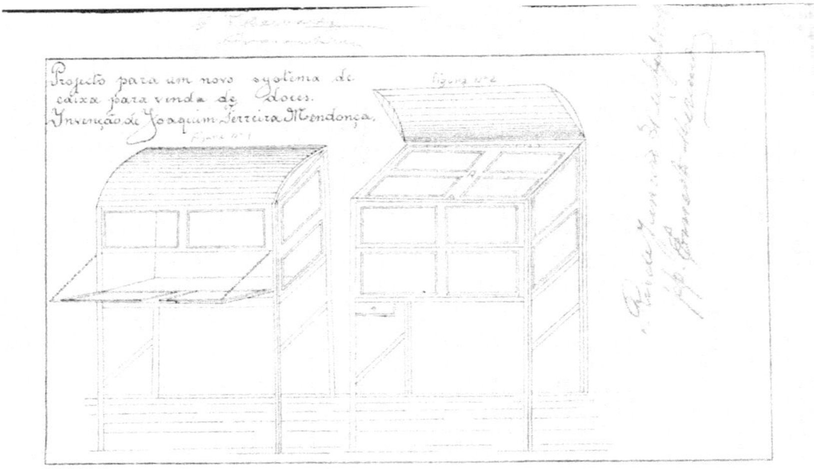

FIGURE 3.4. New system for selling sweets, 1908. Odilo Lorenzo, patent request 4773. Courtesy of Coordenação de Atendimento a Distância, Arquivo Nacional, Rio de Janeiro.

directly off trays and tables, and by the 1880s such goods were presented in glass displays. In 1895 the photographer Marc Ferrez took a picture of a black man in Rio selling sweets off such a table.[46] In 1908 a resident of the city of São Paulo, Joaquim Ferreira Mendonça, resubmitted a patent request that had been in the application process for fifteen years.[47] His design consisted of middle glass layers that would further protect sugary goods from dust and insects and thus improved the traditional tables used for the street selling of sweets (figure 3.4).

The Brazilian industrialist F. Paulo de Freitas had also been trying to patent a "new system of containers for bakeries, street vendors, and other ambulatory businesses" for fifteen years before submitting another request in 1909. The containers he proposed could be made of "wood, zinc, or an impermeable material." The two opposite lateral sides were sliding glass doors used to place a variety of products that "suited bakers and street vendors." His design guaranteed hygiene and food preservation, with containers that were "easy to carry and set up without the help of another person and without sacrificing one's health." Freitas claimed that his mobile device did not demand "the constant effort of muscles and tendons."[48] The same inventor also submitted a patent request for a "system of (mobile or fixed) feet and doors applicable to containers and baskets that bakeries and other ambulatory businesses generally use." Instead of resting containers and baskets directly on the ground, small wheels, or "feet," provided not only easier transportation but also protection from street grime. Therefore, the street vendor could work "without the auxiliary help of a second person" or being "forced to frequent stops and rests because of fatigue and physical exhaustion." Freitas promised that his invention prevented food from spoiling while it also "preserve[d] the health of the vendor," contributing to public health, the common good, and the individual well-being of peddlers.[49]

In 1909 three Brazilian residents of Rio who were public functionaries submitted an application to patent a special type of vending container designed fifteen years earlier. They named this the "Double Turning Box," and it consisted of two parallel boxes with shelves that were connected through a bar resting on the vendor's shoulders to "facilitate transportation." The divisions in each box could be adapted to the product sold, so that the box would be "capable of carrying knick-knacks, fish, meat, bread, sweets, fruits, and more." This vending utility could be made out of wood or metal, the boxes with shelves rotated when settled on the floor, and there was even space for advertisements. The invention was a "symmetrical apparatus, clean and elegant, reflective of hygiene and order." All in all, the device "offered advantages with regard to aesthetics, comfort, and hygiene." It allowed for the comfortable "transport of double the usual weight, distributing weight evenly without straining the vendor, who is now able to preserve a natural posture." The inventors argued that existing vending methods were uncomfortable and unsanitary—meat sat on filthy wooden tables covered with flies, goods for sale were poorly displayed, and fish was overexposed. They claimed that officials disregarded public health and particularly ignored fish vendors. The inventors noted that "when a fish vendor passes by we are all forced to cover our noses with handkerchiefs because of the putrid smell of fish water that causes further deterioration of the fish." Moreover, "because of poor posture, street vendors injure their respiratory, renal, and spinal systems along with their ligaments." The "Double Turning Box" was therefore a solution for these public health and humanitarian concerns.[50]

Municipal officials frequently addressed health concerns in the sale of fresh meat (*carne verde*), which were raised in several patent requests as well. Municipal records illustrate the regular passing of laws regarding sanitation in the city's slaughterhouses.[51] In 1883 and 1898, Augusto Magalhães de Barros Vasconcelos sought to patent a vehicle that would ensure the safe and clean transport of meat from Rio's main slaughterhouse. He proposed a vehicle that could transport other perishable goods such as vegetables, fish, and eggs in a portable icebox that he named the "Excelsior Refrigerator." Vasconcelos engineered the Excelsior refrigerator carriage to transfer meat from the slaughterhouse in São Diogo to private homes and shops. The refrigerator carriage was specially equipped for keeping out the summer heat, which accelerated the deterioration of meat. Its three boxes made of iron or copper could hold twenty kilos of ice and calcium chloride, a chemical used to keep temperatures as low as 10 degrees Celsius. The Excelsior thus enhanced the "safe and efficient nutrition" of Rio's residents.[52]

In 1890, Carlos Freire Vilhalba Alvim and Jorge Alberto Vinhon designed a mobile butcher shop (*açougue volante*) "in order to serve all suburban parishes" and allow residents to buy meat by weight.[53] Their vehicle was another apparatus that could replace the "filthy" tables where meat customarily was sold although the municipality had by then banned them. The ambulatory butcher shop stood on four wheels and had all the necessary appliances such as a marble cutting board, hooks for hanging meat, knives, and even a small basin for hand-washing. The cart was animal-driven, much like the passenger trams of the era. The vendor had the option of remaining seated in the carriage when serving customers, while a pull-out staircase facilitated getting in and out. Another device Vilhalba and Vinhon designed was capable of hooking up to trams, turning public transportation into another site of street commerce. A year later, Benedito Novella e Silva sought to patent an ambulatory meat shop with similar features engineered to distribute meat to the suburban population. Manuel Alves Lobo in 1896 introduced a model with interior air fans that whirled in sync with the carriage's wheels.[54] Between 1889 and 1904, Antônio Ferreira da Silva sought several times to patent a special container made out of zinc for selling meat parts on the street.[55] Patent requests for vehicles, containers, and accessories to store and transport meat generally emphasized hygiene, given public concerns about transporting meat from the unsanitary municipal slaughterhouse.

The ability to move produce between the city's center to its periphery was a common theme that many of the proposed inventions shared. In 1886, José de Freitas Pinheiro sought to patent handcarts that he had designed for street vendors who desired to sell their goods in suburban areas. People who lived on the outskirts of Rio generally had difficulty buying basic goods due to lack of transportation. They could rely on vendors, though, while the main market in Candelária was distant and more expensive. In contrast, Pinheiro's handcarts were a "useful invention . . . practical and industrial," designed to address the daily needs of suburban residents and thus a "great convenience for all working poor."[56] A request in 1891 also focused on taking goods to suburban residents. Pedro Antônio Fagundes, inventor of the "Fagundes System," described the deteriorating effect of Rio's hot tropical climate on meat. He was proposing "a clean and fresh carriage" capable of transporting meat to suburban households and substituting the "filthy and impractical handcarts that to this day have been of deplorable service to the city."[57] Similar to the Excelsior, Fagundes's invention was a cooling system to keep meat fresh and clean while it was transported from the city center to the periphery. Blinds protected meat from the sun and the dusty ride, and the inside of the carriage had all the necessary amenities such as scales and cutting boards.

Many other inventions were designed to keep meat fresh. Although the working poor could only afford meat a few times per week, it was still considered a staple food. In 1898, Benigno Riva and José Stockmeyer applied for a patent for a carriage that was "made with all the principles of good hygiene, ready to sell everything that was necessary for the daily nutrition of the family." They claimed that their vehicle was "a great advantage for housewives, who could save time by easily choosing fresh meat from the comfort of their homes and not having to worry about the lack of domestic help."[58] Other patent requests for vehicles that transported basic household goods linked urban and suburban street commerce while addressing the scarcities in suburban Rio. These new vending technologies were adaptations to the needs of shifting urban and suburban populations that resulted from slavery's decline and the ensuing migrations.

The suburban areas of Rio at the turn of the twentieth century included the northern districts of Inhaúma, Irajá, Jacarepaguá, and Guaratiba popularly known as the *sertão carioca*, the backlands of Rio. The population grew rapidly in these peripheral areas after the abolition of slavery, and the growth stimulated urban development to the extent that it inspired new research. A book was published on the topic in 1936 by the Instituto Histórico e Geográfico Brasileiro; *O sertão carioca* by Magalhães Corrêa examined the various social, cultural, and economic aspects of Rio's suburban periphery. The author dedicated two chapters to rural peddlers and urban and suburban vendors.[59] This 1936 publication demonstrates the commercial connection between central and peripheral Rio, with simple rural and suburban peddlers—and not sophisticated carriages and handcarts—furnishing households with basic goods. Eventually, a distinct vending culture developed in the suburbs that was shaped by rural-urban migrations and ties between the urban center and periphery. Scholars today have described this region in Rio as the interconnected Recôncavo da Guanabara.[60]

Just as many inventors of new vending technologies were concerned with supplying families with basic goods, some vehicles and accessories were created to provide food to the city's workers. In 1891, Victorino de Silveira Sousa Filho and João José Lopes Júnior made a special backpack for the transport of liquids such as soup, broth, cold drinks, and cane juice. The backpack would bring these to "all port warehouses and workplaces" in the city and hence deliver "healthy nutrition that reenergizes and strengthens workers involved in manual labor." The inventors stressed that "if the worker must spend one or two tostões (cents) on ice cream, soups, or beverages, the device ensures the adequate conservation of temperature for street selling, healthy nutrition, and the renewal of hard work."[61] Sousa and Lopes also designed carriages to transport soup and refreshments to workers in Rio's port area. Preoccupation with the health and nutrition of workers reflected a free labor ideology that dignified the nonslave manual worker. In proposals to increase the physical comfort of peddlers, manual labor is not depicted as demeaning or analogous to slavery but rather one more activity in Rio's industrial development.

Technical innovations for modern street commerce included advertising, automatic vending machines, and motorized vehicles. The multiple features that characterized these inventions reflected street commerce as a versatile activity beyond the exchange between seller and consumer. Speed, advertising, and the aesthetic display of goods were all aspects of street selling that transformed urban space into a site where consumer goods were promoted by a new modern and visual experience. Whereas sound characterized older forms of street selling, as peddlers' catchy lines captured the attention of passersby, overcrowded streets now rendered verbal advertising less effective. Proposals emphasized instead the novelty of visual allure, beginning to transform public space as more people occupied the street as consumers.

In 1891, Cateyson Desthur and Sérgio Companheiro submitted a patent request for an invention they had created at least fifteen years earlier. Their "Portable Billboard" was designed to display moving advertisements. Desthur and Companheiro had worked in the field of advertising, using city walls and trams to promote various products. This time they were proposing to take advertising to the street by using "ad men" (*homens-anúncio*) who would wear billboards (*tabuletas*) made of wood or metal. Another name these inventors used for human billboards was the more common "sandwich men" (*homens-sanduíche*) who were able to walk more easily, they claimed, through crowded streets.[62]

The inventors stated that their billboard was "light-weight and very easy to transport" without disturbing public transit. They suggested that sandwich men could wear "the uniform of the company that they were working for to call more attention to themselves." Ads could even be "creatively painted to increase profits." Lighting permitted the wearers to work at night.[63] The use of sandwich men was already a common advertising strategy in European capitals like Paris and London. In 1906, J. E. Coelho de Magalhães merged street selling and advertising in his "Pan-American Cart."[64] An open umbrella for displaying advertisements topped the cart designed for selling refreshments. The vehicle included an icebox, a small basin for washing drinking glasses, fixed Chinese lanterns, iron wheels, and a parasol to protect liquids from the sun.

Valdemar Flor Kathiessen, a naturalized Brazilian citizen who made watches and clocks, submitted in 1891 a request to patent his "Automatic Vendor," an apparatus similar to today's vending machines.[65] Its purpose was to facilitate the sale of small items in train stations and other locations where people "cannot waste time buying small objects of necessity like cigars, cigarettes, etc." from peddlers. The Automatic Vendor released the product after the insertion of a coin into the appropriate slot; although there were other vending machines in the city like it, they were unreliable, according to Kathiessen. His model was of superior quality and did not delay transactions due to the "irregularities of other services." The larger process of mechanized labor was beginning to substitute humans with machines for greater and faster production, and street commerce was no exception. A clockmaker thus seemed to naturally venture into designing a vending machine that saved time.

Belle Époque trends also influenced the modeling of new vending technologies. In 1902, Manuel Antônio Guimarães, a military official who lived in Rio, sought to patent several vehicles that could transport a variety of goods. The vehicles were lightweight and adhered to the principles of "homogeneity, hygiene, simple elegance, and sturdiness."[66] They were decorated to advertise specific products, and the lieutenant emphasized their elegant Parisian quality. Similarly, in 1906, Francisco Falconi, an Italian industrialist who was a resident of Rio, requested to patent his "Yvonette Cart." Vendors who sold flowers, fruits, sweets, and other items of petty commerce would find it comfortable, and customers would find it alluring. The montage-like structure consisted of a miniature Eiffel Tower on top of a box that rested on a tricycle.[67] The street vendor would pedal the tricycle, or it could be motorized. The reproduction of a small Eiffel Tower evoked a popular symbol of European modernity that the inventor hoped would attract customers. The same year, Augusto Fernandes Carreira requested a patent for a vending vehicle that could be run by motor or animal power. Its capacity was greater than the Yvonette Cart, and it could transport larger volumes of bread, pastries, trinkets, and toys, which could all be displayed in a window. He named this vehicle the "Window-Shop Carriage."[68] Articles on display were intended to capture the gaze of passersby, which a few decades later philosopher Walter Benjamin argued was a crucial experience of urban consumer capitalism.[69] These new technologies show how street selling could modernize to appeal to a new type of consumer—the "shopper, committed to making window-shopping capitalism's favorite pastime" and the "flâneur as city stroller, window-shopper and ponderer of modernity."[70]

STREET COMMERCE AND BRAZILIAN MODERNITY

The vending technology developed at the turn of the twentieth century reflected differences between slave society and a consumer culture based on free labor. Inventing a device for street commerce represented an attempt to improve the conditions for both buyers and sellers, as proposed technologies focused on vendors' comfort and buyers' security. Attempting to modernize vending through technical innovation also reflected street commerce as a natural part of city life. Inventors modeled their designs according to Western trends but adapted them for local use. The influx of European immigrants, greater rural-to-urban migration, and an expanding urban periphery influenced their local interpretations of a modern street commerce in a changing slave and postslave city.

Highlighting the humanitarian and hygienic qualities of new vending technologies, inventors demonstrated awareness of a free labor ideology that encompassed efforts to distance street commerce from its slave past. The emphasis on physical comfort and sanitation countered the filthy conditions of the past and corresponded to progressive thought of the times. Proposals erased the slave person and presented a reformed, free peddler who was European in the drawings that accompanied written reports. Not one street seller depicted in these illustrations was brown, black, or female, while the reality on Rio's streets was quite different despite the increased number of European immigrants. In patent requests, it was practice and peddler—rather than the idea of street commerce—that were backward because of connections to slavery.

At the end of the nineteenth century, street commerce shifted from being a fundamental aspect of Rio's urban slave economy to a manifestation of free commerce that municipal officials persistently defended against the inventor Morris Kohn's monopolistic ambitions. Urban reforms that soon followed were not as optimistic about vending, however. But before the influence of Mayor Pereira Passos, efficiency and sanitation could not sacrifice the individual freedom of peddlers, even with the best humanitarian and hygienic intentions. Nineteenth-century Brazilian liberalism had "ideologically filtered" and "contemporized" Western thought—a practice that shaped the transition to free labor. Brazilian critical theorist Alfredo Bosi has used these words to explain how Brazilian political elites resolved the paradox of laissez-faire and slavery by making these compatible and "corporative" and not "out of place".[71] In other words, Brazilian conditions adjusted Western beliefs in economic and political liberalism to limit access to political and economic freedoms according to race, class, and gender. On the one hand, officials approved rational measures that required vendors to use certain vending instruments such as hygienic handcarts and carriages imported from France, but in doing so they limited vendors' preferences and options in a free market. On the other hand, officials rejected Kohn's campaign to gain monopoly over vending technology, claiming it was a hateful practice against the principles of free commerce. Inconsistencies persisted as attempts to regulate street commerce were welcomed or seen as undue limitations on individual liberties and contrary to a general laissez-faire ideology.

The rationalization of urban vending in a transnational context was indeed a process of ideological filtering and contemporization as science, entrepreneurship, and urban development converged locally to improve the quality of basic urban services in Rio. Although inventors—some of them foreign residents in Brazil—fashioned their devices or defended their projects according to European principles, the necessity that justified innovation was grounded in everyday urban life such as the easy mobility of peddlers through crowded streets and the capacity of vehicles to reach peripheral neighborhoods. Street commerce was a flexible activity that could easily serve the needs of a shifting population in packed spaces and new neighborhoods. Street selling—rational or traditional, immigrant or African—was a transnational, diasporic practice. Many patent requests of the period implicitly or explicitly acknowledged international trends and tailored them to local needs and conditions. Proposals also reflected tropical concerns such as selling cold sugarcane juice during hot summer months, a practice that surely would have resonated in other Atlantic port cities such as Salvador and Recife in Brazil and Havana in Cuba.

PART 2

ENDURANCE

CHAPTER 4

A DETRIMENT TO THE LAW

EIGHTEEN MONTHS AFTER the final abolition of Brazilian slavery in 1888, a military coup with positivist and liberal links established the First Republic. A year earlier, Rio's slaves accounted for 9 percent of the total population, but the legacies of slavery still influenced free labor practices. Leaders of the new Brazilian republic aimed to reform a society built around centuries of slavery, but the exclusionary basis for full political citizenship established in 1881 remained. The law divided men into active voter and passive nonvoter citizens, and the literacy requirement alone rendered the majority of Brazilian men passive citizens, nor could women vote. Given limited citizenship and dependent labor relations between patrons and most Brazilian workers at this time, the 1890 Penal Code became a legal instrument for disciplining Rio's popular classes.[1] Consequently, police targeted vendors for street behaviors unrelated to the actual practice of buying and selling. Public disorder and vagrancy, as defined by the new code and influenced by earlier measures, were common grounds for arrest and incarceration regardless of licensed vending practices. In court hearings, judges were less predictable in rulings toward detained vendors, as ideologies of work and honor influenced their decisions to varying degrees.

As the slave past continued to cast a shadow on the nation's political body, so did the collapse of Brazil's monarchical regime. The last Brazilian emperor and empress were generally viewed as slave emancipators, while republican propaganda was disseminated about their "dynastic, hypocritical, and false" abolitionism, arguing that it "compromised the future of the black race."[2] Still, most Afro-descendant workers on the streets of Rio continued to identify as monarchists. Observing the tattoos on people who walked around central Rio in the 1900s, chronicler João do Rio noted their political orientations: "the mermaid encourages talk, the cobra attraction; the fish signifies agility in water, the anchor and star the sailor, the arms of the republic or monarchy political orientation. By the number of royal crowns that I saw, almost all people are monarchists."[3] While monarchist sentiment persisted, street vendors encountered a new republic that was ambivalent toward their work. The new laws sellers navigated on the street and in courts show mixed official attitudes that formalized street vending in the Brazilian capital city.

UNCERTAIN CITIZENSHIP

In 1881, the French biologist Louis Couty (1854–1884), who spent the last eight years of his life in Rio, pronounced the widely quoted statement "O Brasil não tem povo" (Brazil has no people) to convey that he did not see, notes the Brazilian historian José Murilo de Carvalho, "the organized masses composed of small farmers and industrial proletariat that in civilized countries constitute the base of wealth" and the mass electoral base of government.[4] Slavery and racial mixture, Couty implied, had destroyed that possibility. The Brazilian republican Aristides Lobo (1838–1896) later summarized Couty's observation with the term *bestializados*. After witnessing the 1889 inauguration of the First Republic, Lobo saw apathy toward political life in Brazilians that he said "bestialized" them. However, as the Brazilian historian José Murilo de Carvalho points out, "It is worth asking whether this perceived inexistence of the people is more a consequence of the type of people or citizenry sought after" than an inherent anomie.[5] In everyday policing, the apathetic crowd soon became a dangerous element, and vendors were now more vulnerable to the reaches of criminal law.

As a result of the application of the 1890 Penal Code toward the policing of street vendors, more sellers were processed in court with vagrancy and public disorder charges. The detention and court system helped create what James Holston has defined as Brazil's "inclusively inegalitarian citizenship." In examining the historical uses of citizenship in Brazil since 1881, Holston, a political anthropologist, posits that Brazilian "citizenship is a measure of difference and a means of distancing people from one another. It reminds people of what they are not—even though paradoxically, they are themselves citizens—and defines citizens as others."[6] The state thus created a "differentiated citizenship" based on a "gradation of rights" that defined and regulated political, social, and civil spheres, legitimizing differential treatment of citizens based on perceived types. This hegemonic process normalized a culture of individual- and group-based citizenship according to education, property, race, gender, and occupational differences. The popular use of the term *cidadão qualquer*, Holston notes, reflects the lowest type of citizenry, an "anonymous citizen" with no formal identity in family, labor, or community relations yet still an individual citizen that Brazilians recognize.[7]

Differentiated citizenship is not far from what Olívia Gomes da Cunha and Flávio dos Santos Gomes define as the "almost-citizen" (*quase-cidadão*) in Brazil. Almost-citizenship characterizes the status of the postabolition poor, they argue, as a result of the structures that freedom generated. Social marginality was a consequence of almost-citizenship, a type of differentiated citizenship but not an absence of citizenship. Cunha and Gomes maintain that Afro-Brazilians and the working poor in general experienced freedom after slavery as a slippery condition that was not invalidated by notions of black pathology. Citizenship was instead a conditional and "provisional dimension" that structurally and experientially made freedom an incomplete experience.[8] Socioeconomic marginality thus occurred with the process of citizenship building, as Brodwyn Fischer explains in her book *A Poverty of Rights*.[9] Similarly, Holston's "differentiated citizenship" is not a euphemism for "dysfunctional citizenship" or "incomplete modernity" but the basis for an "inclusively inegalitarian citizenship."[10] By characterizing the postabolition poor as almost-citizens, Cunha and Gomes speak to this uneven inclusion, although their discussion seems to focus more on the "almost" than the "citizen" to emphasize a process in which full citizenship remains incomplete.[11]

It was from this position of differentiated or quasi-citizenship that vendors experienced a legal culture of street discipline during Brazil's First Republic. While both the ganho system and criminal law regulated vendors' activities on the street, the shift from ganho regulation to the policing of criminal behavior became more pronounced in the early republican period. Criminality informed police authorities' management of the street, while the judicial process exposed racial thinking and labor ideology that were not necessarily predictable. Charging or discharging peddlers may have fulfilled the mantra of discipline, but judges' decisions did not further criminalize the practice of street selling.

So, as municipal administrators continued to hand out street vending licenses with the appropriate police registration numbers, police enforced the street disciplinary measures of the 1890 Penal Code. During the late slave period, the application of vagrancy laws had begun to deal with unlicensed peddlers and intensified after 1890 as the increasing numbers of vendors held in Rio's detention center reveal. Though street vending was a lawful activity at this time, vendors became an unwanted element of street life that the police removed, even if temporarily, with the help of criminal law. Detention entries for street sellers became more prominent after 1890, pushing street commerce to informal margins.

The 1890 Penal Code replaced the 1830 Criminal Code to rehabilitate a postslave society and discipline a new population of workers in Brazil. The police and the judiciary system used the new penal code to implant ideas about good behavior in republican urban life. Unlike vagrancy, gambling, and certain forms of begging, street vending was not a criminal activity, but as was the case in the late slave period, criminal charges brought against vendors could regulate undesired aspects of street commerce. The 1890 Penal Code thus facilitated street policing, as ideologies of work, race, and gender further formed legal and popular belief systems.[12] Horizontal ties in Rio's traditional vending community and vertical relations in the police and judicial system affected court decisions, revealing official attitudes toward street commerce that were variable and, at best, sympathetic to vendors' freedom to sell.

The registry of entries into Rio's Casa de Detenção demonstrates that being unlicensed usually did not result in the incarceration of vendors and ganhadores. Rather, behaviors associated with begging, inebriation, gambling, capoeira, vagrancy, public disorder, and theft, or violations of the 1890 Penal Code, led to the arrests and detention of a greater number of street sellers. Not carrying a vending license usually resulted in an arrest resolved at the local police station or became an act of vagrancy in detention records. As the 1883 detention records from Santana indicate, police increasingly used antivagrancy laws to arrest unlicensed ganhadores. Holding a license offered little protection from policing that, for instance, deemed ganhadores' walking on sidewalks as disorderly conduct rather than as an infraction of commercial regulation.

Antivagrancy laws targeted the former slaves and poor immigrants who made up most of the participants of street commerce. Article 295 of the 1830 Criminal Code had established compulsory labor as punishment for vagrancy and discipline for those lacking an "honest and useful" occupation. After 1830, forced labor for eight to twenty-four days initiated the process of rehabilitation, though it arguably focused little on true rehabilitation.[13] The 1890 Penal Code further criminalized vagrancy, still aiming to rehabilitate inmates through punishment. An individual could be charged and convicted of vagrancy under Article 399 of the 1890 Penal Code for lacking the required proof of residence, employment contract, or employer testimony. In efforts to rehabilitate convicted vagrants, detainees signed a statement to obtain employment within fifteen days of their release. For the same disciplinary purposes, those between the ages of fourteen and twenty-one were held at labor camps outside the detention center.

Article 399 defined a vagrant as lacking a "profession, trade, means to earn a living, [or] place of residence" and therefore making a living "through illegal occupations" or "morally offensive" means.[14] To avoid such charges, detained street sellers who had weaker ties with patrons and formal employment tended to describe themselves as workers (*trabalhadores*).[15] Declaring that one was a street vendor, a lawful occupation, carried more legitimacy than the general category of *trabalhador* but was still no guarantee of protection against conviction. Participants of street commerce had reason to view themselves as formal workers, especially since the ganho system of the nineteenth century contributed to the growth of street commerce as a legal occupation. However, associations of street commerce with slavery as well as with disorder and vagrancy charges under criminal law led to the delegitimation of peddlers. Street vendors were caught between the uneven recognition of a disappearing ganho system and the stigma that the 1890 Penal Code placed on them. While street vending was a practice that court officials recognized as lawful if licensed, the frequent detention of vendors was a result of policing practices that marginalized their work.

FORMS OF STREET COMMERCE IN TRANSITION

The rationalization of time along with the licensing of vendors and changes in the distribution of goods were part of the larger transition in street commerce. Officials upheld that the closing of business on Sunday was fundamental for modern Christian nations like Brazil. By 1887, most commercial establishments in Rio were closed on Sundays and holidays.[16] Owners who wanted their businesses to remain open on Sundays and holidays contested this regulation by highlighting economic interests as well as ideas of adequate rest for workers.

On 2 November 1890, the Society of Dry and Wet Goods Retailers (Sociedade da União Comercial dos Varejistas de Secos e Molhados) approached municipal officials to request that their stores be allowed to remain open on Sunday until noon. They argued that Sunday, the day when "the capitalist, the public functionary, the worker, the artisan, and the fieldworker have off is exactly the busiest, most profitable day."[17] In their complaint they appealed to the "individual liberty" and "democracy" that the new republic promised, recalling the unjust monopoly they had tolerated under Portuguese and imperial rule. Just "like pharmacies and hotels" remained open on Sundays, the owners of dry and wet goods stores said their industry needed official permission to work on Sundays. Further, they employed ganhadores to distribute their goods, and since vendors were allowed to work on Sundays, the owners of dry goods stores reasoned that they ought to receive the same treatment as vendors' suppliers.

Bakers similarly argued that their establishments should remain open on Sunday mornings, considering residents' desires to buy fresh bread every day. In their appeal to municipal authorities, however, bakery owners sought shorter hours on Sundays than on weekdays. Like the city's dry goods stores bakeries relied on vendors to distribute goods beyond the storefront. Staying open for business on Sunday was crucial for this type of sales, but afternoon hours, they argued, were unnecessary. The laws of 1887 had not adjusted the Sunday or holiday schedules, as bread stores and bakeries officially remained open well beyond one o'clock in the afternoon. In 1890, the board of the Bakers' Protective Society (Diretório da Sociedade Protetora dos Empregados de Padaria e Classes Auxiliares), with headquarters in prosperous Candelária, condemned the daily "twenty-five hour workload of bakeries," during which "workers do not sleep, and many quit their jobs just to be able to sleep."[18] Bakers remained eager to keep their stores open and supply vendors on Sunday mornings but only as late as necessary. Meeting customer demand was as important as honoring a half day of rest in an industry whose ovens were rarely turned off.

Besides the rationalization of time, the formal use of urban space preoccupied officials wanting to modernize food distribution and cleanse the street. An 1892 law required men who sold and delivered bread to carry weight scales on the street. In 1896, the large number of delivery men on the street arrested for not having vending licenses raised the complaints of bakery owners, and the city council passed another law differentiating those who delivered from those who sold. The former could carry bread on the street without a license, but the latter had to be licensed. A municipal ordinance of 14 December 1900 stated that bread baskets had to be covered at all times for hygienic reasons or authorities would fine the vendors and confiscate the baskets. Proper hygiene mattered to both city officials and bakers, who lamented the unclean bread sold on Rio's streets. Perhaps spirited by recent competition, the Bakers' Protective Society in 1902 submitted a list containing the unsanitary bakeries of the capital city that the municipality needed to oversee.[19] Even though municipal officials and business owners agreed on food safety matters, licensing remained a contentious issue since it did not protect bread sellers on the street from arrest and jail time.

The bread industry's resistance to the licensing of its vendors was in part a response to the pressures of demand, inflation, and food shortage. Bread vendors facilitated the distribution of a basic good, and higher licensing fees could result in higher sales prices. Meat and wine were other necessary items the population lacked, according to a letter that "representatives of the people" submitted to the mayor in 1892. The writers argued that basic needs went unmet because of food shortages and monopolistic business practices, pushing them to defend acts of robbery committed out of people's desperation. Inflation had turned basic necessities into luxuries that the "hungry mouths of the working class, the proletariat, the public functionary, and all of those not blessed by fortune" could not afford. Arguing for public health and an end to existing monopolies, the self-proclaimed popular representatives stated that "violating people's right to liberty through the exploitation of hunger" dishonored the most sacred liberty of all—"the freedom to live."[20] Food prices and freight costs decreased during the presidency of Manuel Ferraz de Campos Sales (1841–1913), and some price stability prevailed in Brazil between 1898 and 1902.[21] Still, peddlers persisted as the main providers of basic necessities for many, offering residents cheaper goods than in most stores. Customer demand thus kept peddlers on the street regardless of regulations aiming to remove them.

While popular pressure urged control over rising inflation at the turn of the century and businesses supported food safety reforms, licensing remained a contentious issue. From the perspective of the vending community, licenses were to help protect street sellers from abusive policing, but that did not prove to be a guarantee. José Vaz de Abreu, who managed several vending posts that sold cigars and cigarettes next to the São Gonçalo church returned to municipal offices in 1890 with a license that he had recently purchased. Abreu was worried that his license did not specify the exact number of vending posts he ran at Praça da Aclamação, near the church. Anticipating misunderstanding with the police, Abreu expressed the wish that "nothing happen to me" and requested that the correct number of posts appear on his license.[22]

While many street vending practices were tolerated even if policed, the selling of lottery tickets came under special scrutiny in the early republican years. Before 1888, slaves and ganhadores had not been allowed to sell lottery tickets, which could only be purchased at licensed venues such as botequins, kiosks, and private households. Authorities contended that the street sale of lottery tickets would only encourage slaves to gamble.[23] After 1889, under republican law, individuals were permitted to sell lottery tickets on the street, and in 1895, the national lottery licensed all of its peddlers.[24] Wishing to avoid arrest, some men like João Alves Teixeira promptly renewed their licenses in 1892 to continue selling, but the majority of peddlers remained unlicensed and a nuisance to authorities.

Lottery peddlers on trams and in government buildings alarmed authorities who wanted to regulate this growing line of street commerce. Perhaps as a temporary solution after legalizing the street sale of lottery tickets, the city council resolved on 14 June 1890 not to grant vending licenses to lottery street sellers. Still, municipal records reveal that many peddlers received licenses to sell lottery tickets after that date. In fact, a municipal officer reviewing a license request placed on 14 June 1890 concluded that he "saw no inconvenience in ignoring the new law."[25] In his view, licensing held a better chance at reducing the number of illicit vendors in public areas than not licensing at all.

On 9 July 1890, a resident of Candelária requested that neighborhood police suppress the "daily abuse" of lottery vending in the narrow street of Beco das Cancelas, where peddlers sold illegal lottery tickets from other Brazilian states and Latin American countries.[26] But the police placed blame for their inability to respond on insufficient municipal support. In 1896, a chief of police protested to the mayor that municipal authorities were lenient toward lottery peddlers. He pointed at the many vendors who "infested the hallways and rooms of the municipal building," where they were clearly a "detriment to the law, since the one place where the law should be severely applied is ignored."[27] In 1900, the regulation of lottery vendors, including *jogo do bicho* (animal game) peddlers, continued to facilitate their street selling. Authorities struggled to rein in the very popular yet illicit game throughout the turn of the century.[28] To at least partially address the problem, an officer recommended that the mayor apply the 1895 and 1897 decrees that prohibited illegal lottery selling on Sunday.[29]

Municipal authorities also targeted bookselling on the street in their attempt to restrict unwanted street commerce in the Brazilian capital. An 1891 ordinance declared the Bible as the only book permitted to be sold on Rio's streets due to the large number of unlicensed peddlers selling other types of books. According to officials, selling books other than the Bible was a for-profit enterprise that required a more expensive license, which peddlers largely ignored.[30] The ordinance was meant to eliminate informal booksellers from the street and push them into bookstores. Basic goods like food could be sold on the street, but bookselling was more appropriate for fixed establishments. Street booksellers, however, endured into the twentieth century and are still common in Rio today.

As regulation and policing shifted after the end of slavery, it became rare for peddlers to be held in detention for the simple offense of being unlicensed. Although the police regularly arrested and fined unlicensed street peddlers, detention was usually reserved for those whose behavior was deemed vagrant or disorderly. However, vagrancy and disorder were vague categories that could be applied to inappropriate vending practices or the unwanted presence of a vendor on the street. The arrests and detention of street sellers occurred through enforcement of the 1890 Penal Code even though street commerce was not an illegal practice or criminal activity. Entries to the Casa de Detenção between 1890 and 1902 demonstrate that street commerce was alive and well, while republican officials gazed upon a street that had to be disciplined.[31]

STREET VENDORS IN THE CASA DE DETENÇÃO

Although the ganho system formally endured after 1890, it was no longer central to regulating street vending after the abolition of slavery. Ganhador licenses disappeared from municipal records after 1886, but registry entries of the Casa de Detenção provide insight into the social profiles of street sellers. This shift is indicative of not only the structural changes following the end of slavery but also the movement away from regulating street commerce through the ganho system and toward the more convenient application of the 1890 Penal Code.

Most detainees in 1890–1902 were male, and the average street seller was illiterate, single, white, southern European, and between the years of eighteen and forty-nine.[32] The increased presence of European participants in Rio's street commerce thus continued. Within the small percentage of young married men, Italian males were the majority. A large proportion of the Italians migrated from Cocenza and Salermo, and many who were young became shoe shiners, which had been a predominantly Afro-Brazilian practice. A small number of Portuguese immigrant vendors were married, while Brazilian street sellers were generally unmarried. Urban vending typically absorbed newly arrived immigrants. The striking presence of unmarried Brazilian vendors and young married immigrants suggests that older street sellers eventually found other, maybe better lines of work.

Approximately 60 percent of the detained street sellers in the sample were immigrants from Italy, Portugal, and Spain. A few had migrated from France, Switzerland, Germany, Russia, and other South American countries such as Argentina, Chile, and Bolivia. Syrio-Lebanese men and women from the former Ottoman Empire were also entering Brazil in considerable numbers at this time. Authorities tended to group these immigrants under the generic "Arab" (*árabe*) type. Most African-born vendors were Mina quitandeiros. A small number of African men and women were vendors of sweets; only one African-born man was listed as a ganhador. These figures indicate the continuation of patterns from the ganho system, while European immigrants displaced Brazilian vendors and also became vulnerable to street policing.

In addition to the charge and location of his or her arrest, detention center records list a detainee's name, age, sex, place of residence, occupation, level of literacy, and physical traits such as facial features, hair type, height, clothing, and skin color. Republican authorities continued to use skin color to mark physical racial difference. *Branco* (white) mostly described southern European vendors, but some dark-skinned Italians, Spanish, and Portuguese were considered *morenos*. The term *pardo* designated racially mixed (black and white) Brazilians. Other words that indicated racial mixture were *fula* (having dark skin and mixed heritage) and *acaboclado* (having light brown skin and indigenous heritage). The terms *preto* (black) and *escravo* (slave) had been synonymous, while the use of preto endured to mark skin color and ex-slave status. Brancos made up 66 percent of the 1890–1902 sample of vendors, and pretos were the second largest group (14 percent) at a time when the overall number of blacks in prison was increasing.[33]

Participants in street commerce, peddlers and others, were arrested on similar charges. Quitandeiros often sold fruits and vegetables from tables or stalls or ran *casas de quitanda* (small stores). Shoe shiners, knife sharpeners, vendors of tin wares, and ganhadores were part of the world of street commerce that police officers targeted after abolition. The sellers who were most frequently detained were quitandeiros, sweets vendors, mascates, tinware vendors, and shoe shiners. Newspaper sellers, ganhadores, and peddlers selling lottery tickets followed. Other vulnerable vendors were those who sold fish, bread, fowl, flowers, charcoal, or cigars and cigarettes. The vending community that was policed was hence diverse in occupation, nationality, ethnicity, marital status, and age. The dynamics of slavery and migration had generated a poor class that lived off street commerce in Rio, sharing both spaces and policing experiences.

Young men and women between eighteen and twenty-nine years of age were the most active group in urban vending. Street commerce was an entry point for many young European migrants arriving in the city. Those between thirty and thirty-nine years of age were mostly mascates and ganhadores, and those between forty and forty-nine tended to be quitandeiros and street sellers of various kinds. The oldest participants were quitandeiros, and the overall number of street vendors decreased with age. Quitandeiros had likely found the stability that trading through fixed commerce offered over or in addition to street vending. Southern European immigrants may have recognized the practice of mascataria in Brazil to be similar to that of mascates in their homelands, hence preferring to use that term to describe themselves. Participation in the Brazilian ganho system and licensing also led them to identify as ganhadores.

African-born detainees were older, such as the four Mina men and one Mina woman between seventy and eighty-nine years of age. One Brazilian preto from the state of Sergipe also belonged to this age group. He was likely a former slave from the internal trade that transferred many Northeastern slaves to Southeastern provinces in the mid-nineteenth century. All Minas in the sample were quitandeiros and married, revealing that the aging African-born population was not single or detached from familial and formal economic relations. The immigrant from Sergipe of seventy years of age had probably a more precarious life as an unmarried peddler of flowers in a city far from where he was born. While some Africans prospered, especially those who had casas de quitanda, others evidently found in street selling one of the few opportunities to survive.[34]

Women are mostly absent from the registry entries of the Casa de Detenção for these years. The few detained females who participated in street commerce after 1890 tended to be Brazilian-born quitandeiras, sweets vendors, and mascates. All sweets vendors were pretas or pardas, and half of them were born in the state of Bahia. This is consistent with the prevalence of *tias bahianas* (older black Bahian women) who often sold sweets in early twentieth-century Rio.[35] Like their male counterparts, African Mina and Portuguese women were likely to be quitandeiras, while women of Syrio-Lebanese origin tended to work as mascates. A photograph by Marc Ferrez from 1895 depicts a migrant woman peddling the sewing notions (*miudezas*) that some mascates sold on the street (figure 4.1). In contrast to the slave period, officials noted most mascates after 1890 to be Arab (árabe) or Turkish (*turco*) sellers. Racialization after the abolition of slavery particularly associated mascates with Syrio-Lebanese commerce and sweets vendors with Afro-Brazilians.

Slave and free women street sellers were accustomed to working together in the shared urban spaces of street commerce. This endured in the postabolition period among a female vending population that was racially mixed and otherwise diverse as well. On 18 April 1893, ten female vendors were arrested in Rio's Ilha do Governador on charges of participating in what authorities defined as an orgy. Surprisingly, they were released within days of their arrest because their inappropriate behavior was considered a minor municipal infraction and not criminal activity according to the detention record. Eight of the arrested women were pretas, along with one fula and one parda. Four were from Bahia, three from the city of Rio, one from Ceará state, and another from Africa. Five were vendors of sweets, three were laundresses, and the African Mina woman was a quitandeira. All were unmarried women between the ages of twenty-two and fifty and lived in São José or Candelária. The shared practice of street commerce this time had brought them together in an unusual social setting.

Dividing street occupations according to nationality further reveals the racialization of certain types of vending. Most Italians between the ages of twenty and fifty were quitandeiros and street sellers of vegetables, sweets,

FIGURE 4.1. Vendor of sewing notions, 1895. Photograph by Marc Ferrez. Courtesy of Instituto Moreira Sales, Wikimedia Commons.

newspapers, fish, and lottery tickets. Few were shoe shiners, and one Italian man was listed as a ganhador. Italian peddlers were largely illiterate and the first to take up positions in street commerce that black vendors had traditionally held. Although the street selling of sweets remained mostly an Afro-Brazilian practice, Portuguese and Italian immigrants entered this line of work. Portuguese men, however, generally exercised more profitable trades such as the selling of chicken, fabrics, milk, tin goods, and fruits and vegetables. Portuguese tinware vendors had close connections with suppliers who made tin goods. Spanish immigrants mainly worked as sellers of newspapers, bread, sweets, and fruit. Italians and Spaniards normally held lower positions than Portuguese immigrants in street commerce.

Most Brazilian-born vendors were from the state of Rio, and approximately half were born in the capital city. Those who came from outside the state had mostly migrated from Northeastern states such as Bahia, Pernambuco, Ceará, and Sergipe. Like their female counterparts, it was common for Bahian males to be sweets vendors. Many from Northeast Brazil also sold vegetables and lottery tickets and worked as quitandeiros. Street workers who were born in the city of Rio still tended to be shoe shiners. Europeans had taken up the more profitable business of quitandeiros with the exception of some older African and Brazilian blacks who ran established casas de quitanda.

Disorderly behavior, vagrancy, theft, and physical violence were generally the main charges for vendors' arrests. Vagrancy, disorder, and theft were highest among Brazilian-born detainees. Many were imprisoned for more than one charge, usually in combinations of disorderly behavior, vagrancy, inebriation, and theft. African street sellers were jailed more often for public disorder than for vagrancy, but police officers may have seen little difference between the two. Immigrants were charged more often for physical offenses. Still, it was the general category of public disorder more than vagrancy that associated most street vendors with criminal behavior. Vagrancy implied lack of an occupation, and since vendors were not necessarily out of work, authorities seemed to prefer to charge them with public disorder after 1890.

THE TUMULT OF CITIZENSHIP

The Atlantic port city of Rio, like other global cities "with their concentration of the nonlocal, the strange, the mixed, and the public," was the site for what the anthropologists Arjun Appadurai and James Holston term "the tumult of citizenship."[36] European immigrants entered a city in transition and negotiated shifting structures of labor alongside Brazilians. Both groups participated in a shuffling that redefined labor and social relations after slavery. A shared stage—the capital's city streets—displayed various conflicts and became a site where discipline and resistance constituted new kinds of citizens. In the words of Appadurai and Holston, "Streets combine new identities of territory, contract, and education with ascribed ones of race, religion, culture, and gender. . . . In this process, cities become both the site and the substance not only of the uncertainties of modern citizenship, but also of its emergent forms."[37] A

FIGURE 4.2. Kiosk and newspaper vendors, 1910. Photograph by Augusto Malta, *Quiosque na Rua Estácio de Sá*. Courtesy of G. Ermakoff Casa Editorial, Arquivo Images2You.

set of court cases indicates a streetscape where a vendor's age, gender, race, and ethnic background influenced the legitimization of her or his street commerce and public and private behaviors.

A case from Santana illustrates police and court authorities' attitudes toward vagrancy, minors, and the practice of capoeira, a persecuted martial art linked to black resistance. The criminal charges shed light on the social world surrounding kiosks and newspaper boys at the end of the nineteenth century. Kiosks appeared in Brazil toward the end of the 1870 Paraguayan War and officially remained on Rio's streets until 1911 (figure 4.2). By the turn of the century, in Pedro Vasquez's descriptions, most elites in Rio viewed kiosks as unsanitary places where "cachaça, bread and coffee, fried codfish, sardines, and other delicacies" were sold. Lottery vending attracted "customers leaning about, spitting, dirtying the ground, and talking pornography," as kiosks hosted an underworld of gambling and illicit commerce.[38]

These gathering places on the street gradually disappeared in the early twentieth century, but a chronicle by Escragnolle Dória offers insight into their popularity.[39] Kiosks were modest, open-air botequins that "never lacked flies," he observes, or people "who for only a few vinténs never starved to death." Contrasting ordinary kiosks in Rio to the exotic Asian structures and the "civilized" kiosks of Paris, Escragnolle Dória saw his own country as "popular and prosaic." During the late empire period, kiosks sprang up throughout the city and functioned as "democratic utilities," attracting around their circumferences a diverse spectrum of social types. With time, kiosks developed into two types: those patronized by the upper class and those frequented by the urban poor. Escragnolle Dória recalls that the kiosks on Rua Primeiro de Março and Praça da Constituição (today's Praça Tiradentes) sold lottery tickets, while the kiosks of Campo de Aclamação and Praça da República (former Campo de Santana) near the train station were more plebeian.

The men who worked inside kiosks seemed to be physical extensions of their own establishments, observes the writer. Some were clean and friendly while others were rude and dirty. The proprietors, however, were not actual owners but renters. In 1882, the Companhia Industrial Fluminense managed all 119 kiosks in Rio, and nine years later Camilo da Silva obtained a contract for a twenty-year monopoly. It remains unclear what the company's or da Silva's role was in managing kiosks. Proprietors paid four hundred milréis in rent every year but perhaps purchased supplies from da Silva. After 1889, kiosks were no longer allowed to sell newspapers, books, pamphlets, flowers, sweets, or fruits, but they could still offer cheese, cigarettes, cigars, coffee, refreshments, lottery tickets, alcohol, and certain knick-knacks. Nonetheless, their days were numbered.

Newsboys hung around kiosks along with the other "flies" who raised republican concerns. One July morning in 1893, a popular *café kiosque* of the Praça da República was the site of the arrest of six young men and children charged with vagrancy and capoeira violations.[40] The supposed leader of the group, the minor José Martins, risked a double sentence of four to twelve years in prison because he was also accused of carrying a blade, thereby violating another law targeting armed *capoeiristas*. Although the Casa de Detenção held some minors, the Instituto de Menores (Institute for Minors) of the Casa de Correção across the street had been the traditional destination for youngsters. The historian Carlos Eugênio Líbano Soares finds that group arrests of young capoeiristas such as those at the Praça da República were quite common among detainees at the Instituto de Menores between 1850 and 1890.[41]

According to the police inspector who dealt with the incident at the Praça da República, José Martins had been practicing capoeira with a blade while threatening passersby. The inspector stated that "other known vagrants and capoeiras" were involved until a police officer (*praça*), who had been called by "a citizen" claiming to have been harassed by the capoeiristas, arrested them all. With the help of other officers and "citizen agents," José Martins, other minors, and men who were walking near the kiosk were arrested for *capoeiragem* practicing the illegal martial art of capoeira.[42]

The arrested minors claimed to have been hanging out by the café kiosk and misidentified as capoeiristas, and the older young males were simply walking by. Antônio da Rocha—Portuguese, thirteen years old, illiterate, and a construction worker (*pedreiro*)—explained that he had been walking across the Praça da República when he was suddenly arrested. Jacomo Martins—Italian, nine years old, and a newspaper seller—was at the kiosk when he saw the first arrest take place and seconds later was put under arrest himself. Zeferino Henrique—Brazilian, twenty-one years old, and a sailor—was walking across the Praça da República when he saw a group of capoeira practitioners under arrest; his own arrest soon followed. Zeferino claimed that he did not know the boys, asserting that he was not a vagrant but an "honest worker." Manuel Rodrigues de Sousa—Brazilian, twelve years old, illiterate, and a carpenter—was near the kiosk when he was arrested for being in the wrong place at the wrong time. He argued that he was not a friend of the accused, a capoeirista, or a vagrant.

The supposed leader of the group, José Martins, who was Brazilian, eighteen years old, illiterate, and a resident of the nearby Rua dos Arcos, declared that he was killing time by the kiosk as he sold the morning paper. He was arrested in the act because he was carrying a blade, which he explained was a tool he needed in distributing packed newspapers. Antônio Francisco de Oliveira—Brazilian, eighteen years old, illiterate, and a bread deliveryman—was walking by the kiosk on his way to meet a laundress when he was arrested at the same time as the others, whom he claimed not to know. Antônio de Sousa—Brazilian, eighteen years old, illiterate, and a domestic servant (*copeiro*)—was walking toward the tram stop when he was arrested, and like the others, he insisted that he was not a vagrant but an honest man who lived off his work. While the arrested boys and men were held in detention for days, the minors Artur Cardoso and Manuel Rodrigues de Sousa were soon bailed out by their parents.

In court, Antônio da Rocha, Jacomo Martins, and Antônio de Sousa declared that they indeed had been near a group that was practicing capoeira. However, Zeferino's testimony held that José Martins was drinking coffee by the kiosk and not engaged in capoeira. The three witnesses who appeared in court were low-ranking police officers, and due to a conflict of interest and lack of evidence, the judge eventually released all the accused. The police had also arrested a number of innocent passersby, revealing the social types that authorities identified as capoeiristas or vagrants. By the late nineteenth century, capoeira in Rio had become more than an Afro-Brazilian practice as white immigrants entered its ranks.[43] Imperial law had criminalized capoeiragem, and suspects who wore hats, carried knives, and walked *gingando* (a distinct capoeira move) were quickly arrested. Minors ages ten to fifteen made up 12 percent of Rio's detained capoeiristas; since slave times, many capoeiristas were accustomed to hanging around the Campo de Santana.[44]

Like capoeira, the ganho system was a street practice in transition from the slave period. Rarely did individuals arrested on the street identify as ganhadores after 1888, but the term appeared in the registry entries of the Casa de Dentenção as late as 1905. The capital's municipal government continued to recognize ganhadores as legitimate workers into the twentieth century, as its codes regarding ganho work endured after slavery.[45] In fact, arrested men often chose the term ganhador over the more generic trabalhador to define their occupations to authorities and avoid vagrancy charges.[46]

On 30 July 1899, Antônio José da Silva was arrested for selling stolen chickens and turkeys to José da Costa Fernandes, the Portuguese owner of a casa de quitanda who was arrested for buying the birds.[47] According to the court record, Antônio da Silva was not officially a ganhador or peddler but a construction worker (pedreiro). However, certain aspects of his selling that day are reminiscent of the ganho system's labor arrangements. After several complaints in São Cristovão, the birds were found in the yard of the casa de quitanda at Rua São Luiz Gonzaga 21, which was part of Costa Fernades's home. A married, illiterate man forty-two years of age, the Portuguese quitandeiro stated that at six in the morning he purchased twelve healthy birds from a black man wearing a jacket and without a beard. The seller stressed that the meat was not stolen and belonged to his *patroa* (female patron), "who sent him to sell it on the street." Two days before their arrests, Costa Fernandes bought two turkeys from the same man, who had been trying to sell them "as the patroa had ordered." Suspecting that da Silva was selling stolen poultry, however, the quitandeiro asked a neighbor to keep a watchful eye out for "a black man selling birds" and if he appeared to call the police.

The following day, hoping to sell four birds to the same Portuguese greengrocer, da Silva knocked on the door of the casa de quitanda. Immediately, the neighbor Oscar Martins da Costa found a police officer who was in the vicinity. The officer arrested both peddler and neighbor. Martins da Costa said he did not know the seller but stated that his quitandeiro neighbor Costa Fernandes was a good head of family (*um bom chefe de família*) and an honest man of exemplary behavior incapable of buying stolen goods. The neighbor's remarks reflect a pattern Rockman has traced in early republican Baltimore among the urban poor: "the ideal of the patriarch also figured in the petitions of criminals seeking early release from prison or relief from fines."[48] Costa Fernandes benefited from both patriarchal honor and socioeconomic status in avoiding some jail time. The day following his arrest, business partners bailed him out. In the meantime, the original owners of the stolen birds had come to learn about the incident, and one of them was able to get two turkeys back from the police, as the Portuguese quitandeiro did not object to returning the birds to them.

Although the peddler Antônio da Silva confessed to selling stolen fowl when he was first arrested, the court found him innocent for lack of evidence. The inconsistencies in his declarations shed light on what was probably a manipulation of symbols and values associated with the ganho system that he hoped would legitimize his street selling against theft accusations. Da Silva, a black man, eventually confessed that he had purchased the birds from a *mulatinho* (young mulatto), reducing the person's identity to his physical appearance. He did not know the person's residence, but they had both routinely met at the Largo de Pedregulho for the exchange. Da Silva then carried off the live birds in a covered basket, and once he sold them, he gave the man his share of the money.

At first, da Silva justified his actions by declaring that he was following his patroa's orders, a statement that reflected the practice of ganhadores. It benefited him to say that he was working under the protection of a patron, although such a relationship was unconfirmed. Claiming patronage associated the black vendor with legitimacy in light of the assumption that an unattached black man with no employer was untrustworthy, perhaps vagrant, and possibly dangerous. The patroa did not surface, and da Silva was not bailed out of jail, as far as the record shows, so it is likely that he had been working without a patron from the start.

The street commerce practices of the postabolition period continued to have a public-private dimension. The slaveowning elite perceived the house and the street as necessarily separate from each other, while free and enslaved workers made such boundaries permeable.[49] The interactions between female domestic servants and male street vendors, in particular, connected the house and the street, as republican notions of honor, discipline, and sexuality redefined these spaces. According to the Rio jurist José Viveiros de Castro, "The conquest of civilization [was] the victory of moral ideas over the brutality of instincts" derived from "the vices of slavery" and a Brazilian "sexual temperament" caused by tropical climate, heavy foods, and racial mixture.[50] The historians Martha Abreu and Sueann Caulfield contend that turn-of-the-century jurists considered legal codes to have made some progress in defending women's honor, while the social and demographic transformation following the abolition of slavery made it necessary to reinvigorate the civilizing campaign of the young Brazilian republic.[51] Analyzing related issues, Sueann Caulfield notes that the making of disciplined workers and citizens was dependent on sexual politics and notions of honor, as "the 1890 penal code was one of the several important legal instruments for disciplining the labor force and disseminating a positive ideology of work."[52]

As the state increasingly policed public morality, the 1890 Penal Code specifically criminalized women's *defloramento* (deflowering) as a sexual violation that was an act of seduction, deceit, and fraud.[53] Article 266 made it a crime to harm a person's honor (*pudor*) through threats or violent means that aimed to fulfill lascivious urges. Seduced young women who lost their honor thus appealed to Article 266 to repair the damage through marriage to or imprisonment of the aggressor. If a man did not marry the woman he had deflowered, he risked one to six years in prison. Seduction, deceit, and fraud usually took the form of an unfulfilled marriage promise that preceded many cases of defloramento.[54]

These were the circumstances that created the relationship between José Rodrigues dos Santos, a Portuguese milk vendor, and Maria Rosa Grugel, a *mulata* domestic worker, a decade after the abolition of slavery.[55] A practice inherited from colonial times, most who sold milk in Rio were Portuguese men. Grugel was twenty-three years old and worked for the Montenegro family. Another employer had rented her out to the Montenegros, turning her into a hireling (*alugada*). She lived with her father in Terra Nova, a neighborhood of Inhaúma on the periphery, and commuted to work each day. Working conditions for nonresidential servants had changed little since slave times, nor had the social networks that connected the workers in employers' homes. Within this community, individual honor was linked to family honor, and Grugel's deflowering came to involve family, friends, neighbors, and coworkers in the court process.

On 4 April 1898, Grugel went to the police to declare that Rodrigues had deflowered her. She reported that four months had gone by since the night Rodrigues seduced her and promised to marry her. He delivered milk to the Montenegro household and had courted her and given her a personal bottle of milk to take home every day. One December evening in 1897, Grugel felt that she was coming down with a cold and told Rodrigues at the end of a day's work that she was going back to her father's house. Rodrigues agreed to accompany her, and she accepted "in good faith." Because night was falling, she changed her mind and decided to return to the Montenegro's house. Rodrigues suggested instead that they go to a family home he knew where she could rest alone in a room. She agreed but soon found herself in the room with Rodrigues. She said he deflowered her and "on his knees" asked her to marry him. She agreed, and on New Year's Day 1898 they received her father's blessing.

Four months later, however, Grugel was living with Rodrigues in a rented room, but they remained unmarried. Her father, coworkers, and neighbors were aware of the situation and testified that it was necessary to "repair the damage" that Rodrigues had inflicted on Grugel and her family. It was common for friends and family of deflowered women to become allies in court to defend the honor of individuals, families, and communities. Honor was a public and behavioral matter as well as a physical one. Grugel's coworkers at the Montenegro residence testified on her behalf: Procópia, the twenty-three-year-old cook; Amélia, the twenty-three-year-old maid; and Venâncio, the twenty-eight-year-old butler. They emphasized her "good conduct" and "innocence" as well as her long-term employment. Amélia and Venâncio stated that they knew why Rodrigues did not want to marry Grugel, and it was not because of her age but her skin color. They themselves did not expect a white Portuguese man to marry a *mulata de cor parda* (light-skinned mulata).

The day before Grugel filed charges with the police, Rodrigues had been looking for her and was told by Procópia that she had traveled to Bahia to see some relatives. Grugel returned home that afternoon and argued with Rodrigues about his false intention to marry her. She maintained that living together was not enough and said she had come to distrust his marriage promise. After all, she questioned, would he really marry a mulata? Popular songs of the turn of the twentieth century repeated the old adage that "the white woman is for marriage, the mulata for fornicating, and the black woman for work."[56] Was their relationship a reflection of this? Eventually, Rodrigues confessed to the judge that he did not intend to marry Grugel because she was parda. Impervious to and perhaps even offended by the Portuguese immigrant's revelation and racial prejudice, the judge sentenced Rodrigues to six years in prison for violating Article 266. The judge chose to discipline the immigrant's racist and sexually offensive behavior rather than the mulata's supposed promiscuity. The practice of vending had softened the boundaries between the house and the street, but racial lines were still harder to erase.

UNPREDICTABLE COURTS

The political shift from monarchy to republic placed vendors in new "legal contact zones" with the state.[57] While Rio police were more concerned about regulating inappropriate street behavior than explicit commercial activity, judges expressed mixed attitudes toward discipline. Uncertain evidence and the protection of personhood guided judges' decisions over what might have been the expected racist attitudes. In the legal contact zones of courtrooms, streets, and interactions of offenders, defendants, victims, witnesses, families, friends, and community members, the legacy of slavery continued to mark the world of street commerce. Vendors in courts negotiated with the law primarily as individuals and then as free street sellers. Political more than economic liberalism influenced Brazilian republicanism, and in courts the vendor was first a political individual and second a free worker engaged in free commerce.

Ganho licenses of the latter half of the nineteenth century demonstrate that Afro-Brazilian peddlers were displaced by the significant numbers of immigrants participating in street commerce. However, displacement did not amount to a simple process of substitution. Postabolition labor and racial segmentation influenced Afro-Brazilian marginality, but in the shared history of white immigrants and blacks engaged in street commerce—both vulnerable to policing and detention—the process was uneven and unpredictable. Skin color was not an immediate cause for vagrancy or public disorder charges, as detention records reveal. Authorities who considered vendors a detriment or nuisance to the law could also be offended by dishonorable behavior that transcended gender, ethnic, and racial assumptions.

Just as urban slave society had regulated free and enslaved street labor under the ganho system, the 1890 Penal Code created a similar conditional liberty for street sellers. Thus José Martins's blade for unpacking newspapers made him a criminal capoeira suspect and José Rodrigues dos Santos's courtship of Maria Rosa Grugel a matter for the courts. The judge was understandably unsympathetic toward the racist and sexually offensive behavior of Rodrigues, and his vending activities in a traditional Portuguese occupation were inconsequential. José Martins's practice as a newspaper peddler was, in contrast, central to his release. Even if the police deemed the young newsboy's occupation insignificant, the judge perceived his presence on the street as a logical consequence of his economic activity and not a criminal threat.

CHAPTER 5

AN HONEST OCCUPATION

WHILE THE 1890 PENAL CODE facilitated the policing of street vendors, Pereira Passos during his 1903–1906 term as mayor reinforced the regulatory role of police toward vending in Rio. The sistema de ganho endured, but new regulations linked to urban reforms aimed to eliminate street selling practices perceived as a blot on modernity and progress. New municipal laws confined street commerce to areas where it did not interfere with the mayor's plan for a modern city. In the process, law enforcement relied on criminal law more than established street commerce or ganho labor regulation to deal with the unwanted presence of vendors. Thus it continued to matter little if a street seller was licensed. Being in the wrong place at the wrong time could be enough to bring criminal charges against vendors regardless of their licensed or patronized status. Vendors and their defenders in court resisted criminal charges by emphasizing the legitimacy of street selling as an honest occupation and not a manifestation of vagrancy or public disorder. Selling on the street may have been an unpleasant survival strategy for many, with ties to the slave past, but it was still officially a legitimate line of work in the capital city.

Urban vending practices of the slave past associated with black workers, such as the selling of sweets, fruits, and vegetables, were the most vulnerable to police arrest. Afro-Brazilian shoe shiners were exposed in this way too, as revealed by the arrest records in Rio's *Ocorrências policiais* (Police Occurrences), which were books kept in each district.[1] While most arrests noted in Police Occurrences did not result in vendors being held in the Casa de Detenção, arrest and detention center records are a window on police regulatory practices toward vendors. Street sellers were incarcerated mostly for public disorder and vagrancy charges, with vagrancy being the most common charge in the early 1900s. The cases disputed in court were subject to authorities who applied the worker-vagrant rationale, positioning vendors between the redeeming qualities of legitimate labor and the pathologies of vagrancy.

Judges could decide that accused vendors held no type of formal occupation, as poverty and life on the street delegitimized street selling even among those who were licensed. Vendors who provided evidence of employment or patronage could more effectively claim to be engaged in honorable work, however. An employer or patron defending a vendor in court was therefore crucial for legitimizing the vendor's position. The patron-client relations that had shaped the ganho system endured as an important factor that formalized street commerce. In particular, patrons appeared in court to defend charged vendors, thus bringing together the business interests of street commerce participants. Nowhere in the law was the practice of street commerce unlawful (if licensed), although it was prohibited inside the central districts of Rio in 1903. Nevertheless, vendors held for violating an article of the 1890 Penal Code experienced street selling as if it were an illicit activity. They were targeted for occupying urban space as a result of their trade, but police disassociated their place in the city from their work. Street sellers in their court struggles responded by assuming the legitimacy of their vending practices.

URBAN REFORM

Initiating an era of demolitions to destroy the colonial and slave past of the Brazilian capital, Pereira Passos built a legacy on public works meant to rationalize urban space, transportation methods, and sanitation.[2] It was during this period when street vendors became a targeted nuisance for urban reformers. New municipal codes restricting vending came to coexist with customary practice and old regulations. Further, Pereira Passos intensified the police regulation of street commerce.

Pereira Passos was a presidentially appointed mayor who suspended the municipal council for nearly his entire term when limited suffrage allowed only 20 percent of Rio's population to vote.[3] Restricted civic participation and the demolition of poor neighborhoods resulted in relocating many of the urban poor to the city's periphery, opening spaces for the construction of European-inspired boulevards and neoclassical buildings in central Rio. City officials justified this dramatic overhaul partly by defining crowded population areas as "germ centers" that had to be eliminated. The working poor, however, questioned the intentions of Pereira Passos's public health campaign and protested by revolting against compulsory vaccination in 1904. Forced vaccination, in their view, was one more act of state transgression that was destroying people's private lives.[4] For many, the alternative to losing their homes in the city center was relocating to the outskirts of the city. Naturally, street vendors followed their customers and were themselves among the dislocated.

In 1901, a year before Pereira Passos's appointment, municipal officials initiated reforms to regulate street commerce independently of the ganho system. Decree 830 of 31 October 1901 taxed licensed vendors according to the products they sold. Nineteenth-century law identified mascates as vendors selling superior products, such as fabrics, porcelain, and silverware, but the 1901 decree redefined mascates as ordinary street peddlers. The new law considered all peddlers to be *negociantes ambulantes* (mobile sellers), further formalizing their status. The decree stated that licenses were not transferable and pins had to be visibly worn by vendors. But despite these measures, a mandate anticipated a future direction: mascates and vendors were "absolutely prohibited within the central district," their trade restricted to the semirural periphery. In colonial times, mascates had freely traveled the Brazilian countryside selling their wares, but their presence in the twentieth-century Brazilian capital had become a nuisance as more immigrants took up street vending in downtown areas.[5] The 1901 decree established a tax to regulate the activity of vendors in the newly populated urban periphery.[6]

The Pereira Passos administration maintained this 1901 decree and elevated the license fee for mascates, although it was later decreased. Regulations concerning ganhadores remained unchanged since 1886, but the 1901 law regarding "the service of the ganhador" described them as transporters of small loads (*cargas*) and not sellers. The same law named street vendors as ambulantes or mascates, which further disassociated vending from the ganho system.[7] The formal distancing from the slave past was another effort to erase or demolish the mark of slavery on the city. The registration of ganhadores with the police after 1886 and shifting licensing fees suggest the lower status of ganhadores vis-à-vis ambulantes. Still, all street workers in Rio—ganhadores, ambulantes, and mascates—labored under the shadow of slavery despite this distinction.

The Brazilian capital of the early 1900s was a leading industrial center, but much of its middling population made a living through some form of artisanal occupation. The sistema de ganho had helped connect shops to street commerce, as foreign immigration and the turn to free labor added pressure to the system. Responding to this population shift, Pereira Passos implemented measures to regulate petty commerce. Decree 394, passed in February 1903, tightened licensing procedures and specified locations where street commerce was permitted in the capital. Licenses remained nontransferrable, and the decree revised the licensing of vending vehicles such as carts and tables.[8] Shop owners hiring peddlers to sell food on the street were now required to take out at least two or three licenses, for the patron, the vendor, and the vehicle if necessary. Mascates and street vendors continued to be restricted to selling outside the city center, a condition that benefited the suburban population that found it difficult to access downtown shops.[9] Shopkeepers in central areas who used street vendors to access distant customers were only allowed to operate in the subúrbio; this explains the increased need for vehicles that could travel rough roads revealed in patent requests of the era.

During this period of urban renewal, Pereira Passos particularly targeted "old practices" (*velhas usanças*). In 1903, after his first year in office, new municipal ordinances began to alter economic practices, forms of leisure, and customs rooted in the social and cultural fabric of the city.[10] Pereira Passos stated,

> I started prohibiting the street sale of meat parts, displayed on tables and surrounded by the continuous flight of insects, such a repugnant spectacle. At the same time, I abolished the rustic practice of milking cows on the street, spectacles of waste that nobody, certainly, would qualify as virtuous of a civilized society. . . . I also ordered the immediate extinction of thousands of dogs that wander the city giving it the repugnant appearance of certain Oriental cities. . . . I have put an end to the plague of lottery peddlers who pester people with infernal loud voices, turning the city into a gambling house. Much of my preoccupation has gone into the extinction of public begging, punishing false beggars and preventing real beggars from exposing their miseries on the street.[11]

The mayor aimed to discipline all urban classes, but the burden was heaviest on the poor. Loud and brash peddlers became analogous to the beggars, vagrants, and dogs roaming the city's streets, and such an attitude was reflected in the city's new policing practices.

An excerpt from the American novelist Frank Carpenter's travel book *Round about Rio* (1884) provides a glimpse into the "old customs" that Pereira Passos sought to eliminate.[12] The vendor, like the milk cow, had become an anachronism. A voyeuristic event for the US-born writer, Carpenter was exposed one day to an old practice:

> A waterman with his cart—that is, a barrel of water upon two wheels—next attracted attention and Stacy's sympathy was aroused at seeing this barefooted aquarius tugging at the shaft by the side of his faithful friend and servant, the mule, to help him with what little he could. After the waterman, in logical sequence, came the milkman with his perambulating dairy. He was leading his cow by a rope tied around her horns, and she in turn was dragging her calf, an overgrown hulk of a yearling, by a cord running from the end of her tail to the head of her pampered infant; it is a theory among these

milkmen that the cow will not "give down" unless the calf is present to butt and fumble with her muzzled snout while the dairyman is pursuing his task. Both the calf and the cow hung back stubbornly and wavered as they walked, so that the three formed a procession which, though attenuated, was by no means inconsiderable, and they effectively cleared the sidewalk, driving Robinson and Stacy again into the street. They had the curiosity to watch the milkman until he came to the door of a customer, when he unslung his cup and milked it full, the calf meanwhile interfering with dumb protestations, thrusting his boot-leg muzzle into the tantalizing fluid, while the cow quietly ruminated, probably wondering how it was that this child of hers could drink so much without getting fat.

The ban on public milking took effect in 1903 along with other measures meant to sanitize the distribution of dairy products. A common issue for authorities and customers that resulted in the arrests of many milk vendors was the sale of watered-down milk. Although the exposure of public milking could prevent vendors from mixing water and milk, municipal officials still sought to eliminate, for hygienic and aesthetic reasons, cows from city streets. The municipal ban on street cows had met the resistance of milk sellers since at least 1851, and concerns about milk quality and sanitation were consistent in city council meetings throughout the nineteenth century.[13] By 1912, the city council had prohibited the use of milk tanks (*tanques*) that had come to substitute cows in door-to-door sales; the council now favored the use of glass bottles for milk.[14] Substitution was not easy, and milk sellers protested the lack of municipal support when transitioning to a new vending method, whether the earlier use of tanks or later glass bottles. They also preferred to continue selling through traditional means that ensured a steady client base. Not surprisingly, milk cows still were seen in the streets of Rio in the 1930s, as sellers preferred to risk economic penalties.[15]

Another municipal concern in discussions about a reformed street commerce was the sale of meat (miúdos). In 1903, the municipality prohibited the display of red meat pieces (*miúdos de rezes*) on street tables. The next year an amendment allowed for the street sale of miúdos until ten o'clock in the morning, as long as peddlers transported the meat in closed containers. Restricting the street sale of red meat to morning hours was aimed at preventing the sale of overexposed, deteriorated pieces later in the day. These changes also applied to the sale of poultry, which was restricted to outside the city center. Since little means were available to effectively provide animal protein to many city residents, a number of vending vehicles appeared to facilitate meat distribution in the growing periphery, as reflected in patent requests. Prohibiting the street sale of miúdos in the city center was still difficult to enforce, as unlicensed peddlers tended to sell at cheaper prices. Poor living conditions encouraged the perseverance of street commerce as a way to provide basic goods in all neighborhoods of the city.[16]

While needy customers continued to rely on peddlers, Pereira Passos's new measures toward street commerce increased the regulatory role of the police. Building on the sistema de ganho's reliance on policing, the need to control unlicensed vendors was made explicit in several correspondences (*circulares*) between the municipality and the police. The concern for public health justified police regulation of street commerce. In 1903, Pereira Passos gave vendors up to fifteen days to register the tools and vehicles of their trade with the police. Circulares described the hygienic measures prohibiting shops from displaying goods on outdoor balconies that the police would be responsible for inspecting.[17]

The city council targeted street kiosks too, as they were considered very unsanitary and visually unpleasant. The Companhia de Quiosques, which managed such establishments, was regularly fined for their unsanitary conditions. Eventually, Pereira Passos ordered the destruction of all kiosks, though his tenure as mayor did not witness their complete disappearance from Rio. Kiosks persisted well into the 1920s, with a considerable amount of support from well-to-do residents who wished to preserve the capital's traditions.[18] Other street selling practices became targets of the Pereira Passos reforms. Households were no longer allowed to cultivate the traditional food and herb gardens known as the *fundos de quintal*. Along with the banning of *cargueiros*, who generally carried goods from producers to consumers, such measures became problems for residents in need of food during periods of recession. The rising cost of living was difficult for many of Rio's residents and would only intensify in the next decade, positioning street commerce as a necessary supplier for disadvantaged households.

In efforts to keep the city supplied with basic goods and the streets clean, the Pereira Passos reforms included food distribution through the construction of open-air markets (*feiras livres*) in several neighborhoods. In fact, the most elaborate changes in municipal regulation regarding food distribution concerned the building of new open-air street marketplaces. The mayor, councilmen, and a symbolic *pedra fundadora* (foundation stone) typically inaugurated these marketplaces with ribbon-cutting ceremonies.[19] Having open markets throughout various areas of the city not only aimed to rationalize food supplies but organize the networks of distribution between center and periphery. Most illustrious was the inauguration of the Mercado Municipal (Municipal Market) in 1907 to replace the old downtown Mercado da Can-

FIGURE 5.1. Inauguration of the Municipal Market, 1907. Photograph by Augusto Malta. Courtesy of G. Ermakoff Casa Editorial, Arquivo Images2You.

delária near Guanabara Bay. President Alfonso Pena, leading a group of officials, headed the ceremony to inaugurate the marketplace (figure 5.1). With a wrought-iron gate and space for two hundred stalls, the Mercado Municipal displaced centuries of street selling that had been prevalent in Rio's port area. This landmark of old Rio was demolished in 1962.

Augusto Malta's photographs of smaller market inaugurations displayed as much municipal fervor.[20] The markets were meant to replace informal street selling in traditional places such as the Praça da Harmonia and Praia de Botafogo as well as in neighborhoods including Tijuca, Vila Isabel, and Copacabana. The open-air markets were made possible through federal sponsorship of the Brazilian Cold Storage and Development Company, a London outfit that won exclusive rights over the sale of cooling and storage facilities in Brazil. The contract facilitated the creation of the Companhia Mercado Municipal do Rio de Janeiro, which funded the new building that enclosed the municipal market near the port area. City officials hoped that these marketplaces would naturally make street peddling unnecessary.[21]

As Mayor Pereira Passos and his advisers considered what would constitute proper uses of urban space and commercial activity, restricting peddlers to the peripheral *zona suburbana*, municipal ordinances empowered police to repress street vending, begging, and vagrancy. To that end, the city council prolonged the hours of police work into the night since, officials argued, it was then when most infractions took place.[22] The police consequently gained power over the street "to compensate for the vagueness of the law with respect to petty crimes."[23] Laws concerning street commerce were not vague, however. Specific regulations over the ganho system were still in place, along with vending laws passed in later decades. But the passing of ordinances mattered little if the main goal was to remove disorderly peddlers from the street. Police authorities found the 1890 Penal Code much more effective for that.

The project of urban renewal influenced another turning point in the policing of Rio's streets. The worker-vagrant dichotomy now became a fundamental instrument for criminal identification. The Gabinete de Identificação da Polícia Civil was formed in 1907 to perfect such identification methods.[24] The contingent meaning of vagrancy, varying according to context, allowed for the police to arrest people for diverse street behaviors deemed antisocial.[25] The historian Marcos Bretas observes that "the difficulty in creating efficient demarcations between workers and vagrants generated mistakes in identification, which had repercussions in the press and even in the protests filed with foreign consulates."[26] In a city where a good proportion of the vending population was foreign-born, street vendors were not exempt from misidentification.

Bretas discusses a telling example in his analysis of police and society in early twentieth-century Rio. A newspaper article in *A Notícia* in 1903 condemned the "bad service" of a policeman who arrested the newspaper seller José Maria in São José. At the police station, José Maria was "classified by the inspector as a known thief." Accusing street sellers of being notorious pickpockets was a common and quick way to restrict unwanted street behavior. The writer of the newspaper article described the marker gatuno conhecido as a "worn-out label" (*estafada chapa*) that police used often and conveniently.[27] Consequently, peddlers were arrested without evidence of vagrancy. The term chapa also designated the metal tag worn by licensed vendors, to which the writer alluded in claiming that such a mark of legitimacy was useless in the face of abusive policing. José Maria was held at the police station until nine o'clock at night, when an incoming officer working the night shift recognized him as a newspaper seller who was a "serious and well-mannered boy, in no way a thief or a pickpocket." Wrongful custody had legal consequences, and in this case the officer who carried out the arrest was suspended for eight days.

Throughout the first decades of the twentieth century, peddlers who were arrested, detained, and processed in court contested similarly worn-out labels and argued that they were citizens of the city. The evaluation of arrest, detention, and court records for 1903–1925 provides insight into how vendors responded to street policing and criminal charges. An informal code of behavior coexisted with a formal one, and while the latter excluded the majority of the population from full citizenship, the former became the means for civic and vendor participation in free commerce. Court cases involving street vendors reflected both.

STREET ARRESTS

The arrest records of vendors in Rio during the first decades of the twentieth century shed light on the practice's diverse participants. Reinforced by the Pereira Passos reforms, the street became a site for the quick administration of justice that Brazilians today have popularly termed the "street court" (*tribunal de rua*) to mean authoritarian street policing for which legal recourse is inaccessible to many. In the early 1900s, the administration of justice was generally a three-step process involving the police, the detention center, and the courts. It was on city streets that the majority of the urban working poor experienced the tumult of citizenship, and arrest records reveal peddlers' vulnerabilities. It is not a coincidence that vendors most vulnerable to police arrest tended to have the strongest ties to vending activities of the slave period. Although a racialized policing is evident, poor white immigrant peddlers were similarly vulnerable to street policing and public disorder charges.

Police Occurrences records involving the arrests of 150 peddlers between 1903 and 1925 in Rio give an idea of the early postabolition vending community. The records indicate that the streets of the Pereira Passos era and subsequent administrations adopted the mantra of urban renewal. As in earlier records, individuals' personal data such as name, nationality, place of residence, profession, literacy, and physical characteristics are noted along with the charges and ensuing proceedings of sentencing, medical examination, complaint investigation, and so forth. Most arrests occurred in the city center, which included the São José, Santa Rita, and Santana areas; many vendors were arrested in the outlying neighborhoods of São Cristovão and Gamboa as well. The 1903 law restricted vendors to selling outside the city center; arrests in those central areas demonstrate criminalization of the working poor and marginalization of popular practices.

Between 1890 and 1906—a period of intense urban reform and migration to the Brazilian capital—the population of the city center decreased 50 percent, while the population doubled in neighboring areas such as São Cristovão. The 200 percent increase in semirural peripheral population resulted from the Brazilian rural-to-urban migration that swelled the sertão carioca.[28]

Such population shifts contributed to changes in the city's vending practices. Authorities became increasingly concerned with the unregulated street commerce of the subúrbios as people and police settled in these peripheral areas.[29]

Santana had been Rio's African citadel, but by the early twentieth century much of the African-descent population had moved to Gamboa, north of the city center. Gamboa became an Afro-Brazilian neighborhood that grew as a consequence of demolition and postabolition migration. The area became celebrated for being home to Bahian women who lived near the popular city square Praça Onze and opened their homes to what would become Rio's cradle of samba.[30] Among the most prominent was Tia Ciata (Hilária Batista de Almeida, 1854–1924), a female peddler of sweets who organized musical gatherings that brought together residents from different parts of the city. As arrest and detention records for 1903–1925 demonstrate, street sellers of sweets were mostly Afro-Brazilian, and some like Tia Ciata became famous enough to gain the respect of lower-, middle-, and upper-class customers who protected them from the police.[31]

Several Bahian women set up their vending tables where trams took residents between outlying neighborhoods and the city center. Some of the women relied on children to reach out to customers, and images of these children were popularized in urban culture such as in the traditional samba song "Menino das laranjas" and a 1961 news article discussing the childhood of a tram conductor "having a smile that's all teeth."[32] By the 1930s, Largo da Carioca was a central stop for trams coming from the south zone of the city. The large cement roof under which tram cars were parked earned the name Tabuleiro da Bahiana because it resembled a big vendor's table. By the middle of the twentieth century, passengers were probably familiar with Ary Barbosa's "No tabuleiro da Bahiana," a song performed by the world-renowned Carmen Miranda and others that recalls "o tabuleiro que tinha carurú, vatapá, tapioca e mungunzá," a vending table with a variety of traditional Afro-Brazilian foods. In 1963, the municipality planned to demolish the cement tram stop and substitute trams with buses, ending a long tradition of residents mixing with street types such as peddlers, magicians, musicians, and even fire eaters. The nostalgia generated by the end of trams in Rio resembled the popular reaction to the eliminations of street kiosks in the early 1900s.[33]

The striking transformation of the human and physical environment of the Brazilian capital in the first decades of the twentieth century developed street networks between urban and suburban commerce. Peddlers were everywhere transporting goods between the city center and the urban periphery, as newer and older residents relied on vending's varied occupations.[34] Street commerce was also in the various locations where sellers were arrested: the streets, construction sites, bars, shops, gambling houses, entertainment centers, factories, and rooming houses. Streets were, predictably, the most common places for the arrests of vendors, followed by botequins. Most botequins, like kiosks, were arguably extensions of the street, and police officers routinely inspected them and arrested alleged vagrants, drunks, gamblers, and thieves.

According to Police Occurrences, vagrancy and physical conflict were considered a crime against the common good (*crime contra a fé pública*) or a crime against public order (*crime contra a segurança/tranquilidade*). Theft, which led to the arrests of many street sellers, was a crime against property (*crime contra a propriedade*). A number of peddlers were arrested for crimes of breaching a victim's honor, family, or reputation (*crime contra a honra/família/pudor*), and some were charged with homicide (*crime contra a vida/pessoa*). Although these charges were unrelated to the practices of street commerce, they still show the policing that made vendors vulnerable to arrest. A few individuals were arrested for participating in illegal commerce, which violated property rights. Typically, individuals selling stolen goods or illicit lottery tickets were arrested for illegal commerce rather than for vagrancy or public disorder.

Police Occurrences records of the arrests of vendors do not correspond to the official target that municipal regulation underlined in 1903. Restrictions on the activities of mascates, lottery peddlers, meat vendors, milk sellers, and bread vendors were explicit, but their numbers were the lowest in arrest records. Street sellers of milk, who were typically Portuguese men, were mostly arrested between 1905 and 1910 in the district of Tiradentes, but not once was a milk vendor arrested for walking with a cow. The sample includes only one incident in which a vendor was arrested for selling watered-down milk. Theft, disorder, vagrancy, and inebriation were the most common charges in arrests of milk peddlers. Disorder and vagrancy were vague categories that could apply to these sellers, with or without cows. The street sale of meat was carefully regulated for hygiene. Meat vendors, who were often Portuguese men, were regularly arrested on the street based on unsanitary conditions of their goods.

While few mascates were arrested, according to Police Occurrences, this was not the case for the more general group of *vendedores ambulantes*. Mascates were mainly Syrio-Lebanese men, while ambulantes tended to be Brazilian and southern European, especially Italian. The arrests of peddlers in the Police Occurrences of 1903–1925 continued to reflect turn-of-the-century patterns in Rio's detention center. Accordingly, quitandeiros were the most vulnerable group to arrest, followed by shoe shiners, newspaper sellers, and vendors of sweets. A smaller number of women were arrested, many of them

Afro-Brazilian and residents of Santana, still a heavily policed area that authorities sought to discipline.

African-descended street vendors often specialized in the sale of vegetables, fruits, and sweets, a profile that both arrest and detention records in Rio confirm. Even though several quitandeiros were Italian immigrants, most were Brazilian and African-born vegetable sellers. The few women who were arrested, according to Police Occurrences, were quitandeiras from Portugal or the Brazilian state of Bahia. Vendors of sweets tended to be African-descended men and women from the states of Bahia and Minas Gerais. By 1913 the street bahiana had become widely known for peddling sweets, influencing the publishing of a newspaper cartoon that depicted a bahiana vendor as a symbol of Bahia.[35]

Licensed sweets peddlers were frequently arrested for physical conflict. Along with quitandeiros, sweets sellers were the most common vendors arrested on the street, and police officers tended to record their vending license numbers. There is no explanation as to how incidents of physical conflict related to the practice of street commerce, but court evidence reveals the competitiveness between some sellers of sweets. Along with quitandeiros and sweets sellers, newspaper sellers were often arrested. They were likely to be Italian or Brazilian young men and children; this was a line of work rarely performed by Afro-descendant adults. Petty fighting was a common charge in the arrests of newsboys, as was the allegation of practicing capoeira.

To a lesser extent, vendors selling pastries, sugarcane juice, beer, bread, patties (*empadas*), herbs, knick-knacks, jewelry, gloves, nougat, fish, and wood were arrested. They were largely white Brazilians born in the city of Rio. Shoe shiners, often Afro-Brazilian men born in Rio, were frequently arrested for vagrancy and public disorder. Another reason for their arrest was not paying to ride trams for the purpose of serving passengers. At the police station, officers often confiscated peddlers' belongings such as vending tables, shoeshine stools, and push carts. Records show that Afro-Brazilian vendors usually did not carry valuable objects on them, while Syrio-Lebanese mascates, Portuguese milk sellers, and Italian peddlers had valuables with them like timepieces and money. Although generally poor, immigrant peddlers as a whole were better off than their Brazilian counterparts, who generally worked in lower positions of street commerce.

Individuals whom the police arrested on charges of illegal commerce were not necessarily street vendors by occupation. This type of arrest mostly took place on the street (*via pública*) and in botequins, rooming houses for the working poor (*casas de cômodos*), and places of leisure in Santana and Sacramento. Male, literate, and Portuguese was the typical profile of the person charged with illegal commerce. Few peddlers were arrested on this charge. The men most often charged with illegal commerce were formally employed in activities other than street selling and were literate. Illegal commerce may have been part of street life, but it was generally not practiced by poor and illiterate peddlers. Street sellers of stolen goods usually belonged to the more privileged segments of society.

Examples of illegal commerce charges include a hospital worker buying a stolen Liberty cigar (made in the Sousa Cruz factory) from an individual in a botequim. Both men were caught in the act during a routine police inspection. Another record describes two box-office workers at the theater in Praça Tiradentes arrested for informally selling tickets. Accusations of illegal commerce were also common against jogo do bicho sellers, who were mostly poor and illiterate. Selling goods at night that would be considered legitimate during the day made street vendors more vulnerable to arrest. Such was the case of the Portuguese vendor selling sweets near the Praça Tiradentes after ten o'clock at night. Selling goods at night, clandestinely and outside work hours, had been a common practice since colonial times, as slaves and poor individuals found more freedom of movement at that time when policing was less intense.

Street vending without a license was not considered illegal commerce, however. Instead it was an act of vagrancy or public disorder. Some individuals were arrested for carrying licenses that were in others' names, often because the licenses were stolen. Arrest records indicate that police targeted unlicensed porters and deliverers more often than unlicensed street vendors. Detention records bring to light the opposite. The 1890 Penal Code's foundation for detention seemed more useful than street arrests based on municipal ordinance infractions to deal with unwanted street sellers. Deliverymen were less of a nuisance for street police and therefore could be dealt with through ganho and municipal regulation. Vendors, however, were more numerous and disorderly and hence a great inconvenience for street police. Several deliverymen were arrested for transporting and selling goods in inappropriate locations. These places were outlined in the municipal code and often were arbitrarily decided at the time of arrest. A newspaper article explains what police often considered an inappropriate location: "Every time a police officer runs into a quitandeiro who is selling in one location for an extended period of time, he will fine the seller 10 [milréis]."[36] It seems that any location could become unacceptable to a police officer if a street vendor stayed there long enough.

VAGRANTS OR WORKERS

The association between work ao ganho and vagrancy resulted in the detention of street sellers and ganhadores. The case of "Moleque" (Kid), arrested 9 October 1904, reveals the free labor ideology understood by some street ganhadores.[37] Moleque's real name was Salustiano da Cruz, a twenty-four-year-old, unmarried, and illiterate man from Bahia. The detention center scribe had noted his nickname next to his full name. Along with other personal information, the registry entry at the detention center recorded the man's skin color as black. His repeated detentions for vagrancy in 1904 illustrate the worker-vagrant rationale that influenced both detention and court procedures in which vendors and ganhadores appealed to authorities on the legitimacy of their work.

In 1904, da Cruz was arrested once in Morro da Providência (later known as Morro da Favela), Rio's first informal settlement of shanty houses on a steep hill that were not the beehives (cortiços) of the crowded downtown. His second arrest took place in Santana. In both cases, da Cruz was detained and tried in court with another individual, a friend also accused of vagrancy. Policemen and neighborhood residents described da Cruz and his friend as "notorious pickpockets" and "vagrants" who lacked a home and employment. Instead they would "bum around and disturb whoever they find." Since da Cruz had experienced various stays at the detention center, police argued that his vagrant behavior was incorrigible. His nickname, "Moleque Estafa," which police officials could have used as an epithet, connotes a tendency to tirelessly deceive people.

When da Cruz was first arrested for vagrancy in Rio's Morro da Favela, the court sentenced him to twenty-two and a half days in jail, after which he would have fifteen days to become formally employed or face reincarceration. Stating that he was a "working man" (*homen trabalhador*) with a fixed place of residence—two characteristics that many detainees understood as key to avoiding vagrancy charges—did not work in his favor. The same strategy would be ineffective five months later when Salustiano was put under arrest for vagrancy in Santana. On this occasion, Salustiano specifically stated that he was a ganhador, an occupation that carried more legitimacy than the generic term for worker, trabalhador. A Bahian migrant, da Cruz knew how to earn a living as a ganhador in the city, even if the number of ganhadores had been declining since the end of slavery. Antônio José da Cruz, in 1905, was the last individual at the Casa de Detenção who identified as a ganhador. He was also a black man from Bahia. Both Antônio da Cruz and Salustiano da Cruz had probably worked ao ganho on the streets of Salvador and migrated to Rio to find economic opportunity in the same line of work.[38] Many Afro-Brazilian and European vendors who had worked in the ganho system understood conditions on the street according to nineteenth-century practices, but the protections that the ganho system may have offered them against policing were quickly eroding.

To prove that he had a fixed residence and even admitting that he was behind on rent, Salustiano da Cruz said he rented a room on Rua da Saúde. A "Turkish" woman who managed the casa de cômodos that da Cruz identified as home said da Cruz did not sleep there. This led her to rent out his room to somebody else, emphasizing to the court that she "did not allow just anybody [*qualquer indivíduo*] to rent" from her.[39] Describing him as an undesirable tenant recalls James Holston's cidadão qualquer, a nobody or anonymous citizen with no formal identity rooted in family, labor, or community.[40] Still, Salustiano da Cruz negotiated the terms of his citizenship, declaring in court that he was not just anybody. Aware of the worker-vagrant dichotomy that dominated court decisions, da Cruz stressed that he honorably worked ao ganho.[41] The judge, however, considered him a vagrant due to his repeated detentions and sentenced him to imprisonment and forced labor in the penal colony Dois Rios.[42] Relying on the traditional legitimacy of ganho work proved useless for Salustiano da Cruz in this case.

The court record on Salustiano da Cruz reveals a number of practices that anthropologists and historians have explored in discussing issues of race, citizenship, and labor in postabolition Brazil.[43] The police described him as a "notorious pickpocket," although charges were for vagrancy and not theft. His various incarcerations in the Casa de Detenção demonstrate not only the persistence of alleged vagrancy but also a type of "civic education."[44] The historian Amy Chazkel argues that recurring encounters with the police allowed detainees in Rio's detention center to learn the formal and informal logic of the law and negotiate the terms of their citizenship. The rituals of "social branding" after arrest, such as by physical and medical examinations, gathering of personal data, and fingerprinting, were sites of repression as well as inadvertent teaching moments on civic membership.[45] After repeated detentions and trials for vagrancy, it is not surprising that Salustiano da Cruz continued to repeat that he was a working man with a home. His response reflected a civic education in which he substituted the vagrant for the disciplined worker.

Immigrant peddlers charged with vagrancy sometimes turned to their consulates for help. Deportation was a strategy to deal with immigrant anarchists,[46] and immigrant vendors were vulnerable to deportation as a strategy to clean up the street. A 1926 case from the state of Pará illustrates how the lawyer of a group of detained vendors appealed to habeas corpus to fight deportation charges.[47] The case was widely discussed in the Rio newspaper *Correio da Manhã*, as habeas corpus appeared as a new and modern legal protection for immigrants claiming street vending as a legitimate line of work in Brazil.

Throughout the first decades of the twentieth century, peddlers who were arrested, detained, and tried in court resisted vagrancy charges by appealing to authorities on grounds of their legitimate work and honorable community relations. Detention and court records shed light on what often followed street arrests, and in the sample of individuals held at the Casa de Detenção between 1903 and 1922, 40 percent of vendors were detained for vagrancy.[48] About 80 percent of the detainees were black or racially mixed. Officials often considered Syrio-Lebanese immigrants to be pardos, as Brazilian racial thinking transferred onto European immigrants. Some darker-skinned Italians who were illiterate were also labeled pardos or morenos.[49]

The high incidence of vagrancy charges among poor Brazilians and immigrants reflected 1907 measures of the Gabinete de Identificação da Polícia Civil. The court trials that followed detention in the Casa de Detenção further indicate how the worker-vagrant rationale informed both judicial authorities and defendants. Defendants portrayed street vending as a legitimate practice and vendors as rightful citizens to shape their arguments of urban belonging and citizenship.

Peddlers of various ethnic backgrounds contested vagrancy, public disorder, inebriation, and petty theft charges by claiming that they were honest workers and often heads of household. They emphasized the legitimacy of their work, alluding to honor and discipline. In cases when authorities labeled peddlers "irremediable pickpockets," "everyday drunks," or "habitual vagrants," legal defenders (*curadores*) and their clients raised urban belonging and citizenship as important factors. Such was the case of Laurindo Manuel da Silva, known on the street as "the blind man of Santo Cristo" (*o ceguinho de Santo Cristo*).

Between 1901 and 1911, Laurindo da Silva had several stays in the Casa de Detenção.[50] A poor, blind man charged with vagrancy for living on the street, da Silva "was becoming more and more dangerous," according to the police. His case shows the criminalization of the poor but also of the disabled on the street. Da Silva's legal defender familiar with existing ideas about criminality stated, "The great Italian criminologist Lombroso defines only an individual without occupation or place of residence as a vagrant." Consequently, he argued, da Silva was not a vagrant because he had a home and an occupation in street vending. The judge, however, did not concur and sentenced da Silva to the correctional facility Dois Rios on Ilha Grande. The judge preferred to remove from the street a poor, blind man who was a sore sight for better-off passersby.

Economic crisis, lack of work opportunity, and high cost of living also appeared as reasons for disputing vagrancy charges in court. In the case of a young migrant from Pernambuco, who was arrested along with a minor in 1904, the police inspector claimed that he "knew for a fact that the accused had no type of occupation." The migrant was listed as a vendor, however, in the registry entry of the detention center.[51] A witness agreed that the accused man and minor were "notorious vagrants" and that "by hearsay he knows that they have no occupation or place of residence." The legal defender explained that economic conditions resulted in the precarious living situation of his clients, who were "not vagrants but distressed unemployed young men [*infelizes desempregados*] of the current crisis." Street peddling was hence a result of unemployment and not vagrancy, the defender argued. Eventually, "a variety of circumstances" that perhaps had to do with the vagueness of vagrancy charges led the judge to nullify the case.

Other street sellers had been able to acquire houses in the city during the transition from slavery to freedom. Such proprietors lived off rent and street commerce. The writer João do Rio discusses Afro-Brazilian social mobility in the newspaper chronicle "Negros ricos," in which he displays prevalent racial thinking of the early twentieth century.[52] Rental housing managed by African-descended landlords had origins in the practice that allowed urban slaves to live outside their masters' houses. Many street sellers were able to accumulate resources as ganhadores that allowed them to establish semi-autonomous living conditions. Their residences became centers of resistance, leisure, and music, and a number of them were run by female peddlers, as was the case of the popular Tia Ciata in postabolition Rio.[53]

A dispute between African-born landlords and two Bahian tenants in 1905 illustrates street commerce as a source of Afro-Brazilian wealth in Rio. Antônio Adioi and Maria Emini, an African couple originally from Lagos, rented out a room in their home in Gamboa to Norberto da Silva, a mulatto from Bahia. The landlords noted in their testimony that Norberto da Silva often shared his room with a Bahian girlfriend named Maria da Glória.[54] He worked as a newspaper peddler, and Adioi and Emini were also street sellers who earned additional income by renting out a room in their home. On the night of 20 November 1905 a violent confrontation erupted between landlords and tenants that led to significant property damage. Da Silva had not been paying rent for some months, and after the confrontation, all four—landlords and tenants—ended up in jail to recount their stories in court. The landlords protested that da Silva attacked them first because of his escalating frustration with financial difficulties. The mulatto tenant may have also felt racial prejudice toward an African couple with the privilege of property ownership. The court defended private property over any racial sentiment, however, and the judge acquitted the African couple and declared the Bahian mulatto responsible for property damage and failure to pay rent.

The worker-vagrant rationale also brought under suspicion a variety of street vendors for simply being in public areas of the city. In 1906, João Monteiro and another man were arrested at three o'clock in the morning. Both were charged with vagrancy, fingerprints were collected, and interrogation soon followed. Their court record states that they had been "wandering around" the beach at São Cristovão and were arrested for living under a pile of wood there. João Monteiro, a forty-six-year-old, illiterate, Portuguese man, argued (and the scribe underlined) that "he had an honest occupation being a street peddler of meat."[55] The underlined words emphasized the defender's legal position against charges of vagrancy or unemployment. Monteiro declared that he lived at Rua da Alegria 11, as "he would prove in court." He explained that it was routine for him to return from the slaughterhouse in São Diogo before dawn, after purchasing the meat he would sell later that day. Walking back home, he happened to pass near the pile of wood where the other man may have been spending the night. Both were arrested, but Monteiro was mistaken for a vagrant. Having proof of a place of residence and an occupation, Monteiro was released from detention, as officials knew that meat vendors were usually supplied at the São Diogo slaughterhouse and walked the city in the early morning hours.

Foreign-born immigrants were subject to the same worker-vagrant rationale that informed the arrests of Brazilians. In 1917, the policeman who arrested the young Syrian Miguel Curi on the beach claimed to "personally know" that he was a notorious vagrant, although the registry entry listed him as a mascate. A businessman who was Miguel Curi's patron and supplier came to his defense in court, stressing that the accused was a worker of "exemplary behavior, without leaving much to be desired." This affirming testimony led the judge to conclude that "the accusation of vagrancy is false because [the defendant] is a working young man of good habits."[56] Finding support in patronage was evidently helpful for vendors wishing to legitimize their occupations against vagrancy charges.

The worker-vagrant rationale was not always predictable, as the 1905 conflict between two peddlers of sweets in Rio's Praça da República demonstrates. A case that authorities could have easily dismissed as vagrancy or physical offense was filed instead under Article 329 of the penal code, which related to damaged goods and property. In other words, property rights applied to items sold on the street. Joaquim Maria de Oliveira and Manuel José de Sousa were Brazilian-born peddlers who sold sweets from trays in an area of the Praça da República. A nearby kiosk attracted consumers, so the two vendors routinely stationed themselves close to it. A violent fight between the two erupted around noon on 30 October, according to the Italian witness Eusébio Gentil. The witness stated that de Sousa threw de Oliveira's tray to the ground. Gentil soon called to a civil guard in the vicinity who arrested both peddlers.

According to another witness, the accused de Sousa was in fact the victim. De Sousa claimed in court that de Oliveira had been disturbing him, trying to take over his vending spot (*ponto*). De Sousa had even tried to contact a policeman to settle the dispute properly, but in the absence of one and with de Oliveira's unrelenting harassment, de Sousa decided to take matters into his own hands. In a bout of anger, he threw de Oliveira's tray to the ground. De Sousa's legal defender argued that his client acted in self-defense. Although the judge considered this a plausible motive, de Sousa was not exempt from the charge of property damage.

The court's decision to fine de Sousa for breaking his competitor's vending tray officially recognized vendors' work. As objects of a crime scene, court officials examined the broken tray and ruined sweets to measure their worth. Made of wood and glass, the tray was valued by court officials at 45 milréis. De Sousa was consequently sentenced to one month in jail and fined 5 percent of the property loss. The court estimated the "salary and necessary time for payment of the fine," taking into account that sweets peddlers generally made little over one milréis per day. De Sousa would need at least twenty-seven days of work to be able to repay de Oliveira. Occurring at the height of Pereira Passos's campaign against street commerce that confined peddlers to outside the city's districts, this case demonstrates that the courts treated vendors as formal workers. Although the court record does not note skin color, records from the Casa de Detenção show that most sweets vendors were Afro-Brazilian.

Competitive behavior between peddlers could sometimes result in homicide. These were often reported by a sensationalist press, such as the conflicts between two vendors of meat patties, empadas, in 1913, and two sweets sellers in 1915. The Portuguese sweets vendor Manuel de Ornelias was twenty-five years old and accused the Brazilian vendor Joaquim Brandão of taking away his customers. The Portuguese immigrant claimed that the Brazilian would strategically work the same location, stationing himself there hours before the other arrived, thus reducing the number of customers who bought from de Ornelias. After this occurred several times, de Ornelias, who believed in witchcraft, even resorted to asking a *feiticeiro* (medicine man) to eliminate his competitor. But soon he took matters into his own hands and shot Joaquim in the back when he was serving a customer. A civil guard caught de Ornelias, while Brandão died in the hospital. Upon hearing about his victim's death, de Ornelias, who had been detained, stated to the press, "I am sorry for his death; but he brought it upon himself, since he reduced me to misery."[57] This case reflected the tension between Brazilians and immigrants, particularly Portuguese workers who had prospered in previous times and now felt disadvantaged because of the considerable number of people selling on the street for a living.

A similar altercation took place between two vendors of empadas in 1913 in a botequim on Rua Senador Pompeu in the middle of the night. The botequim was next to a factory where both street peddlers received their supplies and one of them now lived. Resentment had been growing for some time since Benedito "Barão" Alves returned to his supplier with a lesser amount from street sales than his competitor, José Fernandes. This resulted in the termination of Alves's employment. After that, he had been seeking vengeance, which he found when Fernandes entered the botequim to purchase cigarettes and matches. Alves stabbed Fernandes in the stomach with a meat knife and ran away past the empada factory and toward the Morro da Conceição. Fernandes died from his stomach wound while in the Santa Casa da Misericórdia hospital. During that time good police work led to Alves's arrest in another botequim.

Fernandes was an immigrant from Spain who was nineteen years old when he died. Alves was Spanish also and twenty years older. He lived on the top floor of a nearby building that housed the botequim where the stabbing took place. The older Spanish immigrant evidently felt the pressure of a younger generation competing for the same type of work and street space. But the police attributed the murder to an irrational act of violence, as stated in the newspaper *A Época*. The news reporter, however, argued that irrationality was an easy dismissal of something much more serious. "Money, the eternal origin for humanity's weakness and the world's perversity," was the only cause for murder in this case. There was no article in the penal code that spoke to that, the writer lamented, pointing instead at the deeper social problem of marginality.[58] Poverty, inequality, and bad working conditions for immigrants and Brazilians alike made the real fabric of freedom in postabolition Rio.

MARGINALIZING MORE THAN ELIMINATING

Street commerce, an old custom of the Brazilian capital, came to a crossroads in the early 1900s with the Pereira Passos reforms. While new laws were enacted to confine peddling to the city's outskirts and eliminate most street selling from the urban center, vendors resisted official efforts to delegitimize their work. The mayor's aggressive policy toward the eradication of street practices stimulated the policing of vendors, and the 1890 Penal Code became a useful instrument for establishing quick order on the street. Still, municipal ambivalence toward street commerce came out in the regulation of vendors. Officials, on the one hand, could deem street commerce a blot on the Europeanized capital they envisioned. To that end, Pereira Passos enforced the regulatory role of the police on the street. Police officers became notorious for capriciously fining or arresting vendors for vagrancy or public disorder.

On another level, the official creation of open-air markets indicated that the regulation of street commerce and rationalization of urban space coexisted with the increased policing. Buying on the street remained robust, as customers preferred the cheaper products that vendors sold. The building of street markets throughout the city was meant to keep food prices low as well as to rationalize distribution. The Municipal Market was built to do this for central Rio, but it did not succeed in substituting the popular demand for street vendors.

The early twentieth century witnessed municipal initiatives that marginalized street commerce and moved it toward the urban periphery, positioning it in a more vulnerable position vis-à-vis the police. The application of criminal law to unwanted street vendors facilitated this marginalization. The structures of slavery and free labor had coexisted in the ganho system where vendors practiced legitimate work but were a nuisance to policing authorities. In the early twentieth century, the same nuisance justified repeated arrests and detention. Official restrictions on street commerce in Rio thus contributed to its informalization and marginal practices. Regulation could lawfully improve customary practice, or policing could further marginalize vending and associate participants with criminality. The early decades of the twentieth century saw the execution of both trends influencing the informalization of street commerce yet never fully and successfully eliminating it from the capital city.

CHAPTER 6

VENDORS AND THE CITY ASSOCIATE

DURING THE YEARS 1912–1914, the newspaper *A Época* published the activities of organized street vendors in Rio and commented on the issue of policing. The predicament was familiar to the press, as the nineteenth-century Street Occurrences front-page column in the *Gazeta de Notícias* had regularly reported on interactions between police and vendors. Responding to ongoing policing and new municipal regulation, street vendors in 1912 formed the civic and labor association they named the União Protetora de Comércio Volante (Protective Association of Street Commerce). The UPCV defended the economic liberty of all street sellers in the Brazilian capital and nearby Niterói and condemned excessive street policing as a strategy meant to extinguish vending in the city.[1] The legacy of slavery's systematic policing contributed to identifying the street seller as a vagrant and an element of public disorder, but vendors in postabolition Rio turned to organizing to claim urban citizenship and the legitimacy of their work.

On 8 January 1913, the plight of street peddlers made the front page of the evening newspaper *A Noite*. The article "Ficará o Rio sem ambulantes?" (Will Rio be left without peddlers?) announced a possible work stoppage the following day. The newspaper supported street vendors' motives for striking. The writer contemplated whether the Brazilian capital could survive without vendors, estimating that twelve thousand quitandeiros, mascates, fish sellers, and others who "opportunely serve the city of Rio door-to-door" would stop delivering goods. Residents accustomed to buying from peddlers would consequently suffer "great loss." The writer then asks readers to "imagine the absence of the quitandeiro at your door, what awaits the big city with limited resources for provisioning! . . . How will the household head be able to pick the best fish and the freshest greens?" The "exaggerated and unjust" new municipal regulation, he argues, had given vendors "all the reason to protest." Emphasizing that they were crucial for the distribution of basic necessities throughout the city, he declares it a "calamity" that vendors were often fined arbitrarily, a circumstance the new regulation only encouraged.

On January 9, however, vendors did not stop working, and residents purchased goods at their doors as usual. Vendors and their suppliers made the decision to forgo the strike after meeting at the Protective Association of Retail Sellers (Associação Protetora dos Vendedores à Varejo) days before the planned work stoppage. They resolved to negotiate with the mayor instead even if the city council had already passed the regulation concerning street vending. Associated retail sellers included suppliers who provided vendors with goods to sell on the street. The UPCV also met separately to discuss the new measures prompting the stoppage. The UPCV's president, Francisco Gonçalves Vianna Ferraz, a vendor himself, and patrons and suppliers of street commerce drafted a petition asking the mayor to eliminate the new measures and denounce excessive policing. A street peddler named Luiz Ribeiro participated in the discussion and suggested that vendors "resist by not getting licenses since the new law makes it impossible to exercise the vending occupation."[2]

In that same meeting, members agreed to rename the association the União Protetora de Comércio Volante to emphasize the importance of street commerce (*comércio volante*) beyond just street vendors (vendedores ambulantes). The association's first name had been the Protective Association of Street Vendors (União Protetora de Vendedores Ambulantes). The second name purposely included street commerce at large and patrons and suppliers specifically. The next day 287 more individuals enrolled as members, and the UPCV became a growing presence in the city's organized labor and associative life of the early twentieth century. During its brief existence, from 1912 to 1914, the UPCV had an approximate total of 400 members.[3] Suppliers and street sellers of sweets dominated the association, but all types of vendors were invited to join.

The UPCV particularly sought the patronage and protection of small businesses to resist high licensing fees and excessive street policing. Vendors seeking protection in patronage were informed by old practices of mutual aid and the ganho system as well as the more recent activities of trade unionism in the capital city. The UPCV was an attempt to bridge the era of nineteenth-century mutual aid societies and twentieth-century trade unionism that made it feasible for vendors to become active participants in the city's debate over citizenship. To assert their rightful presence in the Brazilian capital, UPCV-affiliated vendors incorporated nineteenth-century traditions that had shaped the work of ganhadores. The patron-client relations that supplied and employed free street sellers had weakened with the decline of the ganho system, and the UPCV aimed to resuscitate these relations in the early postabolition period. The association sought protection in patronage to contend with an allegedly repressive municipality, increased policing, and a changing industry of suppliers. Although restoring unequal dependence between patrons and clients was not street vendors' intention, the protection they desired could not escape this legacy from the slave period.

Vendor organizing, networks between sellers and their suppliers, and a robust customary practice contributed to officials' inability to eliminate street commerce from Rio in the early 1900s. Urban reforms had failed to restrict peddling to outside the city center, while a combination of policing and regulation disciplined the street. The approval of new measures for street commerce in 1924 reflected the strength of customary practice despite increased policing and ongoing restrictive measures. A decade earlier, the UPCV had attempted to negotiate with an ambivalent municipality to prevent vendors from becoming more vulnerable to poverty and the increasingly informal conditions of their trade. Achieving a balance of municipal regulation and policing, street vendors' freedom, and suppliers' interests had been the UPCV's main concern. The 1924 regulations in support of street vending were a long-awaited response for participants in a basic business practice of the capital city.

STREET COMMERCE REGULATION

The 1913 listing of licensing fees for vendors (*impostos de licenças*) was a testament to the failure of Pereira Passos's earlier prohibitive measures against street commerce. The municipality introduced new fees due in January and required payment based on the amount calculated for the type of good destined for street selling. Fees also were increased for registering vehicles.[4] Even though the tax was meant to improve street commerce, the UPCV contended that instead it would encourage more policing that already disregarded the validity of licenses. The real problem for police authorities was not unlicensed street commerce but seeing poor vendors on the street.

The 1913 tax also reflected the urban change resulting from population increase at the turn of the century. The new regulation specifically distinguished between urban and suburban vending, as they were subject to different types of licenses and fees. Vendors and their vehicles were taxed higher in the city center and lower in the subúrbio. The Diretoria Geral da Fazenda regulated the tax for vehicles according to a law passed in 1901 and renewed in 1907 and 1908, after the Pereira Passos regime. This government agency also distributed the license plates and registration numbers that had to be displayed on vehicles and other vending equipment. By this time, pushcarts and vending carriages had become more sophisticated, and storage facilities for them throughout the city that were owned by private companies had to be licensed as well.

The types of goods and vehicles on the 1913 license tax list offer a glimpse into a complex vending landscape that continued to connect established shops with street commerce as well as central and peripheral neighborhoods. Sellers with handcarts working to distribute goods for stables and butcher shops or with pushcarts and carriages under the services of factories and general stores shared the same licensing costs. These vehicles extended the reach of fixed commerce that continued to rely on street peddlers for the distribution of goods. Food growers in rural areas required a vending license that cost less if they remained in the subúrbio. But if they entered central areas of the city they were charged as regular urban peddlers. Downtown shops were taxed as non-producers. Officials in 1913 thus continued to differentiate the diverse vending practices that had existed in the Brazilian capital city during previous decades.

The 1913 license tax was based on and specified where and how vendors could work and what they could sell. Peddlers were not allowed to station themselves in public squares (*logradouros públicos*) and could only sell while walking through them (*venda rápida*). Growers coming from the rural outskirts to sell their produce in the city were exempt from this law, but they were still not allowed to repeatedly set up to sell in the same place. They had to diversify their vending locations throughout the city. Municipal ordinances still required *mercadores ambulantes* (mobile sellers) along with haulers to wear metal pins or post licenses in visible places at all times. The regulation of haulers, who tended to be black workers, remained closest to the norms of the ganho system. Vendors of sweets, baked goods, and cigars and cigarettes were no longer permitted to sell those products from unsealed containers. The hygienic, sealed boxes that patent seekers proposed at the turn of the century were now mandatory. The same held true for vendors of meat parts, who now had to transport their goods in ways that ensured cleanliness. Haulers and candy sellers had to wear uniforms and shoes that improved their physical appearance, thus distancing them from the slave legacy of poorly clothed black sellers or the poverty of street vendors in general. Finally, the 1913 law acknowledged that there were possibly types of vendors not listed in the new regulation, but they still had to follow the same licensing procedures as "second-class" or "small-scale" shops. Linking street vendors to shops acknowledged the ongoing ties between the street and established petty commerce that had shaped supply lines in Rio since the nineteenth century.

These measures showed that officials were meeting the customary practices of urban vending halfway. Peddlers' street cries and loud announcements continued to raise complaints but were allowed and regulated. Vendors who declared their use of cornets, bells, and other sounds to announce their presence paid an additional 50 percent tax when registering their licenses. The rambunctious noise vendors generated was generally undesired, according to complaints published in newspapers. And although the implementation of a higher fee was intended to discourage vendors from using loud instruments, the municipality's decision to regulate rather than prohibit it demonstrates an accommodation to a persisting customary practice. The 1913 law made clear the distinction between milk street sellers and milk deliverymen, exempting the latter from licensing fees if they were not selling on the street. Their exemption was based on the license required for barns with cows. Distinctions were specified in the bread industry as well. The new regulation differentiated those who delivered bread, often by tricycle, from those who sold it on the street. These 1913 nuances were thus acknowledging the customary practices of the meat, milk, and bread industries, which relied on the street for delivery and distribution and whose deliverymen were often harassed as peddlers.

Table 3 in the appendix summarizes the fees that street vendors had to pay in 1913 for selling different types of items. The cost for each license corresponds to the seller's rank and value in the urban vending economy, illustrating a market of consumers who heavily relied on street vendors for all types of items. Group A lists the license fees for selling lower-cost items such as fruits, vegetables, milk, and cheese. Group B lists more valuable goods such as meat, fish, and household supplies. These first two groups included what many would consider to be basic necessities that residents bought on a daily or weekly basis. Group C lists the fees for more exclusive items such as porcelain, crystal, and handmade clothes. The last section, Group D, shows that luxury items such as jewelry and dyes were also a part of street commerce.

In addition, the 1913 license tax list identified the types of shops that often employed street vendors in groups A–D. Haberdasheries (*casas de armarinho*), greengroceries (casas de quitanda), taverns, and botequins had since the nineteenth century hired peddlers, often with vehicles, to distribute goods throughout the city. Haberdasheries mainly sold fabrics for the home such as tablecloths and bedsheets. They relied on *vendedores de fazendas*, mascates who sold door to door. Many casas de quitanda employed quitandeiros and fruit and vegetable peddlers. Taverns and botequins hired a variety of street sellers who sold goods from prepared foods and coffee to cigars and cigarettes. Taverns, which were similar to small restaurants, were bigger than botequins and enjoyed greater business in rural areas. All in all, the new measures reinforced the ties between shops, restaurants, and street commerce.

It was common for peddlers to work into the night, as nocturnal life allowed for movement under less policing. In efforts to repress vending's underground economy, the 1913 license tax ordinance established that the business of peddling (*negócio ambulante*) was only allowed to function from six in the morning to six in the evening. Individual peddlers could still sell on Sundays and on municipal and federal holidays until ten at night. The new regulation was especially meaningful to street sellers of sweets, baked goods, flowers, refreshments, and ice cream, since they frequented churches and public squares on holidays. Street selling of fowl, angu, cigars and cigarettes, fruits, pieces of meat, eggs, bread, plants, and vegetables could only take place until noon on Sunday. In Santo Antônio, Santana, Gamboa, Santa Rita, Sacramento, and the area considered the low city (*cidade baixa*), which included Candelária, São José, Glória, and Santa Teresa, vendors of fowl, red meat, eggs, fish, fruits, and vegetables were permitted to sell any day of the week until midday. The midday curfew on perishable items resulted from ongoing concerns about street commerce and sanitation, as these vendors never completely left the city center.

Peddlers subject to four times the normal fees usually sold valuable goods. These men and women were sellers of shoes, carnival items, lottery tickets, sun umbrellas, cigars and cigarettes, mirrors and paintings, jewelry, porcelain dishes, lamps, crystal and glass, perfume, phonographs, clothes, fabrics, and soap. Growers who lived outside the city and sold from boats in the bay were also listed in this category because they came from rural areas to sell in the city; thus they were charged higher fees.

Police officers could still confiscate vendors' items, followed by a comprehensive audit at the precinct. Officers were permitted to auction off any confiscated perishable goods within the first twenty-four hours, a practice that had been carried out informally. The money from confiscated winning lottery tickets was specifically given to police, the city, and two organizations that provided aid and protection to workers. The police officer who carried out the arrest received 25 percent of the total funds from a winning ticket, 30 percent went to the other policemen involved, and the rest went to municipal coffers and charity. Thus, there was an incentive for street police to confiscate lottery tickets.

MUTUAL AID AND CIVIC LIFE

Vendors' collective organizing in the early twentieth century had origins in the activities of mutual aid societies and the ganho system of the nineteenth century. Street sellers' unsteady relations with suppliers and the municipality influenced their organizing, which was also a statement on the transition from slavery to freedom. The city's milk sellers were involved in associative activities since at least the mid-nineteenth century. In 1913, they resisted another municipal ordinance that altered their customary practice. On 22 January 1913, the daily *Correio da Manhã* reported that milk sellers protested at city hall the recent ban on the milk tanks that had substituted cows in door-to-door selling. The new requirement for milk to be distributed in glass bottles was meant to restore proper nutrition and hygiene that the use of tanks had undermined. The *Correio da Manhã* reported that milk sellers' protests were an act of resistance against urban hygiene; the editors instead endorsed the use of bottled milk.[5] Milk vendors, however, were not as much resisting hygienic reform as they were expressing distrust in municipal support.

Milk vendors had requested that the municipality assist them with the new adoption of bottles. Their association was aware of the need for new hygienic measures and therefore sought public support. Milk vendors feared that they would have to navigate another switch with few resources. Officials had dragged their feet when it came to supplying vendors with milk tanks some years earlier, hence the widespread use of cows being led and milked on the street. Sanitizing milk production and distribution had concerned officials throughout the nineteenth century, and the ban on public milking, along with other measures to sanitize dairy products, took effect in 1903.[6]

The mayor's office redirected milk vendors to meet with the director of Municipal Public Health and the head of milk regulation. In several meetings, milk sellers were "always accompanied by their lawyer Dr. Martins Rodriguez." The outcome, however, did not confirm the municipal support they were hoping for, so the vendors marched to the *Correio da Manhã*'s main office to air their grievances. This newspaper had initiated "the campaign against the falsification or adulteration of milk," prioritizing hygienic reform over milk sellers' interests. It therefore rejected their complaints, recommending instead in an article that the city's "three or four thousand milk vendors . . . adhere to the law" and adopt at once the use of glass bottles.[7] Despite the unwanted outcome for milk sellers, the incident reflects the role of the press as an interlocutor between municipal regulation and organized street vendors.

Luiz Edmundo's *O Rio de Janeiro do meu tempo* (The Rio de Janeiro of my time), first published in 1936, provides a lens onto why the milk seller was "the most shameful of all street vendors" for selling watered-down milk from malnourished cows. Edmundo describes the milk vendor as a male immigrant obsessed with profit and carelessly endangering the lives of children. In addition, "two fearful forces" explained the persistence of these deceitful vendors: first, "an international press that defends the freedom of commerce in a country that still needs immigration," and second, "a political class that needs the approval of the foreign press and silences the defenders of public health."[8]

In other words, the legacy of slavery was keeping Brazil behind. The liberal press's support for the freedom of commerce was the type of protection street vendors sought, but milk vendors did not find it in the *Correio da Manhã*. According to this newspaper, free street commerce "damaged legitimate commerce" of stores and shops.[9]

Vendors and their defenders disagreed. They contended that street commerce was an expression of the economic liberty that the end of the slave era promised. Vendors appealed to economic liberty to protect their trade from overregulation and excessive policing, and they found support in some liberal and progressive papers of Rio. Street sellers also built upon traditional patron-client relations to obtain recognition and create alliances with other civic associations to formalize their presence in the city. It is no surprise, then, that dissenting milk sellers in 1913 were accompanied by their lawyer. Associated workers in general used legal aid and relations with patrons and other unions to advance their cause and leverage their position in the city. Street vendors were no exception.

Rio's mutual aid societies and labor associations of the turn of the twentieth century provided the civic environment for the UPCV to emerge in 1912. Connections between nineteenth-century mutual aid societies and twentieth-century trade unions existed, and recent scholars have moved beyond a teleological explanation to frame these.[10] The UPCV had an associative culture shaped by mutual aid, but this was not a necessary precursor for its organizing. Street commerce's importance to supplying and distributing goods during the slave era transformed vending into a postabolition practice that was heavily policed and regulated. Therefore, poor working conditions and excessive policing primarily influenced the emergence of the UPCV in 1912.

The UPCV developed as a civic association that honored mutual aid and sought relief not from the business interests of patrons and suppliers but a municipality that policed and overregulated vendors. Steady income was difficult for peddlers if constant street policing interrupted their work. The ganho system no longer offered street vendors the same protections of the nineteenth century, and their new civic association aimed to recuperate some of them. To that end, the UPCV sought to renew relations of patronage with suppliers to specifically seek protection from policing and increasing fees and penalties.

In 1860, a law established for the first time the guidelines for civic associations in Brazil. After 1890, associations were listed in the city's official civil registry. During slavery, only free people could belong to associations, thus many former slaves were incorporated into newfound civic membership.[11] The largest labor association in Rio in the nineteenth century, the Liga Operária, was a mutual aid society founded in 1870 and included various occupations. Reaching 1,500 members, it had an "intercategorical" nature organized around the principle of "Equality and Fraternity" and under the motto "One for all and all for one."[12] An extensive network of associations existed alongside the Liga Operária. The civil registry at Rio's Conselho de Estado (State Council) listed more than 180 associations between 1850 and 1900, and historians have counted up to 239 active associations in Rio between 1860 and 1889.[13] Associative life surrounding labor practices in the capital city was thus an important influence in the transition from slavery to freedom, as vendors resorted to organizing to address their grievances.

Most importantly, associative behavior reflected vendors' will to be recognized as legitimate workers. The previous century had witnessed this in the organization of the city's typographers.[14] Civic and abolitionist groups that freed slaves contributed not only to social solidarity but to the expansion of citizenship, creating paths of freedom for slaves after the 1871 Free Womb Law.[15] Workers during this transitional era such as Rio's typographers possibly followed an ideological path in the order of abolitionism, republicanism, and socialism.[16] Their embrace of socialism was arguably a postabolition condition and not just a result of European influences. Street vendors joined a similar struggle to be recognized as legitimate workers, bridging the mutual aid organization of the nineteenth century with the trade unionism of the twentieth century.

The UPCV was hence an important bridge in the transition from the mutual aid societies of blacks and immigrants to the postabolition civic associations formed to secure economic liberty and claim citizenship. Abolitionism and free labor ideology contributed to the complicity between free workers' and slave struggles' for freedom.[17] Mutual aid and civic associations that formed around types of work did not contribute to a uniform class formation, so to understand them as one social class explains little.[18] Associative activities in Rio expanded the politicization of workers, and within this context members of the UPCV understood themselves as a mixed group that represented the interests of all street-commerce participants, including vendors, patrons, and suppliers. Resisting municipal law that repressed street commerce thus required the strategic alliance of a business community long rooted in Atlantic trade and petty commerce.

As the UPCV organized, the municipality adopted a model of governance that incorporated the city's associations. Officials intended to merge what they identified as "public and private assistance," providing welfare for the city's residents through public means and the private partnerships that mutual aid societies offered. Public and private services merged as the municipality integrated the city's associations into public policy. This effort dates back to 1902, when Mayor Pereira Passos requested that the journalist, honorary colone , and adviser to the municipality Francisco Ferreira da Rosa survey Rio's associations. Ferreira listed 181 groups and concluded that 20 percent of the male population in the capital city was associated or organized along occupational religious, or ethnic lines.[19]

In 1913, Mayor Bento Ribeiro (1910–1914) ordered a second and similar survey of the city's associations. His effort was responding to the Campaign against the High Cost of Living (Campanha contra a Carestia da Vida), which the anarchosyndicalist Federação Operária do Rio de Janeiro (FORJ) organized to combat high prices, poor living conditions, and state-sanctioned monopolies.[20] In other words, the same conditions that led to FORJ's activism influenced the municipality to reconsider the role of civic associations in public and private social assistance. In this instance, Mayor Bento Ribeiro requested the lawyer, writer, and journalist Ataúlfo Paiva to research all civic associations that continued to provide mutual aid to the city's residents. Although Paiva's survey was conducted in 1912, the list was not published until 1922.[21] Both administrations' concern with fostering public and private assistance programs resulted in two decrees—in 1903 and 1914—that acknowledged societies providing mutual aid and assistance to its members. Paiva's mapping of the city's associations was to be updated annually and serve in the municipality's fight against poverty.[22]

In 1912, Paiva noted that 421 associations existed in Rio, with a total number of 282,937 members. More than 220 of the groups were mutual aid societies, followed by Masonic and philanthropic groups. The UPCV was among the mutual aid societies he listed, and syndicalist unions that offered protection to its members were also defined as mutual aid societies. Despite this fervent civic life, associations tended to have short lives because of their structural volatility. Hence it is quite remarkable that the short-lived UPCV made it to Paiva's notebook. Most associations did not last more than thirty years, and many dissolved after the first few years of existence. Eventually, the benefits that mutual aid offered, such as pensions and medical insurance, became increasingly dispensable with the expansion of the Brazilian welfare state in the 1930s.

UNIÃO PROTETORA DE COMÉRCIO VOLANTE

A mutual aid society and civic association (*associação de auxílios mútuos e de beneficência*), the UPCV was first headquartered at Rua Visconde de Inhaúma 109, blocks away from the Praça da República. Several associations surrounded the Praça da República since this public square had been central for social protest and remained a center of republic political life.[23] Many associations shared headquarters in traditional two-story buildings (*sobrados*), as was the case for the UPCV. On 14 January 1913, the UPCV announced that it postponed its next meeting because another association was holding its general assembly at the same time in the same space.[24]

The year of Paiva's survey in 1912, the UPCV had one hundred members, all of whom were Brazilian. The survey noted when the UPCV was established (1912) and its mission, which was to provide assistance to all participants of street commerce, including vendors, patrons, and suppliers. Paiva's inquiry into the association's funds, property, membership, and services did not yield specific results. We do not know the number of people who received assistance from the UPCV, but we do know that the association was set up for its members to receive mutual-aid benefits. Inclusion on Paiva's list, at a time when officials questioned the legitimacy of street commerce, is a testament of not only ambivalent municipal attitudes toward street commerce but an organized force that challenged the municipality's restrictions toward urban vending.[25] Other civic associations on Paiva's list that formed around professions, religion, masonry, philanthropy, medical care, and the arts and sciences expanded the political lives of Rio's residents.

The UPCV was registered as a civil society (*sociedade civil*) on 3 January 1913.[26] It was originally founded on 27 May 1912 as the União Protetora de Vendedores Ambulantes. According to the document filed with the civil registry, the UPCV's mission was to "defend the economic interests of members, build schools and libraries, and provide its members with insurance." In addition to medical assistance, the UPCV provided funerary services. Twenty founding members inaugurated the association, with Vianna Ferraz as president. On 31 December 1912, when the association applied for official status as a civil society, the UPCV had one hundred members. The organization's statutes were established on 2 December 1912 and published in the city's *Diário Oficial* on 19 February 1913. Appearance in the *Diário Oficial* formalized the entry of any association into Brazilian civil society and political life.

Admission into the UPCV was contingent on belonging to the "street vending class" and member sponsorship. In this way, the association encouraged alliances between vendors and their suppliers. The UPCV reached out to vendors of all nationalities in Rio and the nearby city of Niterói. A president, vice-president, treasurer, and two secretaries managed the UPCV, and the board was elected annually and represented by the association's lawyer, Alberto Beaumonte. In addition to attending meetings, members were expected to pay monthly dues and a one-time matriculation fee. After six months, members were eligible to receive medical and unemployment benefits as well as financial assistance if arrested or jailed. The latter benefit was especially important since frequent arrests and detentions had been the main reason for organizing in the first place. Members and their immediate families also could attend the association's school and use its library.

The UPCV, like most associations at the time, was affiliated with the larger Confederação Brasileira de Trabalho (CBT, Brazilian Confederation of Labor). If the UPCV dissolved, the CBT or another organization "of progressive thinking" would absorb any of its remaining funds. According to CBT's definition, vendors and even street cleaners were *operários*, skilled workers.[27] Although the UPCV welcomed all nationalities, its Brazilian membership reveals that immigrants preferred to remain unassociated. The UPCV promised protection and insurance but perhaps not as effectively as the private patron-client relations that prevailed in the immigrant vending community. Even if unlicensed, most immigrant peddlers worked directly with suppliers and maintained unofficial patron-client relations with other immigrants. Edmundo explained in his memoir how Portuguese immigrants were instructed in their homeland to take up a Portuguese patron, even if this meant living and working in slavelike conditions. Such was the experience of many vendors known as *caixeiros de venda* who sold cured meat, cheese, and wine on Rio's streets.[28]

The concerns that UPCV members raised reflected their personal origins but also a larger legacy of slavery. Many sold sweets on the streets of Rio, a practice that Afro-Brazilian peddlers had largely carried out since slave times. By the early twentieth century, they had to respond to a separate set of rules from the ganho system. Most outstanding, they no longer needed patrons or sponsors to obtain vending licenses. In 1913, however, UPCV members wished to resuscitate the patronage and protections of the ganho system to deal with what many considered a repressive municipality and police force. They did not want to enforce the dependence between patrons and clients that urban slave society created, however. The result was a mixed understanding of worker, employer, and government relations that drew from nineteenth-century legacies of patronage and early twentieth-century citizenship.

The UPCV thus integrated mutual aid and trade unionism, even if ambiguously, as was also true for other associations in Rio at the time. As in other twentieth-century cities of the Western world, mutual aid societies protected members from some of life's challenges, while labor unions tended to have an anticapitalist agenda.[29] Although the UPCV participated in May Day celebrations and general meetings of the Liga Operária, vendor organizing was not explicitly framed against capitalism but against a state or municipality that sanctioned abusive street policing and overregulation. Street vendors sought the business and support of patrons and suppliers to protect themselves against overregulation and policing. Its main target thus remained the municipality and not private businesses.[30] The UPCV sought the alliance of business partners, as street vendors' distrust of government that policed them turned aspects of the city's anarchosyndicalism into practical strategies of urban citizenship.

Newspapers that supported vendor organizing maintained that street commerce was a crucial institution of urban welfare. They reported incidents of abuses against street vendors, discussed the importance of vending for the distribution of goods, and listed associations' activities. Residents of the capital city, counting on the support of the liberal press, wrote a letter in 1911 to the evening paper *A Noite* denouncing the "unreasonable persecution of street vendors." The authors say they represented the average resident and argue that while members of the city council could afford to buy at the best stores, the majority of city dwellers relied on peddlers—"vegetable peddlers, fish sellers, Middle Eastern vendors of cigarettes and matches, sweets vendors, chicken vendors, mascates, etc."—for daily consumables. In protest, the letter highlights the police "persecution" of vendors as contributing to a "higher cost of living." In the absence of peddlers, many residents were forced to buy at expensive shops that they could not afford.[31] The street vendor thus provided city dwellers with affordable goods.

Another newspaper—*A Época*, "the proletarian voice of the republic"—reported the activities of civic associations and trade unions in its daily section titled "Columna operaria" (Workers column). Although *A Época* editors claimed to not adhere to a specific ideology, they considered it part of the same community as the more syndicalist paper, *Voz do Trabalhador*. "Always progressive," *A Época* was made accessible to all workers in the city regardless of political affiliation.[32] Throughout 1912–1913, the UPCV appeared regularly on *A Época* pages where the Columna operaria listed vendors' grievances. The UPCV's main concern was the overregulation of vendors by the "abusive law" and "absurd policing" that established higher fees and penalties for street sellers. For that reason it encouraged all vendors to join. The policing of street commerce, the association contended, violated the same liberties that the Brazilian republic's constitution established.[33] Low membership and tenuous negotiations with patrons and suppliers were ongoing problems that afflicted the association, but abusive policing and municipal overregulation remained the most-often voiced concerns.

A RIGHT TO THE CITY

The UPCV's organizing was a response to a tragedy of the commons that restricted vendors in public urban space. Individuals often engage in spontaneous collective action to make public goods accessible or manage common-pool resources without an external authority to offer inducements.[34] The UPCV sought to protect, with the wider vending community, the goods that suppliers and street vendors shared. These were the basic necessities that peddlers sold at cheaper prices than those in stores. However, vendors' frequent arrests, which reduced their economic freedom and ability to supply goods, were indeed a tragedy, as residents of Rio explained in their letter to *A Noite* in 1911 and protested against high prices. The UPCV promoted more expansive notions of citizenship and the common good with its declaration that street sellers were legitimate workers and had a right to exercise their trade in a city that demanded what they offered.[35]

Addressing this issue in August 1912, the association's president, Vianna Ferraz, defended the need for all street vendors to organize with their suppliers and connect with other Brazilian associations. The president's call to action stemmed from the association's argument that vendors were "the most unprotected class, without guarantees whatsoever."[36] On 6 September 1912, *A Época* reported that the UPCV met that week to elect its board.[37] On September 7 the association's board was at that year's general assembly with other Brazilian trade unions. The UPCV contributed to the transportation costs in Rio of *A Época* journalists attending the meeting, and the newspaper's publisher thanked the association by sending a bouquet of flowers to its headquarters.[38] The UPCV was also present at the fourth Congresso Operário in October 1912, expressly hosting a partner delegation from the Brazilian Northeast, the Centro Artístico Cearense, an artisans collective from the state of Ceará.[39] Associated vendors also attended the anniversary celebrations of several other associations in the capital city, particularly worker groups active in Rio's port area such as those of sailors and warehouse workers.[40] On 27 May 1913 it was time for the UPCV to celebrate its own one-year anniversary, which deepened the UPCV's roots in Rio's associative life.[41]

Six months after the birth of the UPCV, *A Época*'s Columna operaria reported that several founding members had been expelled for dishonest intentions toward vendors.[42] Vianna Ferraz remained as president along with the association's founding members. By August 4, the paper's list of association meetings gave the UPCV's new address as Rua Senador Eusébio 44, in Gamboa. The frequent change of an association's address was common and reflected structural volatility.[43] In this case the UPCV's move from the Praça da República to the neighborhood of Cidade Nova also indicated a better positioning in an area where Afro-Brazilian sweets vendors lived. The demolition of much of the city center and postabolition migrations had pushed many Afro-descendant residents to settle in this area of Gamboa, particularly the streets surrounding Praça Onze where notable female sweets peddlers such as Tia Cita lived.[44]

Through the Columna operaria the UPCV reminded its members to pay their dues. Having a regular income facilitated their payment of monthly dues and thus the maintenance of an association, but vendors mostly relied on irregular earnings. Their monetary contributions to the UPCV were therefore irregular. Following the May Day meeting in 1913, the UPCV temporarily canceled the initial matriculation fee to increase membership.[45] However, this strategy had little impact on the organization in the long term. Although some street vendors kept bank accounts, depositories generally considered them clients "without professions."[46] Vendors thus found it difficult to enjoy the steady incomes or savings that were needed to support the activities of the UPCV. The association's strategy to ally with patrons and suppliers tried to mitigate the effects of this type of insecurity.

To further legitimize the vending occupation in the Brazilian capital, the UPCV aimed to represent all of those involved in the business of street commerce. On 18 October 1912, the association held a meeting that was attended by vendors and their patrons at Rua General Câmara 203, near the Praça da República. Together they drafted a petition for the city's mayor disputing various measures in the new municipal budget for 1913. The UPCV's board held several discussions with patrons, especially candy and sweets confectioners who supplied peddlers early in the morning at factory gates. Other types of street sellers were supplied at other distribution centers. Vendors who sold fish, poultry, and books worked with suppliers at marketplaces and shops, for example. The awakening of a street market was accompanied by the hubbub of peddlers gathering for their supplies.[47]

On 30 August 1913, the UPCV held a general meeting in which president Vianna Ferraz explained the recent agreement between the association and patrons who supplied sweets to vendors. These were shop owners who provided sweets and ice cream as well as vending carts for transporting these goods (*donos de casas de doces, carrocinhas e sorvetes*). Their addresses were listed in *A Época*'s Columna operaria, mapping a wide presence in Rio. In addition to ensuring a steady supply of goods, contracts with suppliers were intended to protect vendors from abusive policing. Vendors of ice cream and other sweets were especially vulnerable because most were Afro-Brazilian.[48] But could the UPCV offer them the same (or better) protection than the ganho system had offered free ganhadores in the previous century? President Vianna Ferraz seemed to understand members' predicaments since he was a vendor too, but his lighter skin color perhaps revealed a distance from the poor conditions that darker-skinned peddlers shared.[49]

A report on the persecution of sweets peddlers in *A Época* on 4 November 1912 condemned excessive policing that resulted in vendors having to "pay unjust fines and spend days and days in jail without being heard by municipal authorities." An incident involving a sweets peddler walking through the Praça da República toward the train station Central do Brasil was a typical case, the article stated. A passerby had called the vendor when soon a police officer intervened to remove the peddler from the premises. The sweets vendor responded that he was serving a client, but he was still promptly arrested and jailed. The vendor was held at the police station of the Fourteenth Precinct for twenty hours without charges—a case that, in the newspaper writer's assessment, represented "hundreds."[50] An alliance of vendors with patrons and suppliers, UPCV leaders contended, could prevent such abusive policing practices.

Months before the planned work stoppage in January 1913, the UPCV had been trying to organize vendors and patrons. The UPCV's board had participated in several discussions with factory owners, especially confectioners who supplied peddlers with sweets at factory gates. In 1917, the newspaper *Correio da Manhã* reported a fight that took place outside a factory on Rua Hipólito, revealing the hostility that sometimes erupted between peddlers waiting for their supplies.[51] Street sellers usually picked up their supplies early in the morning and then returned after a day's work to hand over an agreed portion of their earnings to their suppliers. Outside the José Baptista factory, vendors were supplied with boxes of sweets to distribute throughout the city. The newspaper reported that business was carried out "with dirty hands" that resulted in "the dangerous cakes . . . that cause the gastrointestinal discomfort of so many victims."[52] The UPCV's alliance with suppliers had the potential to improve hygiene in street commerce.

The frequent arrests and detentions of peddlers added urgency to the UPCV's organizing. A few days before 21 January 1913, soon after the planned work stoppage that did not transpire, a meeting took place in which patrons and suppliers along with vendors revisited the issue of excessive policing. Through a collective effort they would resist abusive street policing and claim their right to work in the city. The UPCV requested that patrons sponsor and cover the membership fees of all the vendors they employed. This was necessary, the board contended, because vendors alone were disadvantaged and powerless.[53] Starting in May 1913, the UPCV had held meetings every Friday of vendors and patrons, and around 20 June 1913 they finally reached a consensus. Along with the secretary of the CBT, suppliers and vendors of sweets had met with the mayor that week to negotiate new terms of street selling.[54] Urgent meetings with patrons were then summoned in July as UPCV leaders argued that the "annihilation of the [street vending] class is now projected."[55] A strike was averted in January, but negotiations with the mayor had fallen through.

Ties between street vending and neighborhood stores had shaped the world of street commerce in Rio since the nineteenth century. In 1902, the Associação dos Empregados no Comércio (Association of Commerce Employees) requested that stores and shops become intermediaries in the vendor licensing process. The regulation of street commerce had to be taken out of the hands of the police. The association organizers described it as a medium in the negotiations between vendors, patrons, and the municipality.[56] While many shops licensed their peddlers, many did not. This created tension among certain groups, such as quitandeiros with established casas de quitanda and owners of shops that sold carnival items. These establishments claimed that not adhering to licensing procedures created an uneven playing field for small shops.[57] For that reason, they chose to save costs and not license their peddlers, especially since policing remained indifferent to vending licenses.

In order to set themselves apart from street commerce, some store owners announced that they did not employ peddlers at all. Such was the case of the Galeries Lafayette, named after a major department store in Paris.[58] The status of a store seemed to decrease if associated with street vending, and some owners avoided the host of issues that usually followed vendors: vagrancy and public disorder charges, jail and court procedures, and increasing fees and fines. For those reasons, the shoe store Casa Lord announced in 1918 that it did not employ peddlers. Vendors selling glass bottles had used the store's name to claim (false) legitimacy when arrested, but Casa Lord publicly announced in a major newspaper that it was not responsible for such peddlers. Their shoe business, the owners affirmed, remained unrelated to the affairs of street commerce.[59]

The UPCV's alliance with patrons went as far as requesting that store owners who specifically dealt with street commerce (*proprietários de casas ambulantes*) hire only vendors who were UPCV members. Patrons hiring non-UPCV vendors would pay a penalty. However, the association was never larger than four hundred people, while many more vendors circulated Rio's streets unlicensed and unassociated. Nonmembers could easily meet supplier demands. Still, the UPCV approved the proposal that patrons hiring non-UPCV vendors pay a fine.[60] Considering that most peddlers in the city were not members of the UPCV made it hard to enforce this norm, especially without alienating patrons.

If throughout 1912–1914 vendors remained reluctant about purchasing vending licenses, the fees to join the UPCV were an additional burden for many. Resisting rising municipal fines and joining an association that also demanded payment disillusioned street sellers who relied on variable earnings. Although the UPCV's activism resulted in the official reduction of licensing costs for sellers of fruits and vegetables, which also helped keep prices low, other types of vendors were not as fortunate.[61] The UPCV protested that high licensing fees were an obstacle for free commerce, usually resulting in a 50 percent reduction of a vendor's earnings. As a result, vendors raised their prices. The UPCV contended that it was consumers who eventually bore the brunt of the fees.

Vendors avoided taking out licenses and sometimes even stole them from one another.[62] Shop owners were hesitant about absorbing the higher costs associated with licenses if this meant little protection from street policing. David Levy's store on Rua Gomes Freire in central Rio licensed all of its peddlers, yet "rare was the day when one of those mascates was not arrested and detained."[63] Owners of many other shops, as one might expect, preferred not to require licenses for their street vendors. As much as the UPCV encouraged licensing, the incentive remained low.

The collaboration with suppliers reflected the endurance of patron-client relations from the ganho system. As with other trade unions of the time, UPCV founders understood much of its work according to the dynamics of late nineteenth-century patronage.[64] Six months after the planned work stoppage and a year after its formation, the UPCV was still trying to get more patrons and suppliers involved. In July 1913, UPCV leaders announced that they wanted to meet with all patrons to address the issue of excessive policing. Earlier that month, the board had encouraged vendors to reach out to their suppliers for greater involvement in the association.[65] The association's press release published in the newspaper on 27 July 1913 declared that patrons and vendors needed to organize to "resist the common enemy." The loss of earnings and the confiscation of goods due to arrests was a burden on patrons, too. Some UPCV members again proposed resisting abusive policing by not paying for the required vending licenses.[66]

Resistance to excessive policing was a recurring discussion in the UPCV meetings of that year; the police persecuted vendors "in a barbarous, inhumane way" and jailed them on vague charges of vagrancy or public disorder.[67] The UPCV asserted that the municipality sanctioned such police behavior.[68] Shortly after vendors' threat to strike in January 1913, police officers in Candelária and São José banned vendors from walking in those areas. A newspaper columnist asked, "Why doesn't the mayor [just] order the immediate prohibition of all street commerce, without even permitting licensed vendors to sell at all? That would be more serious and correct than the persecution of those poor people."[69] Overregulation with excessive policing was analogous to the consequences of prohibiting street commerce.

Meanwhile, a rapidly growing city provided ample opportunities for street selling outside central Rio. By the 1910s, complaints about vendors were also present in the city's suburbs and frequently discussed in *A Época's* Columna operaria and another section titled "Nos suburbios" (In the suburbs). Municipal officials called for the greater regulation of suburban street vendors, while the UPCV condemned the same police interventions there as persecution. On the one hand, authorities condemned relaxed law enforcement in the urban periphery, where fish vendors had no trouble selling their sometimes spoiled goods after the midday curfew.[70] A columnist reported in December 1913 that in Irajá, "Turks, Italians, Spaniards, Polish, and Argentines peddle without a license" in what appeared to be a suburban free trade zone without policing. More than a year later, a writer in the same column asked, "Where are the police?" while at the same time denouncing the persecution of suburban vendors.[71] Peddlers' use of loud cornets and whistles for street selling was also a regular complaint that suburban residents took to the paper.[72] The longer distances and open spaces of the semirural periphery pushed vendors to rely on louder announcements. Still, acknowledging the need for street vendors, suburban residents and many of the city's journalists defended peddlers, "who were undoubtedly honorable men," even if they used "strident sonic apparatuses."[73]

The excessive policing of vendors in the city's center and periphery persisted as the UPCV's main complaint throughout 1912–1914. Even though the association succeeded in gaining the support of several patrons involved in street commerce, by its first anniversary it was not only facing financial difficulties but division among its members as well. Only a few months after the board overhaul in 1912, rumors returned that certain members with leadership positions had to be dropped from the UPCV.[74] A treasurer who started in June 1913 resigned in July.[75] The UPCV still participated in the city's associative life, however. Its members attended the second Congresso Operário, held in September 1913, with the União dos Carregadores composed of fellow street workers who earned a living hauling goods. Vendors and haulers had formed their separate associations but remained close, with shared roots in Rio's ganho system.[76]

The momentum the association enjoyed in early 1913 gradually declined in the following months. At its final meeting, in February 1914, the UPCV members could not reach a consensus, leaving all involved "convinced that the continuation of the association would be impossible."[77] The alliance it fostered with patrons had divided the UPCV, and most members by 1914 believed that "the association would only survive if composed exclusively of vendors, who would have to defend themselves from the exploitations of patrons, police authorities, [and] city council representatives."[78] The alliance with patrons had not protected them from policing or ensured steady supplies. Patrons could afford to ignore street sellers' complaints of ineffective licensing and excessive policing because they had a cheap, daily supply of vendors ready to sell their goods informally. If anything, UPCV patrons now enjoyed greater power as board members trying to secure fewer municipal fees and taxes for themselves.

Although at several meetings members tried to save the association during its last months, the UPCV finally dissolved in 1914. On 7 April 1914, the UPCV called for a meeting that deliberately only included vendors, since "patrons had caused the death of the association."[79] The meeting was held in a building near the Praça da República, a third address, indicating the loss of its more popular location in Cidade Nova. The UPCV did not last beyond this meeting after failing to reproduce the social protections that patronage had offered free street vendors in the ganho system.

By 1914, none of the UPCV's board members were street sellers, and Vianna Ferraz resigned as president. One board member even held several leadership positions in the city's associations and was a member of the National Guard.[80] In other words, street vendors had little ownership in the association they had formed together. But even if the UPCV had lost vendors' trust, it had not destroyed their determination. In 1917, *A Época* reported the existence of another vendors association that was meeting weekly near Largo do Rosário. Peddlers and pushcart sellers composed this new group. After its first appearance, however, this association along with other signs of vendor organizing ceased to appear in the pages of *A Época*.

GREATER REGULATION

The 1913 newspaper headline asking if Rio's peddlers would disappear from the city captured not only residents' anxieties about inconsistent goods distribution but also municipal ambivalence toward street commerce. The earlier Pereira Passos administration tried to eliminate street commerce in the city center, but vendors remained defiant. The complete prohibition of street commerce had been impossible to enforce, so subsequent administrations resorted to improving regulation. A city without peddlers or unclean marketplaces was a nice idea for officials but impractical for residents who had difficult access to transportation and faced rising food prices.

In 1924, the city council passed a comprehensive ordinance listing new fees for different types of street vending.[81] The *imposto de comércio ambulante* was approved just a few years before the implementation of the Plano Agache, a plan to develop the city's southern neighborhoods and port area. Altogether these reforms reflected the 1920s rationalization of urban space. In addition to new licensing fees, street sellers had to follow measures stating where in the city they could sell, along with proper physical appearance and transport methods. Milk vendors, for example, had to wear suit jackets and collared shirt when delivering or selling milk.

The rationalization of time followed concerns about space. The 1924 law included a schedule outlining vendors' work hours, averaging twelve hours per day. Specific weekly and holiday schedules applied to different types of sellers, especially peddlers of sweets, meat, milk, bread, eggs, vegetables, fish, angu, and cigarettes, who served more customers on weekends and holidays. Ganhadores were listed among those participating in street commerce in 1924, a testament to their enduring presence in the postabolition city. Workers ao ganho now specialized in the distribution of goods rather than in street selling, and their hours were restricted. The transition to free labor had officially disassociated street vending from the ganho system, but slave legacies endured in the world of street commerce. The 1924 regulations aimed to even out the playing field for small shops, fixing the prices on items that vendors could not manipulate on the street. Growing urban poverty and policing, however, continued to marginalize street commerce as an informal practice that officials associated with criminality.

REDEFINING URBAN CITIZENSHIP

Vendors' collective efforts to claim their rights to the city and the legitimacy of their work in 1912–1914 reflect a sense of urban belonging and practice of citizenship. The end of slavery and the transition to freedom had put street commerce in the ambiguous position of having a slave past and offering the promise of free labor and free commerce. Authorities had tried to eliminate street vending that was reminiscent of slavery, but complete prohibition as attempted by Pereira Passos was impractical. Regulation was the most effective way to discipline street commerce and vendors. But how that regulation took shape was an issue that vendors negotiated, appealing to the political and economic liberty that slave society had denied many of them and earlier generations. Citizenship for street vendors was as much a political right as an economic freedom.

Creating an alliance with patrons through the UPCV was not intended to restrict that freedom but to protect it. The dynamics of patronage inherited from the ganho system had deeply conditioned street commerce as an economic activity that relied on cooperation between vendors and suppliers. If policing was the main force restricting street commerce, then established patronage on a collective scale could confront it. Although the UPCV failed as an organization, renewing patron-client relations aimed to further legitimize the practice of street commerce in an era when its presence in the city was questioned. As civic activists, associated street sellers challenged the conditional terms of their economic and political freedom. Even if vendors worked in an economy of subsistence, they were not marginal urban dwellers but active participants in the debate over citizenship. Street vendors' associative activities and social networks demonstrated the connectedness of their economic and political lives. Their right to the city embodied a shared urban citizenship that was spatial and interconnected. In particular, vendors' understanding of citizenship and urban belonging was based on relations with suppliers and customers.

CONCLUSION

THE TRANSITION FROM SLAVERY to free labor reorganized street commerce regulation and practice among vendors and suppliers, buyers and sellers, patrons and clients, and vendors and the state. The postabolition period saw the further engagement of Rio's vendors with the era's formulations of freedom, free labor, citizenship, and urban life. Ruptures and continuities shaped this crucial transitional era, while street commerce persisted in the Brazilian capital. Urban residents who consumed goods from everyday peddlers strengthened customary practice, which laws, policing, and vending methods modified as well. The structural and lived experiences of free labor and freedom contributed to the formal and informal ways of street selling. Daily interactions between vendors, suppliers, consumers, and municipal officials, including police and court officials, revealed the underlying formal-informal links of street commerce. These interconnections also defined the shared experiences of enslaved and free street vendors. Enduring patron-client relations, street policing, and organizational and associative strategies further manifested in vendors' claim to urban citizenship, or what has been termed "the right to the city." The ability to occupy physical urban space for street selling was a rights struggle that vendors in Rio related to the defining of citizenship, free labor, and street commerce as a formal type of work or occupation.

The issue of slavery and the turn to free labor were at the center of street commerce practices that prolonged patronage, encouraged urban reform, and expanded the meanings of criminality and citizenship. In the nineteenth century, African slaves and Afro-descendant residents as well as European, Asian, and American immigrants entered the world of urban street commerce and contributed to its endurance. Slave owners, patrons, police officers, court officials, and journalists from their institutional positions influenced the course of street commerce, even if unevenly. Vending's slave past was a shadow on street sellers but not an incapacitating one, especially since urban authorities consistently recognized acceptable aspects of street commerce and some Afro-Brazilian vending practices remained robust. Various actors thus negotiated vending's formal practice. The gradual turn to free labor in the nineteenth century began to change relations between government, petty commerce, street vendors, and modern urban life, and police increasingly were involved as regulators. Vendors resisted stringent policing with traditional support from patrons and newfound citizenship rights. Postabolition patron-client relations and vendors' claim to urban citizenship linked the formal and informal worlds of street commerce and exposed the shared history of slavery and free labor.

This book sheds light on the spatial and professional concerns of vendors' struggle for urban citizenship. Ruptures and continuities from the age of slave emancipation marked vendors' understanding of rights, and although street commerce had been central to the maintenance of urban slavery, it did not end with slavery. Rather, street vending became an important practice in the transition to free labor, almost guaranteeing its continuity. Increased immigration, revised policing, renewed patronage, and a modified institution of urban slavery in the ganho system elongated the life of street vending. More specifically, street commerce in the form of the ganho system in the mid- to late nineteenth century was crucial for gradual abolitionism in Rio. The use of patronage and policing to regulate vending allowed for street commerce to absorb new participants and keep older ones. Remodeling the ganho system as an institution of transition facilitated the continuity of vending practices through extensive urban change. Vendors' key role in supplying residents with basic goods supported their continued presence during watershed moments like the abolition of slavery and the urban reforms of the Pereira Passos administration.

As vending practices adapted to the conditions of freedom, their continuity from the slave period reflected features that particularly took shape during the era of gradual abolitionism. First, established patron-client relations in Rio's petty commerce incorporated free ganhadores and prolonged supply chains and mutual dependence. Those who bought goods from peddlers in 1915 experienced little change from customers of the street commerce that prevailed in 1879. Second, the ganho system's policing of street workers set the precedent for the criminalization of peddlers in the postabolition period. The ganho system's regulation of vending, involving the police, the municipality, and the courts, set the precedent of ambiguity. Street commerce continues to raise ambivalent attitudes among Rio's politicians today who consider vendors to be both a necessity and a nuisance. Yet it is street commerce's participants, usually poor, black, and displaced, who experience continued disadvantages and incomplete freedoms attached to patronage and policing. Sellers in Rio's informal street commerce are generally poor and notably Afro-Brazilian, and street vending is a common line of work among residents in favelas and makeshift neighborhoods. A third continuity in Rio's street vending is thus racial inequality and the racialization of informal practices. Black peddlers continue to be the poorest and most vulnerable vending participants in Rio today, comparable to the Afro-Brazilian sweets vendors that the UPCV tried to protect a century ago.

The role of Rio's ganho system in managing urban slave and free labor is crucial to understanding street commerce's continuities in the slave and post-abolition periods. From its start in slavery, the ganho system relied on patron-client (then specifically master-slave) relations for the administration of street labor and enslaved ganhadores. During the gradual shift to free labor, the municipality adopted the practice of patronage to absorb the growing number of free street workers. While the ganho system declined with slavery, the patron-client relations that shaped vending practices did not. Vendor organizing by the early twentieth century revealed that patronage in Rio's street commerce was alive and well.

The networks of patronage through which vendors secured supplies and licenses were first influenced by the ganho system and then emerging policing methods that marked the transition to free labor. As supply lines changed little, Rio's police became more involved in regulating vendors and the street at the turn of the century. Although the police took the place of patrons when street sellers sought a license after 1886, the vending community was still primarily shaped by patrons who were suppliers and clients who were vendors. Police registration instead of patron sponsorship for acquiring vending licenses emphasized increased policing of street commerce that eventually pushed vendors to resist and organize. On another level, the municipality turned to the civic association that vendors formed in 1912 as well as other mutual aid societies to guide public assistance and piggyback on the private efforts of associated vendors and patrons. Mayor Francisco Pereira Passos initiated this effort in 1905, and Mayor Bento Ribeiro then revised it with a second survey in 1912 of Rio's associative activities. The formal-informal links of street commerce were therefore not just in petty commerce but also in an ambiguous municipal administration that wished to eliminate and at the same time regulate urban vending.

When the municipally administrated ganho system changed licensing rules in 1886, in effect positioning police as the sponsors for vendors to obtain licenses, the state substituted the influence of private patronage with greater policing. The intensified regulatory role of the police marginalized popular practices and informalized relations between vendors and suppliers, as private patrons were unregulated by the ganho system after 1886. While police officers became the new patrons responsible for the licensing of street sellers, policing toward vendors increased regardless of licensing—another example of municipal ambivalence. As a result, Rio's detention center held more street vendors; they commonly were arrested on vagrancy and public disorder charges that criminalized their licensed vending activities. In the shadow of this contradiction, ongoing vendor-supplier relations affected unofficial patronage, while increased policing lessened the protections that street sellers had gained under the ganho system. It is no surprise, then, that to resist policing the UPCV sought to revitalize protections in patronage, which the European immigrant vending community had not lost to the same extent as Afro-Brazilian vendors had.

Vagrancy laws soon replaced the ganho system as a method of regulating unwanted street vendors. The ganho system acknowledged the legitimacy of street commerce, but the application of the 1890 Penal Code facilitated its delegitimization. Policing for criminal activity positioned street commerce as a slave legacy associated with vagrancy and public disorder rather than a socioeconomic practice for distributing goods to urban residents. Criminal laws that restricted the freedom of blacks in Brazil and throughout the Americas after abolition manifested in the policing of free peddlers in Rio. While authorities of a disciplinary republican state saw a backward, slave-based practice in Rio's vending activities, street sellers, court defendants, and associated members of the UPCV argued that free street commerce was instead a manifestation of free labor and postabolition economic freedom.

As the ganho system formed along patron-client lines, customary buying and selling practices influenced the shared experiences of street vending's diverse participants. Even if street sellers chose to remain unlicensed, the supply chains that supported vending still created a shared environment for vendors of African and European descent. The benefits of private patronage, however, were stronger in the European vending community, and the legacy of slavery fell heavier on black street sellers. Street policing was harder on Afro-Brazilians, as the emergence of organized sweets peddlers, who were mostly black, demonstrated in the UPCV. The organizational activities of peddlers in the UPCV thus had a racial dimension with roots in the city's slave past. The policing of all street sellers was widespread in Rio, as the Casa de Dentenção entries illustrate, but the same records show that Afro-Brazilian peddlers selling sweets, fruits, and vegetables were more vulnerable to it. Their persistence in those vending occupations from slave to postabolition times reflected the strength of customary practices that pulled black peddlers to continue to sell through city streets.

The UPCV eventually failed to protect vendors in creating an alliance with patrons and suppliers. By 1912, suppliers of sweets and candy were for the most part confectioners who enjoyed a surplus of peddlers waiting at the gates every morning. The issues that most concerned organized vendors, such as ineffective licensing and excessive policing, were not equally shared by their patrons and suppliers. The goods and earnings lost by the arrest and detention of peddlers were small if suppliers could easily employ available street vendors. In other words, patrons did not need to protect their relations with street sellers to secure profits, whereas vendors argued they were more vulnerable to policing without the protection of patrons. Being dependent on patrons' supplies was less of a concern for peddlers than excessive policing, however, as vending licenses offered little protection from police. Even though patronage reproduced inequalities and dependencies between vendors and suppliers, policing remained the main practice that marginalized vendors. The emergence of the popular term *o rapa*, which peddlers use today to identify the police officers who target street vendors, reveals the ongoing tension between vendors and the state.

As patronage, policing, and racial inequality determined the practice of street commerce, the final abolition of slavery in 1888 involved major ruptures in the development of the city of Rio. The urban reforms that accompanied and followed the Pereira Passos administration dramatically changed central Rio with new street vending routes that included a growing periphery. Most importantly, street vendors took up the benefits of citizenship, although differentiated, that followed the abolition of slavery. Their court defenses in the face of criminal charges and their organizational activities in the UPCV reflected the consequences of the Pereira Passos urban reforms as well as the application of citizenship rights.

The working poor who had once inhabited central areas of Rio increasingly resettled in suburban areas in the early twentieth century. Vendors followed their customer base and often relocated to the urban periphery. Hence patent seekers of the 1900s sought to improve the street vending that connected Rio's established petty commerce downtown and the growing suburbs. Innovative patent requests for new vending technologies reflected still robust urban commerce and the consumer needs of a growing population. Mayor Pereira Passos viewed suburban expansion as an opportunity to repress vending in the city center, which ideally was to be transformed into a Parisian capital, allowing its practice in the outskirts and other less central neighborhoods in 1903. Patent seekers proposed vehicles to develop the trade networks that connected center to periphery and the larger Guanabara Bay area. Even if peddlers in suburban areas sold goods that small farmers produced outside of Rio, most street vendors still relied on supply chains that passed through central Rio.

Despite extensive street selling, municipal code infractions and criminal law violations targeting vendors revealed officials' attitudes about street commerce as a blot on the modern city. The majority of Rio's residents still relied on the affordable goods that street sellers provided. Urban renewal had rerouted their networks, but popular demand persisted. As a result, the municipal outlook after the Pereira Passos administration became less prohibitive and more tolerant toward street commerce. The persistence of street commerce was a consequence of customary practice but also a manifestation of vendors as political and economic actors. The abolition of slavery had led to official disciplinary measures, but the building of citizenship went beyond such categories. The new citizenship rights of vendors, many of whom had been slaves or were descended from slaves, reinforced their struggle for the freedom to sell on the street as residents of the city and practitioners of free commerce.

Vendors' urban citizenship was influenced by the inheritance of nineteenth-century mutual aid societies that led to the creation of the UPCV in 1912. Two more associations appeared in Rio in the 1930s in another attempt to address street sellers' concerns. The organizing of street sellers in Rio continues to this day, with the Sindicato dos Vendedores Ambulantes do Rio de Janeiro in the center city and the Associação dos Vendedores Ambulantes do Flamengo in the Flamengo neighborhood, among others. The vendor associations that appeared in the 1930s shared missions and structures that aligned with those of the mutual aid societies of previous decades. In Brazilian cities the "individualistic spirit of defending the interests of professional group[s]" continued to influence the trade unionism of the 1930s before the expansion of labor legislation under the Estado Novo (1937–1945).[1]

Meat vendors in the Cooperativa de Produção (Transformação) dos Vendedores Ambulantes (Street Vendors Cooperative of Production and Transformation) officially filed with Rio's civil registry on 17 November 1936. All members were Brazilian nationals, and gone were the days when Portuguese men monopolized Rio's meat commerce. The cooperative aimed to transform the selling of meat by "freeing [members] from the heavy commissions that middle men charge."[2] To accomplish this, members agreed to purchase land, build a slaughterhouse, and refrigerate their own meat, only selling to outsiders if economically necessary. Contracts were established between members and the board that allowed vendors to access lines of credit. The cooperative planned to hold a general assembly once a year in February and, like many other mutual aid societies before its time, offered economic assistance after a member's death. Professional interests merged once again with group-based social assistance in the civic participation of Rio's street vendors.

The trade union that appeared on the pages of Rio's civil registry on 29 December 1938, the União dos Negociantes Ambulantes (Union of Mobile Traders), aimed to unite all nonfood street sellers in the capital city and Niterói. The association provided legal counsel and mutual-aid benefits for its members and their families that included economic assistance after their deaths and the organization of a trade cooperative. Founded by Jews who had recently migrated from Europe, the union welcomed all Brazilian vendors and those of other nationalities. If dissolved, according to the association's statutes, remaining funds would be redirected to the Santa Casa da Misericórdia, city hospitals, and other Jewish groups in Rio. Street commerce thus endured as an entry labor practice for new immigrants in the city that encouraged new groups to make alliances with fellow sellers of all nationalities.[3] The right to exercise street occupations based on shared practice, political and economic freedom, and the use of public space thus inspired the ongoing organizational activities of Brazilian and immigrant peddlers into the twentieth century.

Street vendors' selling and associative activities demonstrate not only the connectedness of their economic and political lives but the order and organization of an informal economy that scholars have often deemed chaotic and unstructured. Overregulation and prohibitive measures only resulted in alternatives that vendors devised to continue selling on the street, as John Cross and Hernando de Soto observe for the cases of Mexico City and Lima, Peru, respectively.[4] Street peddlers' informal work thus grew from excessive state regulation and policing, as de Soto particularly emphasizes. Ross shows how most of Mexico City's street vendors are members of trade associations tied to party politics and clientelism. Although Mexico City's vendors have little interest in political allegiances, the formal-informal links of their trade—not with business patrons but with political leaders—facilitates their movement in the Mexican capital. Vendors' negotiations with patrons in political and commercial areas are common in other Latin American cities, although not as extensively or enduringly as in the Mexican case.[5] The long-standing ties that allow street commerce to function as an interrelated formal and informal practice therefore are not specific to Rio or Brazil but a broad Latin American experience as well. Urban slavery and the gradual transition to free labor in the old Brazilian capital did form the particular context of street vending in Rio, nevertheless.

Reifying informal street commerce as an inadequate vestige of slave times only freed Rio municipal officials from responsibility for addressing unsuccessful regulation and persistent urban poverty. Every municipal administration in Rio has attempted to remove illegal street vendors or reform vending practices according to the political tenor of the moment. Populist, socialist, liberal, and neoliberal administrations since the nineteenth century have tolerated street commerce to varying degrees, but the one constant variable has been vendors' endurance and adaptability. The most significant continuity in street commerce, beyond ongoing inequalities, patron-client relations, and policing, is vendors' individual and collective capacity to grow with and adjust to urban change—a modern characteristic, or simply a human one that seeks dignity in work and existence.

Repressive conditions still give rise to alternative forms of urban citizenship today, contributing toward Brazilian democracy as an inevitably unfinished product. In cities, where more than 80 percent of Brazilians live, it is on the margins that poor urban residents come to understand justice and experience citizenship. In peripheral urban communities, informal street vending refines notions of political and economic freedom, still contributing to the ongoing development of citizenship and democracy in Brazil.

APPENDIX

Table 1. Vending occupations of detainees at the municipal Casa de Detenção, 1868–1883

Occupation	Total number	Slave or suspected slave	Free	Male	Female
Amolador (grinder)	1		1	1	
Funileiro (tin products seller)	32		32	32	
Ganhador/a (slave or free earner)	131	47	84	128	3 (1 enslaved)
Limador (knife sharpener)	12		12	12	
Lustrador/engraxate (shoe shiner)	65	9	56	65	
Mascate	37		37	37	
Mascate de livros (peddler of books)	1		1	1	
Quitandeiro/a (greengrocer)	119	57	62	72	47
Vendedor de açúcar (sugar vendor)	1	1		1	
Vendedor de água (water vendor)	1		1	1	
Vendedor de bilhetes (lottery-ticket vendor)	15		15	15	
Vendedor de café (coffee vendor)	5	1	4		5
Vendedor de carne (meat vendor)	1	1		1	
Vendedor de carvão (charcoal vendor)	1		1	1	
Vendedor de doces/balas (sweets/candy vendor)	30	26	4	28	2 (enslaved)
Vendedor de ervas (herbs vendor)	3		3	3	
Vendedor de flores (flower vendor)	2		2	2	
Vendedor de folhas (leafy greens vendor)	20		20	20	
Vendedor de galinhas/pombeiro (poultry vendor)	8		8	8	
Vendedor de jornais/gazetas (newspaper seller)	15		15	15	
Vendedor de leite (milk vendor)	1		1	1	
Vendedor de peixe (fish vendor)	11		11	11	
Volante (peddler)	2		2	2	

Table 2. Charges for arrest, by male/female and slave/free status, 1868–1883

Charge	*Total number*	*Slave or suspected slave*	*Free*	*Male*	*Female*
Begging	1	1		1	
Capoeira	40		40	40	
Contempt	21	17	3	11	9
Curfew violation	1	1		1	
Disorder	143	35	107	121	21
Escaped slave	55	55			
Illegal weapon	4		4	4	
Inebriation	77	52	25	64	12
Military desertion	1		1	1	
Municipal infraction	5	5		5	
No ganhador license	34		34	34	
Obscene behavior	11	6	5	5	6
Physical offense	27	1	26	27	
Presence in casa de zungú	8	2	6	6	2 (enslaved)
Request of master or judge	3	2	1	3	
Theft	39	1	38	37	2 (1 enslaved, 1 free)
Vagrancy	157	5	150	153	2 (1 enslaved, 1 free)

Table 3. Vending license fees, by item, 1913

Group A: 5-30 milréis	
Oil	30
Sand	30
Small rodent animals	20
Angu	10
Baleiro (candy seller) with uniform and shoes	30
Shoe repair	30
Canjica and *carurú* (Northeastern pudding and condiment)	10
Stamps	30
Postcards	30
Charcoal	30
Straw hats	30
Onion	30

Table 3. Continued

Sugarcane juice	30
Sugarcane	30
Ground coffee	30
Confetti and other seasonal carnival goods	30
Goods for funerals	30
Magazines, books, and stamps	25
Artificial flowers	30
Ganhador or carregador with uniform	20
Herbs and medicinal goods	20
Wood	30
Milk	20
Books	25
Ceramic dishware	25
Mingão (pudding)	10
Sweets and *rapadura* (sugar bar)	20
Bar, restaurant, cafe, and street musicians	10
Oilcloth	30
Bread	5
Fish	30
Bread bags and baskets	10
Chemical products for cleaning	30
Cheese	30
Quinquilharias (household gadgets)	30
Refreshments	20
Soap	30
Cloth bags	20
Ice cream	30
Seeds	20
Clogs	25
Fruits and vegetables	30
Glass	20
Group B: 40-80 milréis	
Knife sharpener	40
Poultry	40
Luxurious birds	50
Announcements and flyers	50
Pastries and sweets	50
Caps	40
Toys	50

Table 3. Continued

Fireworks	40
Sun umbrellas	80
Pellets	40
Patties	50
Mirrors and paintings	50
Pottery	40
Natural flowers (sold at theaters)	50
Tinplate, cookware	50
Fruit	50
Ganhador or carregador without uniform	50
Bottles	40
Stone dishware	60
Bedclothes	50
Meat parts (miúdos)	50
Small tables and chairs (wood, rattan)	50
Eggs	40
Photographer	50
Phosphorous matches	80
Barrel organ music	50
Hammocks	50
Brooms	60
Group C: 100-200 milréis	
Fruits transported in carriages/vehicles	100
Porcelain dishware	200
Lamps and crystal goods	200
Office goods	150
Perfumes and fine oils	200
Lace	100
White medical apparel	200
Handmade clothes	200
Bedding	100
Soap	150
Ink setters	100
Group D: 250-500 milréis	
Armarinho (haberdashery)	300
Fazendas (textiles)	300
Jewelry (gold, silver, other metals)	500
Dyes	250

GLOSSARY

Acaboclado: racially mixed person with indigenous heritage or physical traits
Açougue: butcher shop
Angu: cornmeal mush sometimes mixed with pieces of meat
Baleiro/a: (male/female) seller of hard candies (balas)
Barraca: market stall
Bonde: tram
Botequim: small bar or coffee shop
Branco/a: white; male/female with white skin color
Cabra: racially mixed person with light skin color
Caixeiro: salesclerk (at a botequim)
Carne verde: fresh meat
Carregador: hauler, carrier
Capoeirista: practitioner of the Brazilian martial art capoeira
Capoeiragem: the practice of capoeira
Casa de Correção: municipal corrections center
Casa de Detenção: municipal detention center
Casa de pasto: small restaurant
Casa de quitanda: greengrocer's shop
Chapa: metal pin with number that a street seller or ganhador was required to wear
Cigarros: cigarettes
Cesto: basket usually made of wicker
Comércio volante/ambulante: street commerce
Cortiço: beehive-looking urban tenement
Crioulo/a: Brazilian-born slave
Doceiro/a: seller of sweets (doces)
Escravo/a ao ganho: enslaved ganhador, enslaved person who works for earnings (ao ganho)
Engraxate/lustrador: shoe shiner
Fazendas: fabrics
Fiador/a: sponsor or guarantor of a ganhador to attain a license to work
Fugido/a: escaped (slave)
Furto: theft, robbery
Fula: racially mixed person with dark skin color
Funileiro: vendor of tin-plate goods
Galinha/frango: chicken
Ganhador/a: individual who works for earnings, often a day laborer
Ganho: earnings
Ganho system: slavery's urban institution that managed the licensing of ganhadores
Gatuno: thief
Jogo do bicho: animal game of illegal gambling
Jornaleiro: newspaper seller
Kiosque: kiosk

Lavrador/a: rural worker, farm laborer
Leitero/a: seller of milk
Liberto/a: freed male/female slave
Limador: knife sharpener
Mascate: street vendor who sells fabrics, household gadgets, and valuable goods such as jewelry
Mascataria: vending practice of mascates
Matadouro: slaughterhouse
Mercado: market
Milréis: currency in nineteenth-century Brazil up to 1942
Miudezas: sewing notions
Miúdos: cuts of meat
Moreno/a: male/female person with dark skin color
Morro: hill
Negociante: merchant, businessman
Ocupação: occupation in a particular line of work
Operário/a: skilled worker
Padaria: bakery
Passeio: sidewalk
Pardo/a: male/female brown-skinned mulatto
Peixeiro/a: seller of fish
Pedreiro: mason, bricklayer
Pombeiro: vendor of chicken
Postura: municipal ordinance
Preto/a: person with black skin color
Quitandeiro/a: street vendor of fruits and vegetables; greengrocer
Rapa: officer who polices street vendors
Santa Casa da Misericórdia: Catholic brotherhood and hospital
Secos e molhados: dry-and-wet goods store
Sistema de ganho: ganho system
Sorveteiro/a: ice cream seller
Subdelegado: precinct police chief
Subúrbios: suburban areas of Rio, outskirts of the city
Tabuleiro: table for street vending
Tia bahiana: Afro-Brazilian female street seller specializing in Afro-Brazilian foods
Trabalhador/a: worker
Vadiagem: vagrancy
Vadio/a: vagrant
Vendedor/a ambulante: street vendor
Vendedor/a de bilhetes: seller of lottery tickets
Volante: street peddler
Zona Norte: area north of Rio's city center
Zona Sul: area south of Rio's city center with more affluent beachfront neighborhoods
Casa de zungú: house of low-cost rental rooms

NOTES

INTRODUCTION

1. The epigraph translation and others are mine except as indicated. Occorrencias das ruas, *Gazeta de Notícias*, 20 May 1883.

2. Jean-Baptiste Debret, *Viagem pitoresca e histórica ao Brasil* (Rio de Janeiro: Editora Itatiaia, 1989 [1834]); George Ermakoff, *O negro na fotografia brasileira do século XIX* (Rio de Janeiro: Casa Editorial G. Ermakoff, 2004); Gilberto Ferrez, *O Rio antigo de Marc Ferrez* (São Paulo: Ex Libris, 1984).

3. For the case of urban Mexico see Juan Pedro Viqueira Albán, *Propriety and Permissiveness in Bourbon Mexico* (Wilmington, DE: Scholarly Resources, 1997); John C. Cross, *Informal Politics: Street Vendors and the State in Mexico City* (Stanford, CA: Stanford University Press, 1998); Christina Jiménez, "Performing Their Right to the City: Political Uses of Public Space in a Mexican City, 1880–1910s," *Urban History* 33, no. 3 (2006): 435–456; Sandra Mendiola, *Street Democracy: Vendors, Violence, and Public Space in Late Twentieth-Century Mexico* (Lincoln: University of Nebraska, 2017).

4. Museu Histórico Nacional (MHN), "Pelas ruas e calçadas—Comércio informal e ambulante ontem e hoje," traveling exhibit, 2006, http://www.museuhistoriconacional.com.br/mh-i-01e.htm.

5. Lúcio Kowarick, *Trabalho e vadiagem: A origem do trabalho livre no Brasil* (São Paulo: Editora Brasilense, 1987).

6. Fernando Gralha de Sousa, "Augusto Malta e o olhar oficial: Fotografia, cotidiano e memória no Rio de Janeiro—1903/1936," *História, imagem e narrativas* 2, no. 1 (2006): 7.

7. Elinor Ostrom, Basudeb Guha-Khasnobis, and Ravi Kanbur, eds., *Linking the Formal and Informal Economy* (Oxford, England: Oxford University Press, 2006).

8. Afonso Henriques de Lima Barreto, "A barganha," in *Lima Barreto: Contos completos*, ed. Lilia Moritz Schwarcz (São Paulo: Companhia das Letras, 2010).

9. Juliana Barreto Farias, Carlos Eugênio Líbano Soares, and Flávio dos Santos Gomes, *No labirinto das nações: Africanos e identidades no Rio de Janeiro, século XIX* (Rio de Janeiro: Arquivo Nacional, 2005); Mary C. Karasch, *Slave Life in Rio de Janeiro, 1808–1850* (Princeton, NJ: Princeton University Press, 1987).

10. Zephyr L. Frank, *Dutra's World: Wealth and Family in Nineteenth-Century Rio de Janeiro* (Albuquerque: University of New Mexico Press, 2004).

11. Leslie Bethell, *The Abolition of the Brazilian Slave Trade* (Cambridge, England: Cambridge University Press, 1970).

12. Eduardo Spiller Pena, *Pajens da casa imperial: Jurisconsultos, escravidão e a lei de 1871* (Campinas: Editora da Unicamp, 2001).

13. For a discussion of citizenship as political and spatial right see Henri Lefebvre, *Writings on Cities*, trans. and ed., Eleonore Kofman and Elizabeth Lebas (Oxford, England: Blackwell, 1996); Eugene J. McCann, "Space, Citizenship, and the Right to the City: A Brief Overview," *GeoJournal* 58 no. 2–3 (2002): 77–79; Marc Purcell, "Excavating Lefebvre: The Right to the City and Its Urban Politics of the Inhabitant," *GeoJournal* 58, no. 2–3 (2002): 99–108.

CHAPTER 1

1. Camillia Cowling, *Conceiving Freedom: Women of Color, Gender, and the Abolition of Slavery in Havana and Rio de Janeiro* (Chapel Hill: University of North Carolina Press, 2013); Richard Graham, *Feeding the City: From Street Market to Liberal Reform in Salvador, Brazil, 1780–1860* (Austin: University of Texas Press, 2010); Cecília Moreira Soares, "As ganhadeiras: Mulher e resistência em Salvador no século XIX," *Afro-Ásia* 17 (1996): 67; Luiz B. Mott, "Subsídios à história do pequeno comércio no Brasil," *Revista de História* 53, no. 105 (1976): 81–106.

2. Marilene Rosa Nogueira da Silva, *Negro na rua: A nova face da escravidão* (São Paulo: Editora Hucitec, 1988), 90.

3. Ira Berlin, *Slaves without Masters: the Free Negro in the Antebellum South* (New York: New Press, 2007), xxvii.

4. Escravos ao ganho e escravidão 1833–1841, 6-1-43, Arquivo Geral da Cidade do Rio de Janeiro (hereafter AGCRJ); Africanos livres ao ganho 1855–1880, 38-1-31, AGCRJ. Items from the AGCRJ are cited by their folder names and hyphenated call numbers.

5. Richard Wade, *Slavery in the Cities: The South 1820–1860* (New York: Oxford University Press, 1967), 48.

6. Sergio A. Fridman and Samuel Gorberg, *Mercados no Rio de Janeiro, 1834–1962* (Rio de Janeiro: S. Gorberg, 2003), 9.

7. Juliana Barreto Farias, "Descobrindo mapas dos minas: Alforrias, trabalho urbano e identidades, 1800–1915," in *No labirinto das nações*, by Farias, Carlos Soares, and Gomes, 105–148; M. Silva, *Negro na rua*; Luiz Carlos Soares, "Os escravos de ganho no Rio de Janeiro século XIX," *Revista Brasileira de História* 8, no. 16 (1988): 107–142.

8. Kirsten Schultz, *Tropical Versailles: Empire, Monarchy, and the Portuguese Royal Court in Rio de Janeiro, 1808–1821* (New York: Routledge, 2001), 45.

9. Karasch, *Slave Life in Rio de Janeiro*, 185–213.

10. Carlos Kessel and Karen Worcman, *Um balcão na capital: Memórias do comércio na cidade do Rio de Janeiro* (Rio de Janeiro: Senac, 2003), 14.

11. Fridman and Gorberg, *Mercados no Rio de Janeiro*, 6; "Mendigos ao ganho," *O Philantropo*, 15 June 1849.

12. Guilherme de Castro, "Requerimento encaminhado ao Ministério do Império, solicitando o pagamento de 30$080, devido a seu escravo, pelo tratamento de pedreiro feito por dois meses nas obras da Carioca," C-0757,029, Manuscritos, Biblioteca Nacional (hereafter BN); Theotônio José Dantas, "Requerimento encaminhado ao Ministério do Império, solicitando ser indenizado pela morte de seu escravo Daniel, que trabalhava como pedreiro no Arsenal da Guerra e faleceu tentando apagar o incêndio do edifício das Obras Públicas em 30 de junho de 1852," C-0768,004, Manuscritos, BN.

13. Wade, *Slavery in the Cities*, 48–50, 54.

14. Leila Mezan Algranti, *O feitor ausente: Estudo sobre a escravidão urbana no Rio de Janeiro* (Petrópolis, Brazil: Editora Vozes, 1988).

15. Código de Posturas, Illustríssima Câmara Municipal, 1838 (Rio de Janeiro: Emp. Typ. Douze de Dezembro, Dep. Brito, Impressor da Casa Imperial, 1838); Posturas da Câmara Municipal do Rio de Janeiro, 1839 (Rio de Janeiro: Typ. Imp. e Nac., 1839).

16. Adelino Magalhães, "Ambulantes de ontem," in *Obras completas*, vol. 2 (Rio de Janeiro: Livraria Editôra Valverde, 1946), 472–473.

17. Código de Posturas, Illustríssima Câmara Municipal, 1854 (Rio de Janeiro: Emp. Typ. Douze de Dezembro, Dep. Brito, Impressor da Casa Imperial, 1854).

18. The milréis (one thousand réis) used in Brazil at the turn of the twentieth century was the equivalent of approximately $1.40 in 2016 US currency.

19. João José Reis, "'The Revolution of the Ganhadores': Urban Labor, Ethnicity, and the African Strike of 1857 in Bahia, Brazil," *Journal of Latin American Studies* 29 (May 1997): 355–393.

20. Sandra Lauderdale Graham, *House and Street: The Domestic World of Servants and Masters in Nineteenth-Century Rio de Janeiro* (Cambridge, England: Cambridge University Press, 1988).

21. Escravos ao granho 1851–1855, folios (hereafter fls.) 22–24, 6-1-29, AGCRJ.

22. The inspector of the district of Lagoa informed municipal authorities in 1841 that he did not apply ganho law in his jurisdiction because slaves there were mainly domestic or agricultural workers, so he believed ganho law was irrelevant in that location; Escravos ao ganho e escravidão 1833–1841, fl. 45, 6-1-43, AGCRJ.

23. The full names of enslaved men and women born in Africa were usually composed of European first names, then second names designating African "nations," such as Antônio Mina. A slave's last name signaling an African nation was in reality a Europeanized name of the African coastal slave port or area of origin, such as Mina, Benguela, and Congo.

24. Escravos ao ganho 1846–1850, fl. 2, 6-1-45, AGCRJ.

25. Candelária 1870–1888, fls. 31–32, 9-2-37, AGCRJ.

26. Fridman and Gorberg, *Mercados no Rio de Janeiro*, 1–10; Henry Chamberlain, *Vistas e costumes da cidade e arredores do Rio de Janeiro em 1819–1820* (Rio de Janeiro, 1943 [1820]).

27. Posturas da Câmara Municipal, 1839.

28. Comércio de peixe e indústrias de pesca 1851–1859, fls. 10, 12, 17, 45, 61-3-16, AGCRJ.

29. Quoted in L. Soares, "Os escravos de ganho," 114.

30. Mercado da Candelária 1886–1889, fls. 30–31, 61-2-27, AGCRJ; Fridman and Gorberg, *Mercados no Rio de Janeiro*, 11–34.

31. Barracas, barracões e barraquinhas 1846–1865, fls. 24–26, 58-3-36, AGCRJ.

32. Victorino de Silveira Sousa Filho, João José Lopes Júnior, Privilégios Industriais (hereafter PI) 6245, Arquivo Nacional (hereafter, AN).

33. Gêneros alimentícios 1850–1879, fls. 2–3, 59-1-45, AGCRJ.

34. Posturas da Câmara Municipal, 1839; Código de Posturas, 1854.

35. Gêneros alimentícios 1850–1879, fls. 2–3, 43, 59-1-45, AGCRJ.

36. Fridman and Gorberg, *Mercados no Rio de Janeiro*, 42–46.

37. Gêneros alimentícios 1850–1879, fls. 49–52, 59-1-45, AGCRJ.

38. R. Graham, *Feeding the City*; Maria Isaura Pereira de Queiroz, "Viajantes, século XIX: Negras escravas e livres no Rio de Janeiro," *Revista do Instituto de Estudos Brasileiros* 28 (1988): 53–76; Maria Odila da Silva Dias, "Nas fimbrias da escravidão urbana: Negras de tabuleiro e de ganho," *Estudos Econômicos* 15 (1985): 89–109; L. Soares, "Os escravos de ganho," 116; Cecilia Soares, "As ganhadeiras."

39. Horatio Hale, "Vocabularies and notes based on material collected by Horatio Hale from enslaved African-Brazilians," Manuscript 7235, National Anthropological Archives, Smithsonian Institution, Washington, DC.

40. Cecilia Soares, "As ganhadeiras," 60–61.

41. Ibid. See also Gwendolyn Midlo Hall, *Slavery and African Ethnicities in the Americas: Restoring the Links* (Chapel Hill: University of North Carolina Press, 2005).

42. Dias, "Nas fimbrias da escravidão urbana," 91.

43. Cecilia Soares, "As ganhadeiras"; Maria Odila da Silva Dias, *Power and Everyday Life: The Lives of Working Women in Nineteenth-Century Brazil*, trans. Ann Frost (New Brunswick, NJ: Rutgers University Press, 1995).

44. Karasch, *Slave Life in Rio de Janeiro*, 42.

45. Joaquim Manuel de Macedo, *Um passeio pela cidade do Rio de Janeiro* (Rio de Janeiro: Livraria Garnier, 1991 [1862]), 237–238.

46. Ibid.

47. Barracas, barracões e barraquinhas 1846–1865, fls. 13, 17, 19, 20, 58-3-36, AGCRJ.

48. Barracas em Botafogo 1860, fls. 1–2, 58-3-77, AGCRJ.

49. Queixas e reclamações 1861–1879, fl. 129, 49-1-24, AGCRJ.

50. Flávio dos Santos Gomes and Carlos Eugênio Líbano Soares, "'Dizem as quitandeiras . . .': Ocupações e identidades étnicas em uma cidade escravista: Rio de Janeiro, século XIX," *Acervo: Revista do Arquivo Nacional* 15, no. 2 (2002): 3–16.

51. Comércio de peixe e indústria de pesca 1851–1859, 61-3-16, AGCRJ.

52. Comércio de gelo 1842–1862, 58-4-41, AGCRJ.

53. Comércio de madeiras, 58-4-81, AGCRJ.

54. Comércio de café 1848–1887, fls. 6–7, 58-4-42. AGCRJ.

55. Ibid., fl. 31.

56. João José Reis, "Identidade e diversidade étnicas nas Irmandades Negras no tempo da escravidão," *Tempo* 2, no. 3 (1996): 7–33; Karasch, *Slave Life in Rio de Janeiro*, 134–5.

57. Comércio de fumo 1831–1903, 58-4-28, AGCRJ.

58. Ademir Gebara, *O mercado de trabalho livre no Brasil, 1871–1888* (São Paulo: Brasiliense, 1986); Joseli Maria Nunes Mendonça, *Entre a mão e os anéis: A lei dos sexagenários e os caminhos da abolição no Brasil* (Campinas: Editora da Unicamp, 1999); Pena, *Pajens da casa imperial*.

59. R. Graham, *Feeding the City*, 3.

60. Ganhadores livres, 44-1-31, AGCRJ; Africanos livres ao ganho, 38-1-31, AGCRJ.

61. Ganhadores livres, 44-1-27, AGCRJ.

62. Africanos livres, 44-1-28, 38-1-29, 44-1-31, AGCRJ.

63. Carnes verdes, volantes de carnes e miúdos 1855–1903, 53-4-12, AGCRJ. The meaning of *miúdos* varies. Here it is meat parts.

64. Ferrez, *O Rio antigo de Marc Ferrez*.

65. Luis Felipe de Alencastro, "Proletários e escravos: Imigrantes portugueses e cativos africanos no Rio de Janeiro, 1850–1872," *Novos Estudos* (July 1988): 30–56; population figures are cited from Alencastro's appendix.

66. Farias, "Descobrindo mapas dos minas," 126; Escravos ao ganho, 6-1-59, AGCRJ.

67. João José Reis, "'The Revolution of the Ganhadores': Urban Labor, Ethnicity, and the African Strike of 1857 in Bahia, Brazil," *Journal of Latin American Studies* 29 (May 1997): 355–393.

68. Thomas Holloway, *Policing Rio de Janeiro: Repression and Resistance in a 19th-Century City* (Stanford, CA: Stanford University Press 1993), 253.

69. Ganhadores livres, 44-1-27, 44-1-29, AGCRJ.

70. Fridman and Gorberg, *Mercados no Rio de Janeiro*, 9.

71. Stuart Hall, "Negotiating Caribbean Identities," in *New Caribbean Thought*, ed. Brian Meeks and Folke Lindahl (Trinidad and Tobago: University of the West Indies Press, 2001).

72. Maurício de Almeida Abreu, *Evolução urbana do Rio de Janeiro*, 4th ed. (Rio de Janeiro: Prefeitura do Rio de Janeiro, 2006), 59–67. For urban reform in early twentieth-century Rio see also, Teresa Meade, *"Civilizing Rio": Reform and Resistance in a Brazilian City, 1889–1930* (University Park: Pennsylvania State University Press, 1997).

73. Gomes and Soares, "'Dizem as quitandeiras . . . ,'" 13.

74. M. Silva, *Negro na rua*, 48–49, 55.

75. In Brazilian cities, masters commonly allowed male slaves to live in rented rooms in separate houses; João José Reis, *Slave Rebellion in Brazil: the Muslim Uprising of 1835 in Bahia*, trans. Arthur Brakel (Baltimore, MD: Johns Hopkins University Press, 1993).

76. Gladys Sabina Ribeiro, *A liberdade em construção: Identidade nacional e conflitos antilusitanos no Primeiro Reinado* (Rio de Janeiro: Reluma Dumará, 2002); Gladys Sabina Ribeiro, *Mata Galegos: Os portugueses e os conflitos de trabalho na República Velha* (São Paulo: Editora Brasiliense, 1989).

77. R. Graham, *Feeding the City*, 34. For the city of Salvador, Graham explains that small stores had direct connections with trade from Portugal, which supplied them with traditional Portuguese consumer goods.

78. Comércio de pão 1841–1907, 58-4-36, AGCRJ.

79. Leila Duarte, *Pão e liberdade: Uma história de padeiros escravos e livres na virada do século XIX* (Rio de Janeiro: Fundação de Amparo à Pesquisa do Rio de Janeiro, 2002).

80. Ganhadores livres 1880, 1885, 1886, 1887, 44-1-3, AGCRJ.

81. Martha Abreu, *O império do divino: Festas religiosas e cultura popular no Rio de Janeiro, 1830–1900* (Rio de Janeiro: Editora Nova Fronteira, 1999).

82. Posturas da Câmara Municipal, 1870 (Rio de Janeiro: Eduardo e Henrique Laemmert, 1886). This publication includes revisions to the work of ganhadores under the title "Sobre o serviço de ganhador" (March 1882), 24.

CHAPTER 2

1. "O trabalho," *O Trabalho*, 11 May 1868.

2. Marcos Luiz Bretas, "What the Eyes Can't See: Stories from Rio de Janeiro's Prisons," in *The Birth of the Penitentiary System: Essays on Criminology, Prison Reform, and Social Control, 1830–1940*, ed. Carlos Aguirre and Ricardo Salvatore (Austin: University of Texas Press, 1996).

3. Occorrencias das ruas, *Gazeta de Notícias*, 4 March 1883.

4. Occorrencias das ruas, 23 January 1883.

5. Precisa-se (help-wanted ad section), *Gazeta de Notícias*, 19 January 1880. The use of the term *menino* (boy) indicates the child's free status, whereas the term *molequinho* or *molequinha* generally refers to a male or female slave child; Kátia M. de Queirós Mattoso, *To Be a Slave in Brazil, 1550–1888*, trans. Arthur Goldhammer (New Brunswick, NJ: Rutgers University Press, 1986).

6. Leila Mezan Algranti, "Slave Crimes: The Use of Police Power to Control the Slave Population of Rio de Janeiro," *Luso-Brazilian Review* 25, no. 1 (Summer 1988): 27–48.

7. Alencastro, "Proletários e escravos"; Aluísio Azevedo, *The Slum*, trans. David H. Rosenthal (New York: Oxford University Press, 2000); Marcelo Badaró Mattos, "Trabalha-

dores escravizados e livres na cidade do Rio de Janeiro na segunda metade do século XIX," *Revista do Rio de Janeiro* 12 (2004): 229–251; Jaime Rodrigues, "Ferro, trabalho e conflito: Os africanos livres na fábrica de Ipanema," *História Social*, no. 4/5 (1996/1997): 29–42; Artur José Renda Vitorino, "Escravismo, proletários e a greve dos compositores tipográficos de 1858 no Rio de Janeiro," *Cadernos Arquivo Edgar Leuenroth* 6, no. 10/11 (1999): 71–106

8. M. Mattos, "Trabalhadores escravizados e livres," 234.

9. Flávio dos Santos Gomes and Antônio Luigi Negro, "Além de senzalas e fábricas Uma história social do trabalho," *Tempo Social, Revista de Sociologia da Universidade de São Paulo* 18, no. 1 (2006): 217–240.

10. Seth Rockman, *Scraping By: Wage Labor, Slavery, and Survival in Early Baltimore* (Baltimore, MD: Johns Hopkins University Press, 2009), 11.

11. Sidney Chalhoub, *Visões da liberdade: Uma história das últimas décadas da escravidão na corte* (São Paulo: Companhia das Letras, 1990); Keila Grinberg, *Liberata, a lei da ambigüedade: As ações de liberdade da Corte de Apelação do Rio de Janeiro no século XIX* (Rio de Janeiro: Relume, Dumara, 1994).

12. Keila Grinberg, "Slavery, Liberalism, and Civil Law," in *Honor, Status, and Law in Modern Latin America*, ed. Sueann Caulfield, Sarah C. Chambers, and Lara Putman (Durham, NC: Duke University Press, 2005), 122.

13. Holloway, *Policing Rio de Janeiro*, 231.

14. Alexandra K. Brown, "'A Black Mark on Our Legislation': Slavery, Punishment, and the Politics of Death in Nineteenth-Century Brazil," *Luso-Brazilian Review* 37, no. 2 (2000): 103–104.

15. Precisa-se, *Gazeta de Notícias*, January-December 1883.

16. Precisa-se, *O Bonde*, 11 February 1881.

17. Precisa-se, *Gazeta de Notícias*, 19 January 1880.

18. Precisa-se, *Gazeta de Notícias*, 6 April 1883.

19. Rockman, *Scraping By*, 186–187.

20. Occorrencias das ruas, *Gazeta de Notícias*, 12 February 1883.

21. Occorrencias das ruas, 11 April 1883.

22. Occorrencias das ruas, 20 May 1883.

23. Brasil Gerson, *História das ruas do Rio de Janeiro* (Rio de Janeiro: Editora Sousa, 1954).

24. Occorrencias das ruas, *Gazeta de Notícias*, 4 March 1883. The original reads, "Que outros Srs. Subdelegados cumpram o que manda a lei ou que o Sr. subdelegado do 2° distrito de Santana deixe que alí, como em toda parte, possa cada um carregar a sua cruz, não a sua sogra, ainda não a sua carga as costas."

25. Occorrencias das ruas, 12 March 1883.

26. Occorrencias das ruas, 8 March 1883.

27. Occorrencias das ruas, 7 March 1883.

28. Occorrencias das ruas, 12 February 1883.

29. Occorrencias das ruas, 10 March 1883.

30. Occorrencias das ruas, 26 February 1883.

31. Carlos Aguirre and Ricardo Salvatore, "Birth of the Penitentiary System in Latin America: Toward an Interpretive Social History," in *Birth of the Penitentiary System in Latin America: Essays on Criminology, Prison Reform, and Social Control, 1830–1940*, ed. Carlos Aguirre and Ricardo Salvatore (Austin: University of Texas Press, 1993), 9. Also see Brown, "'Black Mark on Our Legislation.'"

32. Bretas, "What the Eyes Can't See," 104.

33. Holloway, *Policing Rio de Janeiro*, 16–17.

34. Ibid., 289.

35. Amy Chazkel, "Social Life and Civic Education in the Rio de Janeiro City Jail," *Journal of Social History* 42, no. 3 (2009), 697–783.

36. "Onde termina a rua" (Where the street ends) originally appeared as a newspaper chronicle by João do Rio in 1904, later becoming a chapter in his book *A alma encantadora das ruas*, first published in 1908. Also see Bretas, "What the Eyes Can't See," 113.

37. Thomas Holloway, "Punishment in Nineteenth-Century Rio de Janeiro: Judicial Action as Police Practice," in *Reconstructing Criminality in Latin America*, ed. Carlos A. Aguirre and Robert Buffington (Wilmington, DE: Scholarly Resources, 2000), 101–103.

38. The collections of registry entries are in books titled "Livros da Casa de Detenção" in the Arquivo Público Estadual do Rio de Janeiro (APERJ). The books that make up this sample are numbers 3956, 3957, 3965, 3969, 3989, 4042, 4052, 4059, 4312, 5418, 5419, 5436, and 5454.

39. Holloway, *Policing Rio de Janeiro*, 231.

40. Gomes and Soares, "'Dizem as quitandeiras . . . .'"

41. Sandra Lauderdale Graham, "Slavery's Impasse: Slave Prostitutes, Small-Time Mistresses, and the Brazilian Law of 1871," *Comparative Study in Society and History* 33, no. 4 (1991): 669–694. For a recent study on Rio's businesswomen during the nineteenth century's second half see Kari Zimmerman, "'As Pertaining to the Female Sex': The Legal and Social Norms of Female Entrepreneurship in Nineteenth-Century Rio de Janeiro, Brazil," *Hispanic American Historical Review* 66, no. 1 (2016): 39–72.

42. Amy Chazkel, *Laws of Chance: Brazil's Clandestine Lottery and the Making of Urban Public Life* (Durham, NC: Duke University Press, 2011).

43. Manuel de Mello and Paulo José de Faria Brandão, *Catálogo dos livros do Gabinete Portuguez de Leitura no Rio de Janeiro* (Rio de Janeiro: Typographia Commercial de F. de O. Q. Regadas, 1858).

44. Carlos Eugenio Líbano Soares, *A capoeira escrava e outras tradições rebeldes no Rio de Janeiro, 1808–1850* (São Paulo: Editora da Unicamp, 2002).

45. Gomes and Soares, "'Dizem as quitandeiras . . . .'"

46. Queixas e reclamações 1880–1889, fl. 7, 49-1-33, AGCRJ.

47. Carlos Eugênio Líbano Soares, *Zungú: Rumor de muitas vozes* (Rio de Janeiro: Arquivo Público do Estado do Rio de Janeiro, 1998), and "O reino do Zungú," *Nossa História* 3, no. 29 (2006): 46–49; Graham, "Slavery's Impasse," 672.

48. Occorrencias das ruas, *Gazeta de Notícias*, 26 March 1883.

49. Occorrencias das ruas, 18 March 1883.

50. Livro 3969, Casa de Detenção, APERJ.

51. Holloway, "Punishment in Nineteenth-Century Rio de Janeiro," 104. For a detailed description on the formation and abolition of the Urban Guard see chapter 6 of Holloway's *Policing Rio de Janeiro*.

CHAPTER 3

1. Walter Goebel and Saskia Schabio, eds., *Beyond the Black Atlantic: Relocating Modernization and Technology* (New York: Routledge, 2006), 5.

2. The patent requests discussed in this chapter are from the Arquivo Nacional collec-

tion Privilégios Industriais for the years 1875–1919. The Arquivo Público was where individuals registered all patent requests at the turn of the century. An applicant would deposit a copy of his or her request in the Arquivo Público while another copy was submitted to the Ministério da Indústria, Viação e Obras Públicas through the Sociedade Auxiliadora da Indústria Nacional. The Arquivo Público notified the applicant upon approval, stamping a copy of the patent request with the ministry's acceptance number.

3. Paulo Vieira de Sousa, patent request 0380, Privilégios Industriais (hereafter PI), Arquivo Nacional (hereafter AN).

4. Julyan Peard, *Race, Place, and Medicine: The Idea of the Tropics in Nineteenth-Century Brazilian Medicine* (Durham, NC: Duke University Press, 2000).

5. Brazilian abolitionist discourse was strongly influenced by British antislavery activists who defined their cause as a humanitarian campaign. Brazilian abolitionist Joaquim Nabuco represented this British influence, writing *O abolicionismo* in London in 1863 (Brasília: Fundação Universidade de Brasilia, 2003). See also Charles Martial Allemand-Lavigerie, *Crusade against the Slave-Trade: Oration . . . at the Meeting of the Anti-Slavery Society Held in Prince's Hall London, Tuesday, July 31st, 1888* (London: LSE Pamphlets, 1888).

6. Joaquim Nabuco, *Campanha abolicionista no Recife: Eleições de 1884* (Recife, Brazil: Fundação Joaquim Nabuco, Editora Massangana, 1988).

7. Joaquim Nabuco, *Abolitionism: The Brazilian Antislavery Struggle*, trans. and ed. Robert Conrad (Urbana: University of Illinois Press, 1977 [1883]).

8. In Antônio Manuel Bueno de Andrade, "A abolição em São Paulo," *Revista do Arquivo Municipal* 77 (1941): 263.

9. Nabuco, "Reformas Sociaes!" in *Campanha abolicionista no Recife*. Also see his speech "Escravidão e trabalho" in the same book.

10. George Reid Andrews, *Blacks and Whites in São Paulo, Brazil, 1888–1988* (Madison: University of Wisconsin Press, 1991); Thomas Skidmore, *Black into White: Race and Nationality in Brazilian Thought* (Durham, NC: Duke University Press, 1993).

11. Kohn's years of birth and death are unknown to the author. The most reliable published source, Egon Wolff and Frieda Wolff, identifies Kohn in Brazil during the late imperial period, a time when "several of his inventions were honored with the presence of Emperor Dom Pedro II." After 1891, Kohn, "the entrepreneur of so many innovations during Imperial Brazil, becomes annoyed with deferred patent requests and disappears from Brazil, returning probably to his native country, the United States"; Wolff and Wolff, *Judeus nos primórdios do Brasil-República: Visto especialmente pela documentação no Rio de Janeiro* (Rio de Janeiro: Edição da Biblioteca Israelita H. N. Bialik, Centro de Documentação, 1979), 67–69.

12. Morris Kohn, patent request 087, PI, AN; Morris N. Kohn, registro (hereafter reg.) 20952, livro 100, fls. 175–177, Junta Commercial, AN.

13. For a study on Brazilian investments in technology during the imperial period see Teresa Cribelli, *Industrial Forests and Mechanical Marvels: Modernization in Nineteenth-Century Brazil* (New York: Cambridge University Press, 2016).

14. Morris Kohn, reg. 14656, livro 673, AN.

15. Wolff and Wolff, *Judeus nos primórdios do Brasil-República*, 67–69. See also entries for Morris N. Kohn in Benjamin Franklin Ramiz Galvão, *Catálogo. Exposição Nacional, 1875* (Rio de Janeiro: Typographia e Lithographia Carioca, 1875).

16. Morris N. Kohn, reg. 20952, livro 100, fls. 175–177, Junta Commercial, AN. Kohn and Silva's company, Empresa de Engraxadores, was officially licensed in 1879. The patent allowed the company to distribute materials for nine years; after that, the company could

renew its license if Kohn became responsible for one-third of the investments that had been fronted by Silva.

17. Requerimento e mais papeis de Morris N. Kohn, administrador da Empresa Ambulante Doméstica—e de Jeronymo Maximo Romano—sobre carrocinhas hygiênicas para condução de gêneros alimentícios e cadeiras de engraxates, Gêneros alimenticios 1887–1890, 59-2-2, AGCRJ.

18. Acta da 19ª Seção Ordinária, 28 July 1887, Gêneros alimenticios 1887–1890, 59-2-2, AGCRJ.

19. Ibid.

20. Ibid.

21. Câmara Municipal do Rio de Janeiro, *Posturas da Illustríssima Câmara Municipal 1870* (Rio de Janeiro: Eduardo e Henrique Laemmert, 1870), AGCRJ.

22. Gêneros alimentícios 1887–1890, 59-2-2, AGCRJ.

23. Ibid., fls. 7–9.

24. Ibid.

25. Morris Kohn, patent request 6410, PI, AN. Most patent requests included manual designs of the invention. None are available for Kohn (that I saw) in the Arquivo Nacional in Rio.

26. Morris Kohn, patent request 9032, PI, AN.

27. Queixas e reclamações 1890–1899, fls. 131–132, 49-1-33, AGCRJ.

28. Morris Kohn, patent request 0270, PI, AN.

29. Sandra Lauderdale Graham, "The Vintém Riot and Political Culture: Rio de Janeiro, 1880," in *Riots in the Cities: Popular Politics and the Urban Poor in Latin America 1765–1910*, ed. Silvia M. Arrom and Servando Ortoll (Wilmington, DE: Scholarly Research, 1996).

30. Luis Gastão Escragnolle Dória, "Kiosques," *Revista da Semana*, 1 August 1925.

31. The inflation of food prices was related to the fall in price of coffee, Brazil's major export product at the time; Eulália Maria Lahmeyer Lobo, *História do Rio de Janeiro: Do capital comercial ao capital industrial e financeiro*, vol. 2 (Rio de Janeiro: Ibmec 1978).

32. Everardo Backheuser, "Comércio ambulante e ocupações de rua no Rio de Janeiro," *Revista Brasileira de História* 6, no. 1 (January-March 1944): 3–34. Backheuser asserts that the practices of street commerce at the time had changed little from the nineteenth century.

33. Antônio Silveira de Sousa, patent request 1190, PI, AN.

34. Paulo Vieira de Sousa, patent request 0380, PI, AN.

35. Manuel Moreira Dias, patent request 0838, PI, AN.

36. Artur Araújo, patent request 8478, PI, AN.

37. Manuel Antônio Guimarães, patent 3312, PI, AN.

38. Debret, Engenho manual, in *Viagem pitoresca e histórica ao Brasil.*

39. Debret, Vendedor de suco de cana, in *Viagem pitoresca e histórica ao Brasil.*

40. Antônio Jacques Junot, patent request 9110, PI, AN.

41. Carlos Augusto de Castro e Silva, patent request 1270, PI, AN.

42. Comércio de pão 1841–1907, fls. 34 and 170–171, 58-4-36, AGCRJ. In 1895 the municipality officially declared that delivering bread was not a part of street commerce; Código de Posturas: Leis, decretos, editaes e resoluções da Intendencia Municipal do Distrito Federal, Decreto Legislativo no. 410, 8 June 1897. Compilação feita por ordem da prefeitura, pela repartição do Arquivo Geral. Prefeito Dr. Henrique Valladares (Rio de Janeiro: Typographia Mont'Alverne. Rua do Ouvidor 82, 1894), AGCRJ.

43. Comércio de pão 1895–1913, fls. 26, 31–32, 35–36, 59-1-32, AGCRJ.

44. Projeto de uma caixa para doces, 1907 (desenho), patent request 4743, PI, AN.

45. Odilo Lorenzo, patent request 4773, PI, AN.

46. Ferrez, Vendedor de doces, in *O Rio antigo de Marc Ferrez.*

47. Joaquim Ferreira Mendonça, patent request 8226, fl. 53, PI, AN.

48. F. Paulo Freitas, patent request 5377, PI, AN.

49. F. Paulo Freitas, patent request 7959, PI, AN.

50. Artur Pitágoras Toval Conrado, José Werneck Massena, Manuel José de Lacerda, patent request 5501, PI, AN.

51. Câmara Municipal do Rio de Janeiro, Posturas da Illustríssima Câmara Municipal 1870; Francisco Agenor de Noronha Santos, *As freguesias do Rio antigo* (Rio de Janeiro: O Cruzeiro, 1965).

52. Augusto Magalhães de Barros Vasconcelos e Guimarães Rovira, patent request 2158, PI, AN.

53. Carlos Freire Vilhalba Alvim and Jorge Alberto Vinhon, patent request 0623, PI, AN. Vilhalba Alvim also made handcarts and vending accessories.

54. Benedito Novella da Silva, patent request 0811, PI, AN; Manuel Alves Lobo, patent request 1622, PI, AN.

55. Antônio Ferreira da Silva Porto, patent request 3696, PI, AN.

56. José de Freitas Pinheiro, patent request 0208, PI, AN.

57. Pedro Antônio Fagundes, patent request 783, PI, AN.

58. Benigno Rios and José Stockmeyer, patent request 7117, PI, AN.

59. Magalhães Corrêa, *O sertão carioca* (Rio de Janeiro: Edição do Instituto Histórico Brasileiro, 1936).

60. Mariza de Carvalho Soares and Nelson Rosa Bezarra, eds., *Escravidão africana no Recôncavo da Guanabara (séculos XVII-XIX)* (Rio de Janeiro: Editora da UFF, 2011).

61. Victorino de Silveira Sousa Filho and João José Lopes Júnior, patent request 6245, PI, AN.

62. Cateyson Desthur and Sergio Companheiro, patent request 0789, PI, AN.

63. Ibid.

64. J. E. Coelho de Magalhães, patent request 8567, PI, AN.

65. Valdemar Flor Kathiessen, patent request 0898, PI, AN.

66. Manuel Antônio Guimarães, patent request 3284, PI, AN.

67. Francisco Falconi, patent request 4518, PI, AN.

68. Augusto Fernandes Carreira, patent request 4526, PI, AN.

69. Walter Benjamin, *The Arcades Project* (Cambridge: Belknap Press, 2002).

70. Esther Leslie, "Ruin and Rubble in the Arcades" in *Walter Benjamin and the Arcades Project*, ed. Beatrice Hanssen (London: Continuum, 2006), 91.

71. Alfredo Bosi, *Dialética da colonização* (São Paulo: Companhia das Letras, 1992).

CHAPTER 4

1. Marcos Luiz Bretas, *Ordem na cidade: O exercício cotidiano da autoridade policial no Rio de Janeiro, 1907–1930* (Rio de Janeiro: Rocco, 1997); Luís Antônio F. de Sousa, Fernando Afonso Salla, and Marcos César Alvarez, "A sociedade e a lei: O Código Penal de 1890 e as novas tendências penais na Primeira República," *Justiça e História* 3, no. 6 (2003): 1–33.

2. "Treze de maio," *Gazeta de Notícias*, 13 May 1889, quoted in Antônio Silva Jardim,

Propaganda republicana, 1888–1889 (Rio de Janeiro: Fundação Casa Rui Barbosa, 1978), 353–354.

3. João do Rio, *A alma encantadora das ruas*, 109.

4. José Murilo de Carvalho, *Os bestializados: O Rio de Janeiro e a república que não foi* (São Paulo: Companhia das Letras, 1987), 66.

5. Ibid., 68.

6. James Holston, *Insurgent Citizenship: Disjunctions of Democracy and Modernity in Brazil* (Princeton, NJ: Princeton University Press, 2007), 5.

7. Holston, *Insurgent Citizenship*, 4.

8. Olívia Maria Gomes da Cunha and Flávio dos Santos Gomes, eds., *Quase-cidadão: Histórias e antropologias da pós-emancipação no Brasil* (Rio de Janeiro: Fundação Getúlio Vargas, 2007), 7–15. The question the historian Thomas Holt first asks and the editors of *Quase-cidadão* emphasize as crucial for the study of people of color in postemancipation societies is "Liberty for what?"; Holt, *The Problem of Freedom: Race, Labor, and Politics in Jamaica and Britain, 1832–1938* (Baltimore, MD: Johns Hopkins University Press, 1992). Also see Rebecca J. Scott, Frederick Cooper, and Thomas C. Holt, *Beyond Slavery: Explorations of Race, Labor, and Citizenship in Postemancipation Societies* (Chapel Hill: University of North Carolina Press, 2000); Hebe Maria Mattos, *Das cores do silêncio: Os significados da liberdade no sudeste escravista, Brasil século XIX* (Rio de Janeiro: Nova Fronteira, 1998).

9. Brodwyn Fischer, *A Poverty of Rights: Citizenship and Inequality in Twentieth-Century Rio de Janeiro* (Stanford, CA: Stanford University Press, 2008).

10. Holston, *Insurgent Citizenship*, 14.

11. Cunha and Gomes, *Quase-cidadão*.

12. Sidney Chalhoub, *Trabalho, lar e botequim: O cotidiano dos trabalhadores no Rio de Janeiro da Belle Époque* (São Paulo: Brasiliense, 1986).

13. Holloway, *Policing Rio de Janeiro*.

14. Código Penal de 1890, Senado Federal, Brazil, http://legis.senado.leg.br/legislacao/ListaTextoIntegral.action?id=50260&norma=66049.

15. Carlos Eugênio Líbano Soares, "Os últimos malungos: Moradia, ocupação e criminalidade entre libertos africanos, 1860–1900," in *No labirinto das nações*, by Farias, Soares, and Gomes, 165.

16. Gêneros alimentícios 1887–1890, fls. 7–9, 59-2-2, AGCRJ.

17. Comércio varejista 1890, 5-1-27, AGCRJ.

18. Comércio de pão 1841–1907, fls. 121–123, 58-4-36, AGCRJ.

19. Ibid., fls. 148–149.

20. Representação popular dirigida ao prefeito contra a exploração do comércio e carestia de gêneros alimentícios, Gêneros alimentícios 1892, 59-2-8, AGCRJ; Representação popular sobre a carestia de gêneros com os pareceres do Intendente Julio Silveira Lobo e o advogado da Intendência Municipal Dr. João Capistrano Bandeira Mello, Gêneros alimentícios 1892, 59-2-10, AGCRJ.

21. Lobo, *História do Rio de Janeiro*, vol. 2.

22. Comércio de fumo 1831–1903, fl. 143, 58-4-28, AGCRJ.

23. Loterias e bilhetes de loterias 1841–1856, fls. 9–13, 46-2-3, AGCRJ.

24. Jogos, rifas, e loterias 1895–1913, 45-2-49, AGCRJ.

25. Loterias e bilhetes de loterias 1874–1895, fl. 14, 46-2-4, AGCRJ.

26. Ibid., fls. 17–18.

27. Loterias 1890–1899, fl. 20, 46-1-47, AGCRJ.

28. Chazkel, *Laws of Chance.*

29. Jogos 1874–1911, fl. 121, 45-2-30, AGCRJ.

30. Comércio de livros 1848–1891, 58-4-43, AGCRJ; Alessandra El Far, *Páginas de sensação: Literatura popular e pornográfica no Rio de Janeiro (1870–1924)* (São Paulo: Companhia das Letras, 2004).

31. Maria Tereza Chaves de Mello, *A república consentida* (Rio de Janeiro: Fundação Getúlio Vargas, 2007).

32. This chapter's sample of registry entries from the Casa de Detenção for 1890–1902 includes books numbered 063, 317, 3960, 3972, 3982, 4218, 4317, 4322, 5414, 5415, 5453, 6333, s/n Homens 6/2-4/19/1895, s/n Homens 26/4-21/6/1897, s/n 20/1-27/2/1898, s/n Mulheres 1898–1899, 907, and s/n Menores de 21, 1892–1896.

33. Sam Adamo, "The Broken Promise: Race, Health, and Justice in Rio de Janeiro, 1850–1940" (PhD diss., Columbia University, 1983), 205.

34. João do Rio, "Negros ricos," *Gazeta de Notícias*, 13 May 1905.

35. Roberto Moura, *Tia Ciata e a pequena África no Rio de Janeiro* (Rio de Janeiro: Funarte, 1983).

36. Arjun Appadurai and James Holston, introduction to *Cities and Citizenship*, ed. Appadurai and Holston (Durham, NC: Duke University Press, 1999), 2.

37. Ibid., 23.

38. Pedro Vasquez, *Fotógrafos no Rio de Janeiro: Victor Frond, George Leuzinger, Marc Ferrez e Juan Gutierrez* (Rio de Janeiro: Dazibao, 1990), 22.

39. Escragnolle Dória, "Kiosques." In smaller Brazilian cities like Belém old kiosks remained throughout the twentieth century.

40. José Martins (1895), 8ª Pretoria Criminal, OR 128, AN.

41. Carlos Eugênio Líbano Soares, *A negrada instituição: A capoeira no Rio de Janeiro, 1850–1890* (Rio de Janeiro: Prefeitura do Município do Rio de Janeiro, Biblioteca Carioca, 1994).

42. Influenced by republican discourse, police officers began to use the title "citizen"; Holloway, *Policing Rio de Janeiro*, 244. In this case, individuals who were citizens but not police officers initiated the arrests of capoeiristas.

43. Soares, *A negrada instituição.*

44. Carlos Eugênio Líbano Soares, "A capoeira escrava no Rio de Janeiro, 1863–1882," in *Escravidão: Ofícios e liberdade*, ed. Jorge Prata de Sousa (Rio de Janeiro: Arquivo Público do Estado do Rio de Janeiro, 1998).

45. Livro da Casa de Detenção S/N Homens, 1905/1906, 11/10/1905–21/2/1906, Arquivo Público do Estado do Rio de Janeiro (hereafter APERJ); Boletim da Intendência Municipal, 1906 (Rio de Janeiro: Typographia Rua Sete de Setembro, 1906).

46. Carlos Soares, "Os últimos malungos," 165.

47. Antônio José da Silva (1899), 10ª Pretoria Criminal, 7C 111, AN.

48. Rockman, *Scraping By*, 161.

49. Graham, *House and Street.*

50. In Martha Abreu and Sueann Caulfield, "50 Years of Virginity in Rio de Janeiro: Sexual Politics and Gender Roles in Judicial and Popular Discourses, 1890–1940," *Luso-Brazilian Review* 30 (Summer 1993): 47–74.

51. Ibid.

52. Sueann Caulfield, *In Defense of Honor: Sexual Morality, Modernity, and Nation in Early Twentieth-Century Brazil* (Durham, NC: Duke University Press, 2000), 49.

53. Ibid., 34–35.

54. Ibid., 39.

55. José Rodrigues dos Santos (1898), 8ª Pretoria Criminal, OR 683, AN.

56. Martha Abreu, "*Mulatas*, *Crioulos*, and *Morenas*: Racial Hierarchy, Gender Relations, and National Identity in Postabolition Popular Song (Southeastern Brazil, 1890–1920)," in *Gender and Slave Emancipation in the Atlantic World*, ed. Pamela Scully and Diana Patton (Durham, NC: Duke University Press, 2005), 267–288.

57. For a discussion on the concept of "legal contact zones" see Gilbert M. Joseph's preface to *Crime and Punishment in Latin America: Law and Society since Late Colonial Times*, ed. Carlos Aguirre, Gilbert M. Joseph, and Ricardo D. Salvatore (Durham, NC: Duke University Press, 2001), ix-xii.

CHAPTER 5

1. The database "Ocorrências policiais" at the Centro de Pesquisa em História da Cultura in Campinas, São Paulo state, offers a selection from the repository of the Secretaria da Polícia Civil in Rio.

2. Oswaldo Porto Rocha, *A era das demolições: Cidade do Rio de Janeiro, 1870–1920* (Rio de Janeiro: Biblioteca Carioca, 1983).

3. Sueann Caulfield, "The Making of the Carioca Working Class: Social History of Rio de Janeiro during the First Republic," *Luso-Brazilian Review* 28, no. 2 (1991): 99–105.

4. Meade, "*Civilizing Rio*"; Jeffrey Needell, "The Revolta contra a Vacina of 1904: The Revolt against Modernization in Belle-Époque Rio de Janeiro," *Hispanic American Historical Review* 67, no. 2 (May 1987): 233–269.

5. José Alípio Goulart, *O mascate no Brasil* (Rio de Janeiro: Conquista, 1967).

6. Decreto n. 830 de 31 de outobro de 1901, Regula o Exercício da Profissão de Mascate, Boletim da Intendência Municipal, Diretoria Geral do Interior e Estatística, October-December 1901 (Rio de Janeiro, 1902).

7. Ibid.

8. Jaime Larry Benchimol, *Pereira Passos, um Haussman tropical: A renovação urbana da cidade do Rio de Janeiro no início do século XX* (Rio de Janeiro: Prefeitura da Cidade do Rio de Janeiro, Biblioteca Carioca, 1990), 280–281.

9. The policing of vendors due to violations of space rather than occupational practice during periods of urban renewal was not uncommon to the Americas, as Pablo Piccato illustrates for the case of Mexico City; Piccato, "Urbanistas, Ambulantes, and Mendigos: The Dispute for Urban Space in Mexico City, 1890–1930," in *Reconstruction Criminality in Latin America*, ed. Carlos A. Aguirre and Robert Buffington (Wilmington, DE: Scholarly Resources, 2000), 113–148.

10. Maria Clementina Pereira Cunha, *Ecos da folia: Uma história do carnaval carioca entre 1880–1920* (São Paulo: Companhia das Letras, 2001).

11. In Benchimol, *Pereira Passos*, 277–8.

12. Frank De Yeax Carpenter, *Round about Rio: A Novel* (Chicago: Jansen, McClurg, 1884), 178–179. Charles Granville Hamilton describes this work "as fiction, but it is primarily a travel book with a thin sugar-coating"; "English Speaking Travelers in Brazil, 1851–1887," *Hispanic American Historical Review* 4, no. 4 (1960): 533–546.

13. José Alípio Goulart, "Alguns dados sobre o comércio ambulante do leite no Rio de Janeiro do século XIX," *Revista do Instituto Histórico e Geográfico Brasileiro* 263 (1954): 1–40.

14. "Leiteros ambulantes," *Correio da Manhã*, 22 January 1912.

15. Luiz Edmundo, *O Rio de Janeiro do meu tempo* (Rio de Janeiro: Conquista, 1957). Edmundo's book was first published in 1938.

16. Benchimol, *Pereira Passos*, 278.

17. Ibid., 279.

18. Escragnolle Dória, "Kiosques."

19. Augusto Malta's photographs depicting feiras livres are held in the Malta collection at AGCRJ.

20. Augusto Malta, Fotografias, AGCRJ.

21. Benchimol, *Pereira Passos*, 283; Fridman and Gorberg, *Mercados no Rio de Janeiro.*

22. "Posturas e leis circulantes e editaes da Polícia Militar," Boletim da Intendência Municipal, Diretoria Geral da Polícia Administrativa, Arquivo e Estatística (Rio de Janeiro, 1903).

23. Chazkel, "Social Life and Civic Education," 56.

24. Berenice Brandão, *A polícia e a força policial no Rio de Janeiro* (Rio de Janeiro: Pontífica Universidade Católica do Rio de Janeiro, 1981), 253.

25. Olívia Maria Gomes da Cunha, *Intenção e gesto: Pessoa, cor e a produção cotidiana da (in)diferença no Rio de Janeiro* (Rio de Janeiro: Arquivo Nacional), 32.

26. Marcos Luiz Bretas, *A guerra das ruas: Povo e polícia na cidade do Rio de Janeiro* (Rio de Janeiro: Arquivo Nacional, 1997), 101–102.

27. From *A Notícia*, 24 July 1930, quoted in Bretas, *A guerra das ruas*, 103–104.

28. Maurício Abreu, *Evolução urbana do Rio de Janeiro*, 87; Corrêa, *O sertão carioca.*

29. Cristiane Regina Miyasaka, "Viver nos subúrbios: A experiência dos trabalhadores de Inhaúma (Rio de Janeiro, 1890–1910)," master's thesis, Universidade Estadual de Campinas, 2008.

30. Marc Hertzman, *Making Samba: A New History of Music and Race in Brazil* (Durham, NC: Duke University Press, 2013); Moura, *Tia Ciata*; Mônica Pimenta Velloso, "As tias bahianas tomam conta do pedaço: Espaço e identidade cultural no Rio de Janeiro," *Estudos Históricos* 3, no. 6 (1990): 207–228.

31. Moura, *Tia Ciata.*

32. "Jaú é a boa passagem do bonde Penha," *Jornal do Brasil*, 4 August 1961.

33. "Fim de uma tradição: Bondes da Praia Vermelha extintos," *O Jornal*, 29 September 1962; "Taboleiro da Bahiana, ponto final da Poesia," *O Jornal*, 31 January 1963; "Acabou-se o din din seu condutor," *Correio da Manhã*, 9 March 1963; "O taboleiro agora sem finalidade será derrubado para favorecer o tráfego," *Correio da Manhã*, 22 May 1963.

34. Corrêa, *O sertão carioca.*

35. Cartoon, *Jornal do Brasil*, 19 Janeiro 1913.

36. "Ficará o Rio sem ambulantes?" *A Noite*, 8 January 1913.

37. Salustiano Cruz (1904), 8ª Pretoria Criminal, OR 3553, AN; Livro da Casa de Detenção, s/n Homens, 25/7/1904–20/10/1904, APERJ.

38. Livro da Casa de Detenção, s/n Homens, 1905/1906, 11/10/1905–21/2/1906, APERJ; João José Reis, "De olho no canto: Trabalho de rua na Bahia na véspera da abolição," *Afro-Ásia* 24 (2000): 199–242.

39. Salustiano Cruz (1904), 8ª Pretoria Criminal, OR 3553, AN.

40. Holston, *Insurgent Citizenship*, 5–9.

41. For the debate on workers and vagrants discussed in the Brazilian Chamber of Deputies see Chalhoub, *Trabalho, lar e botequim.*

42. Salustiano Cruz (1904), 8ª Pretoria Criminal, OR 3553, AN. For more on Dois Rios prison see Myrian Sepúlveda dos Santos, "Os porões da república: A colônia correcional de Dois Rios entre 1908 e 1930," *Topoi* 7, no. 13 (2006): 445–447. Built in 1903 off the southern coast of the state of Rio, Dois Rios on the island of Ilha Grande was built to contain the so-called undesirable citizens of the First Republic.

43. Chazkel, "Social Life and Civic Education"; O. Cunha, *Intenção e gesto*; Cunha and Gomes, *Quase-cidadão*; Holston and Appadurai, *Cities and Citizenship*.

44. Chazkel, "Social Life and Civic Education."

45. Ibid. Chazkel borrows the term "social branding" from Olívia Cunha's *Intenção e gesto*.

46. Columna operaria, *A Época*, 26 October 1913.

47. "O 'habeas corpus' aos vendedores ambulantes da estação Great Western," *Correio da Manhã*, 17 August 1926.

48. A sample of twenty-seven books has registry entries from the Casa de Detenção for 1903–1922, in the APERJ.

49. Jeffrey Lesser, *Negotiating National Identity: Immigrants, Minorities, and the Struggle for Ethnicity in Brazil* (Durham, NC: Duke University Press, 1999).

50. Laurindo Manuel da Silva, 1911, 9ª Pretoria Criminal, TZ 1707, AN.

51. The Portuguese word *tipo* (type) is underlined in the original document Samuel Vieira da Cunha, 1904, 8ª Pretoria Criminal, OR 3315, AN.

52. "Negros ricos". Gazeta de Notícias. 13 May 1905. Also see Juliana Barreto Farias, "João do Rio e os africanos: Raça e ciência nas crônicas da Belle Époque carioca," *Revista de História* 162 (2010): 243–270.

53. Moura, *Tia Ciata*.

54. Antônio Adioi, 1905, 8ª Pretoria Criminal, OR 3983, AN.

55. Underlined in the Portuguese original document. Manuel José de Sousa, 1905, 8ª Pretoria Criminal, OR 4276, AN.

56. Miguel Curi, 1917, 5ª Pretoria Criminal, 70.2538, AN. In the detention center's registry entry, Miguel Curi is listed as a mascate, but in the court process interrogation he is noted as having no occupation or place of residence.

57. "Entre doceiros" *A Época*, 25 December 1915.

58. "A obra do despeito," *A Época*, 14 November 1913.

CHAPTER 6

1. Columna operaria, *A Época*, 5 January 1912. The original spelling *columna operaria* is retained.

2. Columna operaria, *A Época*, 6 January 1913.

3. Columna operaria, *A Época*, 8 January 1913.

4. "Imposto de licenças," *Annaes do Conselho Municipal, Septembro/Novembro* (Rio de Janeiro: Of. Typ. Paiz, 1913).

5. "Leiteros ambulantes," *Correio da Manhã*, 22 January 1913.

6. Benchimol, *Pereira Passos*, 279–281.

7. "Leiteros ambulantes," *Correio da Manhã*, 22 January 1913.

8. Edmundo, *O Rio de Janeiro de meu tempo*, 58, 59, 60, 61.

9. "Leiteros ambulantes," *Correio da Manhã*, 22 January 1913.

10. Cláudio Batalha, "Vida associativa: Por uma nova abordagem da história institu-

cional nos estudos do movimento operário," *Anos 90* 5, no. 8 (1997): 91–99; Cláudio Batalha, "Os desafios atuais da história do trabalho," *Anos 90* 13, no. 23/24 (2006): 87–104; Cláudio Batalha, "Sociedades de trabalhadores no Rio de Janeiro do século XIX: Algumas reflexões em torno da formação da classe Operaria," *Cadernos Arquivo Edgar Leuenroth* 6, no. 10/11 (1999): 43–68; Maria Cecília Velasco e Cruz, "Puzzling Out Slave Origins in Rio de Janeiro Port Unionism: The 1906 Strike and the Sociedade de Resistência dos Trabalhadores em Trapiche e Café," *Hispanic American Historical Review* 82, no. 2 (2006): 205–245.

11. Sidney Chalhoub, "Solidariedade e liberdade: Sociedades beneficientes de negros e negras no Rio de Janeiro na segunda metade do século XIX," in *Quase-cidadão*, ed. Cunha and Gomes.

12. Marcelo Badaró Mattos, "Trajetórias entre fronteiras: O fim da escravidão e o fazer-se da classe trabalhadora no Rio de Janeiro," *Revista Mundo do Trabalho* 1, no. 1 (2009): 51–64.

13. Cláudia Viscardi, "Experências da prática associativa no Brasil (1860–1880)," *Topoi* 9, no. 16 (2008): 117–136; Ronaldo Pereira de Jesus, "Associativismo no Brasil do Século XIX: Repertório crítico dos registros de sociedades no Conselho de Estado (1860–1889)," *Locus: Revista de História* 13, no. 1 (2007):144–170.

14. David P. Lacerda and Ronaldo Pereira de Jesus, "Dinâmica associativa no século XIX: Socorro mútuo e solidariedade entre livres e libertos no Rio de Janeiro Imperial," *Revista Mundos do Trabalho* 2, no. 4 (2010): 126–142. M. Mattos, "Trajetórias entre fronteiras," 58.

15. Chalhoub, "Solidariedade e liberdade."

16. M. Mattos, "Trajetórias entre fronteiras," 61.

17. Ibid., 55; M. Mattos, "Trabalhadores escravizados e livres," 245.

18. Viscardi, "Estratégias populares de sobrevivência," 33–34.

19. Francisco Ferreira da Rosa, *Rio de Janeiro* (Rio de Janeiro: Edição Oficial da Prefeitura, 1905).

20. Meade, *Civilizing Rio*, 140–141.

21. Prefeitura do Distrito Federal, *Assistência pública e privada no Rio de Janeiro: História e estadística* (Rio de Janeiro: Typografia do Anuário do Brasil, 1992).

22. Cláudia Viscardi, "Estratégias populares de sobrevivência: O mutualismo no Rio de Janeiro republicano," *Revista Brasileira de História* 29, no. 58 (2009): 291–315.

23. Cláudio Batalha, "A geografia associativa: Associações operárias, protesto e espaço urbano no Rio de Janeiro da Primeira República," in *Trabalhadores na cidade*, ed. Elciene Azevedo, Jefferson Cano, Sidney Chalhoub, and Maria Clementina Pereira Cunha (Campinas, Brazil: Editora da Unicamp, 2009).

24. Columna operaria, *A Época*, 14 January 1913.

25. Ataúlfo Paiva, Prefeitura do Distrito Federal, *Assistência pública e privada no Rio de Janeiro (Brasil): História e estatística* (Rio de Janeiro: Typ. do Anuário do Brasil, 1922).

26. 1° Ofício de Registro de Títulos e Documentos (J-Z), fl. 222, AN.

27. Cláudio Batalha, "Identidade da classe operária no Brasil (1880–1920): Atipicidade ou legitimidade?" *Revista Brasileira de História* 12, no. 23/24 (1992): 111–124.

28. Edmundo, *O Rio de Janeiro do meu tempo*, 359.

29. Michel Ralle, "A função da proteção mutualista na construção de uma identidade operária na Espanha (1870–1910)," *Cadernos Arquivo Edgar Leuenroth* 6 no. 10/11 (1999): 15–38.

30. Columna operaria, *A Época*, 30 August 1912.

31. "A perseguição aos vendedores ambulantes não é razoâvel," letter to the editor, *A Noite*, 24 Nov 1911.

32. Columna operaria, *A Época*, 1 September 1912.

33. Columna operaria, *A Época*, 5 January 1913.

34. Elinor Ostrom, "A Behavioral Approach to the Rational Choice Theory of Collective Action," *American Political Science Review* 92, no. 1 (March 1998): 1–22.

35. On people's use of public space as a foundation for urban citizenship see, Lefebvre, *Writings on Cities*; McCann, "Space, Citizenship, and the Right to the City"; Purcell, "Excavating Lefebvre."

36. Columna operaria, *A Época*, 30 August 1912.

37. Columna operaria, *A Época*, 6 September 1912.

38. Columna operaria, *A Época*, 7 September 1912.

39. Columna operaria, *A Época*, 26 October 1912.

40. Columna operaria, *A Época*, 26 October 1912 and 3 May 1913.

41. Columna operaria, *A Época*, 29 May 1913.

42. Columna operaria, *A Época*, 26 December 1912.

43. Batalha, "A geografia associativa."

44. Bruno Carvalho, *Porous City: A Cultural History of Rio de Janeiro (from the 1810s Onward)* (Liverpool, England: Liverpool University Press, 2013); Moura, *Tia Ciata*.

45. Columna operaria, *A Época*, 7 May 1913.

46. "A caixa econômica," *A Noite*, 28 May 1914.

47. "O despertar no mercado," *A Época*, 18 Agosto 1912; "Em Nictheroy," *A Época*, 23 October 1918; "O que nos disse um livreiro ambulante," *A Época*, 28 December 1918; "Porque o peixe nos envenena," *A Época*, 13 December 1917.

48. Edmundo, *O Rio de Janeiro do meu tempo*.

49. Photograph of Vianna Ferraz and other leaders in Rio's associative life, Columna operaria, *A Época*, 27 May 1913.

50. Columna operaria, *A Época*, 4 November 1912.

51. "Eram amigos . . . esmurraram-se no interior d'uma fábrica de doces," *Correio da Manhã*, 25 February 1917.

52. "A população envenenada," *A Noite*, 24 January 1912.

53. Columna operaria, *A Época*, 21 January 1913.

54. Columna operaria, *A Época*, 20 June 1913.

55. Columna operaria, *A Época*, 21 July 1913.

56. "Associação dos Empregados no Comércio do Rio de Janeiro," *Gazeta de Notícias*, 28 February 1902.

57. Reclamações, *Correio da Manhã*, 18 June 1908; Diversos, *Gazeta de Notícias*, 3 February 1903.

58. Precisa-se, *A Noite*, 6 February 1914.

59. Declarações, *Correio da Manhã*, 2 April 1918.

60. Columna operaria, *A Época*, 23 July 1913.

61. "A reducção das licenças dos mercados ambulantes," *A Época*, 28 February 1913.

62. Notas policiais, *A Época*, 17 August 1919.

63. "Os mascates em apuros," *A Época*, 1 February 1914.

64. Lacerda and Pereira de Jesus, "Dinâmica associativa no século XIX."

65. Columna operaria, *A Época*, 7 July 1913.

66. Columna operaria, *A Época*, 1 March 1913.
67. Columna operaria, *A Época*, 5 January 1913.
68. Columna operaria, *A Época*, 6 April 1913.
69. Columna operaria, *A Época*, 18 January 1913.
70. Nos suburbios, *A Época*, 12 November 1913. The original spelling *Nos suburbios* is retained.
71. Nos suburbios, *A Época*, 3 December 1913 and 29 March 1915.
72. Prefeitura, *A Época*, 30 May 1917; Nos suburbios, *A Época*, 11 May 1919.
73. Providências! *A Noite*, 11 June 1913.
74. Columna operaria, *A Época*, 19 January 1913.
75. Columna operaria, *A Época*, 6 June 1913 and 1 July 1913.
76. "2° Congresso Operário Brasileiro," *A Época*, 14 September 1913.
77. "Os mascates em apuros," *A Época*, 1 February 1914.
78. Ibid.
79. Columna operaria, *A Época*, 7 April 1914.
80. Columna operaria, *A Época*, 6 January 1914.
81. "Imposto de comércio ambulante," Boletim da Camara Municipal, Prefeitura do Distrito Federal, Secretaria do Gabinete do Prefeito, 1924 (Rio de Janeiro, 1924), 70–74.

CONCLUSION

1. Michael Conniff, *Urban Politics in Brazil: The Rise of Populism* (Pittsburgh, PA: University of Pittsburgh Press, 1981), 78.
2. Cooperativa de Produção (Transformação) dos Vendedores Ambulantes, Registro de Sociedades Civís, vol. 27, 581–600, 16/10/1936–17/11/1936, no. 600, AN.
3. União dos Negociantes Ambulantes, Registro de Sociedades Civís, vol. 38, 801–824, 07/10/1938–11/05/1938, no. 811, AN.
4. Cross, *Informal Politics*; Hernando de Soto, *The Mystery of Capital: Why Capitalism Triumphs in the West and Fails Everywhere Else* (New York: Basic Books, 2003).
5. Cross, *Informal Politics*; Sally Roever, "Street Trade in Latin America: Demographic Trends, Legal Issues and Vending Organisations in Six Cities," in *Street Vendors in the Global Urban Economy*, ed. Sharit Bhowmix (London: Routledge, 2010).

BIBLIOGRAPHY

ARCHIVES, COLLECTIONS, AND LIBRARIES

Arquivo Geral da Cidade do Rio de Janeiro (AGCRJ)
  Biblioteca
  Miscellaneous files
Arquivo Edgar Leuenroth (AEL), Campinas
  Periódicos do século XIX
  Periódicos do século XX
Arquivo Nacional (AN), Rio de Janeiro
  Junta Comercial
  Pretorias criminais
  Privilégios industriais
  Registro de sociedades civís
  Registro de títulos e documentos
Arquivo Público do Estado do Rio de Janeiro (APERJ)
  Livros da Casa de Detenção
Biblioteca Nacional (BN), Rio de Janeiro
  Manuscritos: Escravidão
  Periódicos
Centro de Pesquisa em História Social da Cultura (Cecult), Campinas
  Ocorrências policiais
George Ermakoff Casa Editorial, Arquivo de Imagens, Images2You, Rio de Janeiro
Instituto Histórico e Geográfico Brasileiro (IHGB), Rio de Janeiro
Instituto Moreira Salles (IMS), Rio de Janeiro
  Fotografias: Marc Ferrez
Museu Histórico Nacional (MHN), Rio de Janeiro
  Fotografias: Comércio ambulante, Marc Ferrez, Juan Gutierrez, Augusto Malta
National Anthropological Archives, Smithsonian Institution, Washington, DC
Real Gabinete Português de Leitura, Rio de Janeiro

NEWSPAPERS AND MAGAZINES OF THE PERIOD, RIO DE JANEIRO

O Apostolo
O Artista
A Calçada Elegante
Correio da Manhã
Diário do Rio de Janeiro
Diário Oficial
A Época
Gazeta de Notícias
O Jornal
Jornal do Commercio
Jornal do Brasil
A Noite
O Paiz
O Panificador
O Philantropo
Revista da Semana
Rua do Ouvidor
O Trabalho
Trabalho e Direito
A Voz do Trabalhador

SECONDARY SOURCES

Abreu, Martha. *O império do divino: Festas religiosas e cultura popular no Rio de Janeiro, 1830–1900*. Rio de Janeiro: Nova Fronteira, 1999.

———. "*Mulatas*, *Crioulos*, and *Morenas*: Racial Hierarchy, Gender Relations, and National Identity in Postabolition Popular Song (Southeastern Brazil, 1890–1920)." In *Gender and Slave Emancipation in the Atlantic World*, edited by Pamela Scully and Diana Patton. Durham, NC: Duke University Press, 2005.

———. "Slave Mothers and Freed Children: Emancipation and Female Space in Debates on the 'Free Womb' Law, Rio de Janeiro 1871." *Journal of Latin American Studies* 28 (1996): 567–580.

Abreu, Martha, and Sueann Caulfield. "50 Years of Virginity in Rio de Janeiro: Sexual Politics and Gender Roles in Judicial and Popular Discourses, 1890–1940." *Luso-Brazilian Review* 30, no. 1 (1993): 47–74.

Abreu, Maurício de Almeida. *Evolução urbana do Rio de Janeiro*. 5th ed. Rio de Janeiro: Instituto Municipal de Urbanismo Pereira Passos, 2006.

Adamo, Sam. "The Broken Promise: Race, Health, and Justice in Rio de Janeiro, 1890–1940." PhD diss., Columbia University, 1983.

Aguirre, Carlos, and Ricardo Salvatore. *The Birth of the Penitentiary System in Latin America: Essays on Criminology, Prison Reform, and Social Control, 1830–1940*. Austin: University of Texas Press, 1996.

Aguirre, Carlos, Gilbert M. Joseph, and Ricardo D. Salvatore. *Crime and Punishment in Latin America: Law and Society since Late Colonial Times*. Durham, NC: Duke University Press, 2001.

Alencastro, Luiz Felipe de. "Proletários e escravos: Imigrantes portugueses e cativos africanos no Rio de Janeiro, 1850–1872." *Novos Estudos* 21 (1988): 30–56.

Algranti, Leila Mezan. *O feitor ausente: Estudo sobre a escravidão urbana no Rio de Janeiro*. Petrópolis, Brazil: Vozes, 1988.

———. "Slave Crimes: The Use of Police Power to Control the Slave Population of Rio de Janeiro." *Luso-Brazilian Review* 25, no. 1 (Summer 1988): 27–48.

Allemand-Lavigerie, Charles Martial. *Crusade against the Slave Trade: Oration . . . at the Meeting of the Anti-Slavery Society Held in Prince's Hall London, Tuesday, July 31st, 1888*. London: LSE Pamphlets, 1888.

Andrews, George Reid. *Blacks and Whites in São Paulo, Brazil, 1888–1988*. Madison, WI: University of Wisconsin Press, 1991.

Appadurai, Arjun, and James Holston, eds. *Cities and Citizenship*. Durham, NC: Duke University Press, 1999.

———. Introduction to *Cities and Citizenship*, edited by Appadurai and Holston.

Azevedo, Aluísio. *The Slum*. New York: Oxford University Press, 2000. Originally published as *A Favela* in 1895.

Backheuser, Everardo. "Comércio ambulante e ocupações de rua no Rio de Janeiro," *Revista Brasileira de Geografia* 6 (January-March 1944): 3–34.

Batalha, Cláudio. "Os desafios atuais da história do trabalho." *Anos 90* 13, no. 23/24 (2006): 87–104.

———. "A geografia associativa: Associações Operárias, protesto e espaço urbano no Rio de Janeiro da Primeira República." In *Trabalhadores na cidade*, edited by Elciene Azevedo,

Jefferson Cano, Sidney Chalhoub, and Maria Clementina Pereira Cunha. Campinas, Brazil: Editora da Unicamp, 2009.
———. "Identidade da classe operária no Brasil (1880–1920): Atipicidade ou legitimidade?" *Revista Brasileira de História* 12, no. 23/24 (1992): 111–124.
———. *O movimento operário na Primeira República*. Rio de Janeiro: Editora Zahar, 2000.
———. "Sociedades de trabalhadores no Rio de Janeiro do século XIX: Algumas reflexões em torno da formação da classe operária." *Cadernos Arquivo Edgar Leuenroth* 6, no. 10/11 (1999): 43–68.
———. "Vida associativa: Por uma nova abordagem da história institucional nos estudos do movimento operário." *Anos 90* 5, no. 8 (1997): 91–99.
Benchimol, Jaime Larry. *Pereira Passos, um Haussmann tropical: A renovação urbana da cidade do Rio de Janeiro no início do século XX*. Rio de Janeiro: Prefeitura da Cidade do Rio de Janeiro, Biblioteca Carioca, 1990.
Benjamin, Walter. *The Arcades Project*. Cambridge, MA: Belknap Press, 2002.
Berlin, Ira. *Slaves without Masters: The Free Negro in the Antebellum South*. 2nd ed. New York: Pantheon, 2007.
———. "The Structure of the Free Negro Caste in the Antebellum United States." *Journal of Social History* 9, no. 3 (1976): 297–318.
Bethell, Leslie. *The Abolition of the Brazilian Slave Trade*. Cambridge, England: Cambridge University Press, 1970.
Bosi, Alfredo. *Dialética da colonização*. São Paulo: Companhia das Letras, 1992.
Brandão, Berenice. *A polícia e a força policial no Rio de Janeiro*. Rio de Janeiro: Pontífica Universidade Católica do Rio de Janeiro, 1981.
Brandão, Paulo José de Faria, and Manuel de Mello. *Catálogo dos livros do Gabinete Portuguez de Leitura no Rio de Janeiro*. Rio de Janeiro: Typographia Commercial de F. de O. Q. Regadas, 1858.
Bretas, Marcos Luiz. *A guerra das ruas: Povo e polícia na cidade do Rio de Janeiro*. Rio de Janeiro: Arquivo Nacional, 1997.
———. *Ordem na cidade: O exercício cotidiano da autoriedade policial no Rio de Janeiro, 1907–1930*. Rio de Janeiro: Rocco, 1997.
———. "What the Eyes Can't See: Stories from Rio de Janeiro's Prisons." In *The Birth of the Penitentiary System: Essays on Criminology, Prison Reform, and Social Control, 1830–1940*, edited by Carlos Aguirre and Ricardo Salvatore. Austin: University of Texas Press, 1996.
Brown, Alexandra K. "'A Black Mark on Our Legislation': Slavery, Punishment, and the Politics of Death in Nineteenth-Century Brazil." *Luso-Brazilian Review* 37, no. 2 (2000): 95–121.
Carpenter, Frank De Yeax. *Round about Rio: A Novel*. Chicago: Jansen, McClurg, 1884.
Carvalho, Bruno. *Porous City: A Cultural History of Rio de Janeiro (from the 1810s Onward)*. Liverpool, England: Liverpool University Press, 2013.
Carvalho, José Murilo de. *Os bestializados: O Rio de Janeiro e a república que não foi*. São Paulo: Companhia das Letras, 1987.
Caulfield, Sueann. *In Defense of Honor: Sexual Morality, Modernity, and Nation in Early Twentieth-Century Brazil*. Durham, NC: Duke University Press, 2000.
———. "The Making of the Carioca Working Class: Social History of Rio de Janeiro during the First Republic." *Luso-Brazilian Review* 28, no. 2 (1991): 99–105.
Chalhoub, Sidney. "Solidariedade e liberdade: Sociedades beneficientes de negros e negras no

Rio de Janeiro na segunda metade do século XIX." In *Quase-cidadão*, edited by Cunha and Gomes.

———. *Trabalho, lar e botequim: O cotidiano dos trabalhadores no Rio de Janeiro da Belle Époque*. São Paulo: Brasiliense, 1986.

———. *Visões da liberdade: Uma história das últimas décadas da escravidão na corte*. São Paulo: Companhia das Letras, 1990.

Chamberlain, Henry. *Vistas e costumes da cidade e arredores do Rio de Janeiro em 1819–1820*. Rio de Janeiro: Livraria Kosmos, 1943 [1820].

Chazkel, Amy. *Laws of Chance: Brazil's Clandestine Lottery and the Making of Urban Public Life*. Durham, NC: Duke University Press, 2011.

———. "Social Life and Civic Education in the Rio de Janeiro City Jail." *Journal of Social History* 42, no. 3 (2009): 697–731.

Conniff, Michael. *Urban Politics in Brazil: The Rise of Populism*. Pittsburgh, PA: University of Pittsburgh Press, 1981.

Corrêa, Armando Magalhães. *O sertão carioca*. Rio de Janeiro: Edição do Instituto Histórico e Geográfico Brasileiro, 1936.

Cowling, Camillia. *Conceiving Freedom: Women of Color, Gender, and the Abolition of Slavery in Havana and Rio de Janeiro*. Chapel Hill: University of North Carolina Press, 2013.

Cribelli, Teresa. *Industrial Forests and Mechanical Marvels: Modernization in Nineteenth-Century Brazil*. New York: Cambridge University Press, 2016.

Cross, John C. *Informal Politics: Street Vendors and the State in Mexico City*. Stanford, CA: Stanford University Press, 1998.

Cruz, Maria Cecília Velasco e. "Puzzling Out Slave Origins in Rio de Janeiro Port Unionism: The 1906 Strike and the Sociedade de Resistência dos Trabalhadores em Trapiche e Café." *Hispanic American Historical Review* 82, no. 2 (2006): 205–245.

Cunha, Maria Clementina Pereira. *Ecos da folia: Uma história do carnaval carioca entre 1880–1920*. São Paulo: Companhia das Letras, 2001.

Cunha, Olívia Maria Gomes da. *Intenção e gesto: Pessoa, cor e a produção cotidiana da (in)diferença no Rio de Janeiro*. Rio de Janeiro: Arquivo Nacional, 2002.

———. "Learning to Serve: Intimacy, Morality, and Violence." *Hispanic American Historical Review* 88, no. 3 (2008): 455–491.

Cunha, Olívia Maria Gomes da, and Flávio Gomes dos Santos, eds. *Quase-cidadão: Histórias e antropologias da pós-emancipação no Brasil*. Rio de Janeiro: Fundação Getúlio Vargas, 2007.

Debret, Jean-Baptiste. *Viagem pitoresca e histórica ao Brasil*. Rio de Janeiro: Editora Itatiaia, 1989 [1834].

Dias, Maria Odila da Silva. "Nas fímbrias da escravidão urbana: Negras de tabuleiro e de ganho." *Estudos Econômicos* 15 (1985): 89–109.

———. *Power and Everyday Life: The Lives of Working Women in Nineteenth-Century Brazil*. Translation by Ann Frost. New Brunswick, NJ: Rutgers University Press, 1995.

Duarte, Leila. *Pão e liberdade: Uma história de padeiros escravos e livres na virada do século XIX*. Rio de Janeiro: Fundação de Amparo à Pesquisa do Rio de Janeiro, 2002.

Edmundo, Luiz. *O Rio de Janeiro do meu tempo*. 2nd ed. Rio de Janeiro: Conquista, 1957.

Ermakoff, George. *O negro na fotografia brasileira do século XIX. Rio de Janeiro: Casa Editorial G. Ermakoff, 2004.*

Far, Alessandra El. *Páginas de sensação: Literatura popular e pornográfica no Rio de Janeiro (1870–1924)*. São Paulo: Companhia das Letras, 2004.

Farias, Juliana Barreto. "Descobrindo mapas dos minas: Alforrias, trabalho urbano e identidades, 1800–1915." In *No labirinto das nações*, by Juliana Barreto Farias, Carlos Eugênio Líbano Soares, and Flávio dos Santos Gomes. Rio de Janeiro: Arquivo Nacional, 2005.

———. "João do Rio e os africanos: Raça e ciência nas crônicas da Belle Époque carioca." *Revista de História* 162 (2010): 243–270.

Farias, Juliana Barreto, Carlos Eugênio Líbano Soares, and Flávio dos Santos Gomes. *No labirinto das nações: Africanos e identidades no Rio de Janeiro, século XIX*. Rio de Janeiro: Arquivo Nacional, 2005.

Ferrez, Gilberto. *O Rio antigo de Marc Ferrez*. São Paulo: Ex Libris, 1984.

Fischer, Brodwyn. *A Poverty of Rights: Citizenship and Inequality in Twentieth-Century Rio de Janeiro*. Stanford, CA: Stanford University Press, 2008.

Frank, Zephyr. *Dutra's World: Wealth and Family in Nineteenth-Century Rio de Janeiro*. Albuquerque: University of New Mexico Press, 2004.

Fridman, Sergio A., and Samuel Gorberg. *Mercados no Rio de Janeiro, 1834–1962*. Rio de Janeiro: S. Gorberg, 2003.

Galvão, Benjamin Franklin Ramiz. *Catálogo. Exposição Nacional, 1875*. Rio de Janeiro: Typographia e Lithographia Carioca, 1875.

Gebara, Ademir. *O mercado de trabalho livre no Brasil, 1871–1888*. São Paulo: Brasiliense, 1986.

Gerson, Brasil. *História das ruas do Rio de Janeiro*. Rio de Janeiro: Sousa, 1954.

Goebel, Walter, and Saksia Schabio, eds. *Beyond the Black Atlantic: Relocating Modernization and Technology*. New York: Routledge, 2006.

Gomes, Flávio dos Santos, and Carlos Eugênio Líbano Soares. "'Dizem as quitandeiras . . .': Ocupações e identidades étnicas em uma cidade escravista: Rio de Janeiro, Século XIX." *Acervo: Revista do Arquivo Nacional* 15, no. 2 (2002): 3–16.

Gomes, Flávio dos Santos, and Antônio Luigi Negro. "Além de senzalas e fábricas: Uma história social do trabalho." *Tempo Social, Revista de Sociologia da USP* 18, no. 1 (2006): 217–240.

Goulart, José Alípio. "Alguns dados sobre o comércio ambulante do leite no Rio de Janeiro do século XIX." *Revista do Instituto Histórico e Geográfico Brasileiro* 263 (1954): 1–40.

———. *O mascate no Brasil*. Rio de Janeiro: Conquista, 1967.

Graham, Richard. *Feeding the City: From Street Market to Liberal Reform in Salvador, Brazil, 1780–1860*. Austin: University of Texas Press, 2010.

Graham, Sandra Lauderdale. *House and Street: The Domestic World of Servants and Masters in Nineteenth-Century Rio de Janeiro*. New York: Cambridge University Press, 1988.

———. "Slavery's Impasse: Slave Prostitutes, Small-Time Mistresses, and the Brazilian Law of 1871." *Comparative Study in Society and History* 33, no. 4 (1991): 669–694.

———. "The Vintém Riot and Political Culture: Rio de Janeiro, 1880." In *Riots in the Cities: Popular Politics and the Urban Poor in Latin America 1765–1910*, edited by Silvia M. Arrom and Servando Ortoll. Wilmington, DE: Scholarly Research, 1996.

Grinberg, Keila. *Liberata, a lei da ambigüedade: As ações de liberdade da corte de apelação do Rio de Janeiro no século XIX*. Rio de Janeiro: Relume Dumara, 1994.

———. "Slavery, Liberalism, and Civil Law." In *Honor, Status, and Law in Modern Latin America*, edited by Sueann Caulfield, Sarah C. Chambers, and Lara Putman. Durham, NC: Duke University Press, 2005.

Hall, Gwendolyn Midlo. *Slavery and African Ethnicities in the Americas: Restoring the Links*. Chapel Hill: University of North Carolina Press, 2005.

Hall, Stuart. "Negotiating Caribbean Identities." In *New Caribbean Thought*, edited by Brian Meeks and Folke Lindahl. Trinidad and Tobago: University of the West Indies Press, 2001.

Hamilton, Charles Granville. "English Speaking Travelers in Brazil, 1851–1887." *Hispanic American Historical Review* 4, no. 4 (1960): 533–546.

Hertzman, Marc. *Making Samba: A New History of Music and Race in Brazil*. Durham, NC: Duke University Press, 2013.

Holloway, Thomas. *Policing Rio de Janeiro: Repression and Resistance in a 19th-Century City*. Stanford, CA: Stanford University Press, 1993.

———. "Punishment in Nineteenth-Century Rio de Janeiro: Judicial Action as Police Practice." In *Reconstructing Criminality in Latin America*, edited by Carlos A. Aguirre and Robert Buffington. Wilmington, DE: Scholarly Resources, 2000.

Holston, James. *Insurgent Citizenship: Disjunctions of Democracy and Modernity in Brazil*. Princeton, NJ: Princeton University Press, 2007.

Holt, Thomas. *The Problem of Freedom: Race, Labor, and Politics in Jamaica and Britain, 1832–1938*. Baltimore, MD: Johns Hopkins University Press, 1992.

Jardim, Antônio da Silva. *Propaganda republicana (1888–1889)*. Rio de Janeiro: Fundação Casa Rui Barbosa, 1978.

Jiménez, Christina. "Performing Their Right to the City: Political Uses of Public Space in a Mexican City, 1880–1910s." *Urban History* 33, no. 3 (2006): 435–456.

Joseph, Gilbert M. Preface to *Crime and Punishment in Latin America: Law and Society since Late Colonial Times*, edited by Carlos Aguirre, Gilbert M. Joseph, and Ricardo D. Salvatore. Durham, NC: Duke University Press, 2001.

Karasch, Mary C. *Slave Life in Rio de Janeiro, 1808–1850*. Princeton, NJ: Princeton University Press, 1987.

Kessel, Carlos, and Karen Worcman. *Um balcão na capital: Memórias do comércio na cidade do Rio de Janeiro*. Rio de Janeiro: Senac, 2003.

Kowarick, Lúcio. *Trabalho e vadiagem: A origem do trabalho livre no Brasil*. São Paulo: Editora Brasilense, 1987.

Lacerda, David P., and Ronaldo Pereira de Jesus. "Dinâmica associativa no século XIX: Socorro mútuo e solidariedade entre livres e libertos no Rio de Janeiro Imperial." *Revista Mundos do Trabalho* 2, no. 4 (2010): 126–142.

Lefebvre, Henri. *Writings on Cities*. Translated and edited by Eleonore Kofman and Elizabeth Lebas. Oxford, England: Blackwell, 1996.

Leslie, Esther. "Ruin and Rubble in the Arcades." In *Walter Benjamin and the Arcades Project*, edited by Beatrice Hanssen. London: Continuum, 2006.

Lima Barreto, Afonso Henriques de. *Lima Barreto: Contos completos*. Edited by Lilia Moritz Schwarcz. São Paulo: Companhia das Letras, 2010.

Lobo, Eulália Maria Lahmeyer. *Historia do Rio de Janeiro: Do capital comercial ao capital industrial e financiero*. Vol. 2. Rio de Janeiro: Ibmec, 1978.

Macedo, Joaquim Manuel de. *Um passeio pela cidade do Rio de Janeiro*. Rio de Janeiro: Livraria Garnier, 1862.

Magalhães, Adelino. *Obras completas*. Vol. 2. Rio de Janeiro: Livraria Editora Valverde, 1946.

Mattos, Hebe Maria. *Das cores do silêncio: Os significados da liberdade no sudeste escravista, Brasil século XIX*. Rio de Janeiro: Nova Fronteira, 1998.

Mattos, Marcelo Badaró. "Trabalhadores escravizados e livres na cidade do Rio de Janeiro na segunda metade do século XIX." *Revista do Rio de Janeiro no.* 12 (2004): 229–251.

———. "Trajetórias entre fronteiras: O fim da escravidão e o fazer-se da classe trabalhadora no Rio de Janeiro," *Revista Mundo do Trabalho* 1, no. 1 (2009): 51–64.

Mattoso, Kátia M. de Queirós. *To Be a Slave in Brazil, 1550–1888*. Translation by Arthur Goldhammer. New Brunswick, NJ: Rutgers University Press, 1986.

McCann, Eugene J. "Space, Citizenship, and the Right to the City: A Brief Overview." *GeoJournal* 58 no. 2–3 (2002): 77–79.

Meade, Teresa. *"Civilizing Rio": Reform and Resistance in a Brazilian City, 1889–1930*. University Park: Pennsylvania State University Press, 1997.

———. "'Living Worse and Costing More': Resistance and Riot in Rio de Janeiro, 1890–1917." *Journal of Latin American Studies* 21 (1986): 241–266.

Mello, Maria Tereza Chaves de. *A república consentida*. Rio de Janeiro: Fundação Getúlio Vargas, 2007.

Mendiola, Sandra. *Street Democracy: Vendors, Violence, and Public Space in Late Twentieth-Century Mexico*. Lincoln: University of Nebraska, 2017.

Mendonça, Joseli Maria Nunes. *Entre a mão e os anéis: A lei dos sexagenários e os caminhos da abolição no Brasil*. Campinas, Brazil: Editora da Unicamp, 1999.

Miyasaka, Cristiane Regina. "Viver nos subúrbios: A experiência dos trabalhadores de Inhaúma (Rio de Janeiro, 1890–1910)." Master's thesis, Universidade Estadual de Campinas, 2008.

Mott, Luis B. "Subsídios à história do pequeno comércio no Brasil." *Revista de História* 53, no. 105 (1976): 81–106.

Moura, Carlos Eugênio Marcondes de. *A travessia da Calunga Grande: Três séculos de imagens sobre o negro no Brasil (1637–1899)*. São Paulo: Editora da USP, 2000.

Moura, Roberto. *Tia Ciata e a pequena África no Rio de Janeiro*. Rio de Janeiro: Funarte, 1983.

Museu Histórico Nacional (MHN). "Pelas ruas e calçadas—Comércio informal e ambulante ontem e hoje." Traveling exhibit. 2006. http://www.museuhistoriconacional.com.br/mh-i-o1e.htm.

Nabuco, Joaquim. *O abolicionismo*. Brasília: Fundação Universidade de Brasilia, 2003 [1863].

———. *Abolitionism: The Brazilian Antislavery Struggle*. Translated and edited by Robert Conrad. Urbana: University of Illinois Press, 1977 [1883].

———. *Campanha abolicionista no Recife: Eleições de 1884*. Recife, Brazil: Fundação Joquim Nabuco, Editora Massangana, 1988.

Needell, Jeffrey. "The Revolta contra a Vacina of 1904: The Revolt against Modernization in Belle-Époque Rio de Janeiro." *Hispanic American Historical Review* 67, no. 2 (May 1987): 233–269.

Ostrom, Elinor. "A Behavioral Approach to the Rational Choice Theory of Collective Action." *American Political Science Review* 92, no. 1 (March 1998): 1–22.

Ostrom, Elinor, Basudeb Guha-Khasnobis, and Ravi Kanbur, eds. *Linking the Formal and Informal Economy*. Oxford: Oxford University Press, 2006.

Paiva, Ataúlfo. Prefeitura do Distrito Federal. *Assistência pública e privada no Rio de Janeiro: História e estadística*. Rio de Janeiro: Typografia do Anuário do Brasil, 1992.

Peard, Julyan. *Race, Place, and Medicine: The Idea of the Tropics in Nineteenth-Century Brazilian Medicine*. Durham, NC: Duke University Press, 2000.

Pena, Eduardo Spiller. *Pajens da casa imperial: Jurisconsultos, escravidão e a lei de 1871*. Campinas, Brazil: Editora da Unicamp, 2001.

Pereira de Jesus, Ronaldo. "Associativismo no Brasil do século XIX: Repertório crítico dos registros de sociedades no Conselho de Estado (1860–1889)." *Locus: Revista de História* 13, no. 1 (2007): 144–170.

Picatto, Pablo. "Urbanistas, Ambulantes, and Mendigos: The Dispute for Urban Space in Mexico City, 1890–1930." In *Reconstructing Criminality in Latin America*, edited by Carlos A. Aguirre and Robert Buffington. Wilmington, DE: Scholarly Resources, 2000.

Purcell, Marc. "Excavating Lefebvre: The Right to the City and Its Urban Politics of the Inhabitant." *GeoJournal* 58 no. 2–3 (2002): 99–108.

Queiroz, Maria Isaura Pereira de. "Viajantes, século XIX: Negras escravas e livres no Rio de Janeiro." *Revista do Instituto de Estudos Brasileiros* 28 (1988): 53–76.

Ralle, Michel. "A função da proteção mutualista na construção de uma identidade operária na Espanha (1870–1910)," *Cadernos Arquivo Edgar Leurenroth* 6 no. 10/11 (1999): 15–38.

Reis, João José, ed. "De olho no canto: Trabalho de rua na Bahia na véspera da abolição." *Afro-Ásia* 24 (2000): 199–242.

———. "Identidade e diversidade étnicas nas irmandades negras no tempo da escravidão." *Tempo* 2, no. 3 (1996): 7–33.

———. "'The Revolution of the Ganhadores': Urban Labor, Ethnicity, and the African Strike of 1857 in Bahia, Brazil." *Journal of Latin American Studies* 29, no. 2 (1997): 355–393.

———. *Slave Rebellion in Brazil: The Muslim Uprising of 1835 in Bahia*. Translation by Arthur Brakel. Baltimore, MD: Johns Hopkins University Press, 1993.

Ribeiro, Gladys Sabina. *A liberdade em construção: Identidade nacional e conflitos antilusitanos no Primeiro Reinado*. Rio de Janeiro: Reluma Dumará, 2002.

———. *Mata galegos: Os portugueses e os conflitos de trabalho na República Velha*. São Paulo: Editora Brasiliense, 1989.

Rio, João do. *A alma encantadora das ruas*. São Paulo: Companhia das Letras, 1997 [1908].

Rocha, Oswaldo Porto. *A era das demolições: Cidade do Rio de Janeiro, 1870–1920*. Rio de Janeiro: Prefeitura da Cidade do Rio de Janeiro, Biblioteca Carioca, 1983.

Rockman, Seth. *Scraping By: Wage Labor, Slavery, and Survival in Early Baltimore*. Baltimore, MD: Johns Hopkins University Press, 2009.

Rodrigues, Jaime. "Ferro, trabalho e conflito: Os africanos livres na fábrica de Ipanema." *História Social*, no. 4/5 (1996/1997): 29–42.

Roever, Sally. "Street Trade in Latin America: Demographic Trends, Legal Issues and Vending Organisations in Six Cities." In *Street Vendors in the Global Urban Economy*, edited by Sharit Bhowmix. London: Routledge, 2010.

Rosa, Francisco Ferreira da. *Rio de Janeiro*. Rio de Janeiro: Edição Oficial da Prefeitura, 1905.

Santos, Francisco Agenor de Noronha. *As freguesias do Rio antigo*. Rio de Janeiro: O Cruzeiro, 1965.

Schultz, Kirsten. *Tropical Versailles: Empire, Monarchy, and the Portuguese Royal Court in Rio de Janeiro, 1808–1821*. New York: Routledge, 2001.

Scott, Rebecca J., Frederick Cooper, and Thomas C. Holt. *Beyond Slavery: Explorations of Race, Labor, and Citizenship in Postemancipation Societies*. Chapel Hill: University of North Carolina Press, 2000.

Silva, Gonçalo Ferreira da. *A briga do rapa com o camelô*. Chapbook. Rio de Janeiro: Academia Brasileira de Literatura de Cordel, 1988.

Silva, Marilene Rosa Nogueira da. *Negro na rua: A nova face da escravidão*. São Paulo: Hucitec, 1988.

Skidmore, Thomas. *Black into White: Race and Nationality in Brazilian Thought*. Durham, NC: Duke University Press, 1993.

Soares, Carlos Eugênio Líbano. *A capoeira escrava e outras tradições rebeldes no Rio de Janeiro, 1808–1850*. Campinas, Brazil: Editora da Unicamp, 2002.

———. *A negrada instituição: A capoeira no Rio de Janeiro, 1850–1890*. Rio de Janeiro: Prefeitura do Município do Rio de Janeiro, Biblioteca Carioca, 1994.

———. "O reino do Zungú," *Nossa História* 3, no. 29 (2006): 46–49.

———. "Os últimos malungos: Moradia, ocupação e criminalidade entre libertos africanos, 1860–1900." In *No labirinto das nações*, by Juliana Barreto Farias, Carlos Eugênio Líbano Soares, and Flávio dos Santos Gomes. Rio de Janeiro: Arquivo Nacional, 2005.

———. *Zungú: Rumor de muitas vozes*. Rio de Janeiro: Arquivo Público do Estado do Rio de Janeiro, 1998.

Soares, Cecília Moreira. "As ganhadeiras: Mulher e resistência em Salvador no século XIX." *Afro-Ásia* 17 (1996): 57–71.

Soares, Luiz Carlos. "Os escravos de ganho no Rio de Janeiro século XIX." *Revista Brasileira de História* 8, no. 16 (1988): 107–142.

Soares, Mariza de Carvalho, and Nelson Rosa Bezarra, eds. *Escravidão africana no Recôncavo da Guanabara (séculos XVII-XIX)*. Rio de Janeiro: Editora da UFF, 2011.

Soto, Hernando de. *The Mystery of Capital: Why Capitalism Triumphs in the West and Fails Everywhere Else*. New York: Basic Books, 2003.

Sousa, Fernando Gralha de. "Augusto Malta e o olhar oficial: Fotografia, cotidiano e memória no Rio de Janeiro—1903/1936." *História, imagem e narrativas* 2, no. 1 (2006): 72–93.

Sousa, Luís Antônio F. de, Fernando Afonso Salla, and Marcos César Alvarez. "A sociedade e a lei: O Código Penal de 1890 e as novas tendências penais na primeira República," *Justiça e História* 3, no. 6 (2003): 1–33.

Vasquez, Pedro. *Fotógrafos no Rio de Janeiro: Victor Frond, George Leuzinger, Marc Ferrez e Juan Gutierrez*. Rio de Janeiro: Dazibao, 1990.

Velloso, Mônica Pimenta. "As tias bahianas tomam conta do pedaço: Espaço e identidade cultural no Rio de Janeiro." *Estudos Históricos* 3, no. 6 (1990): 207–228.

Viqueira Albán, Juan Pedro. *Propriety and Permissiveness in Bourbon Mexico*. Translation by Sonya Lipsett-Rivera and Sergio Rivera Ayala. Wilmington, DE: Scholarly Resources, 1997.

Viscardi, Cláudia. "Estratégias populares de sobrevivência: O mutualismo no Rio de Janeiro republicano." *Revista Brasileira de História* 29, no. 58 (2009): 291–315.

———. "Experências da prática associativa no Brasil (1860–1880)." *Topoi* 9, no. 16 (2008): 117–136.

Vitorino, Artur José Renda. "Escravismo, proletários e a greve dos compositores tipográficos de 1858 no Rio de Janeiro." *Cadernos Arquivo Edgar Leuenroth* 6, no. 10/11 (1999): 71–106.

Wade, Richard. *Slavery in the Cities of the South, 1820–1860*. New York: Oxford University Press, 1964.

Wolff, Egon, and Frieda Wolff. *Judeus nos primórdios do Brasil-República: Visto especialmente pela documentação no Rio de Janeiro*. Rio de Janeiro: Edição da Biblioteca Israelita H. N. Bialik, Centro de Documentação, 1979.

Zimmerman, Kari. "'As Pertaining to the Female Sex': The Legal and Social Norms of Female Entrepreneurship in Nineteenth-Century Rio de Janeiro, Brazil." *Hispanic American Historical Review* 66, no. 1 (2016): 39–72.

INDEX

Numbers in italics refer to maps.